W9-AJP-754

5203
Wor

World Book
Discovery Science Encyclopedia

Space

WORLD
BOOK

a Scott Fetzer company
Chicago
www.worldbook.com

For information about other World Book publications, visit our
website at www.worldbook.com or call
1-800-WORLDBK (967-5325).

For information about sales to schools and libraries, call
1-800-975-3250 (United States); **1-800-837-5365** (Canada).

World Book, Inc.
233 N. Michigan Ave.
Chicago, IL 60601
U.S.A

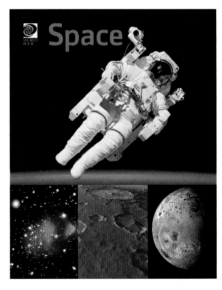

Library of Congress Cataloging-in-Publication Data

Encyclopedia of space.
     p. cm. -- (World Book discovery science encyclopedia)
   Summary: "An introduction to space, including information about the astronomical
bodies that make up the universe, noted astronomers, astronomical devices, and the
history of space exploration, including explorers and space probes. Features include
drawings, diagrams, photographs, and activities"--Provided by publisher.
   Includes index.
   ISBN 978-0-7166-7523-5
   1. Astronomy--Encyclopedias, Juvenile. 2. Space sciences--Encyclopedias,
Juvenile. 3. Outer space--Exploration--Encyclopedias, Juvenile. I. World Book, Inc.
II. Series: World Book discovery science encyclopedia.
QB14.E533 2013
520.3--dc23
                                    2012051083

Printed in China by Shenzhen Donnelley
Printing Co., Ltd., Guangdong Province
1st printing July 2013

Front Cover:
© NASA; M. Markevitch, D. Clowe, NASA/
ESO/Magellan/U of Arizona;
© Stocktrek/Alamy; NASA/JPL/U of Arizona

Back Cover:
© Purestock/Alamy; © Photo Resource
Hawaii/Alamy; © Margaret Bourke-White,
Time & Life Pictures/Getty

Staff

How to use World Book Discovery Science Encyclopedia

http://bit.ly/13kOpzd

- Hundreds of illustrations
- Guide words
- Phonetic spellings
- Related article lists
- Experiments and activities
- QR codes

World Book Discovery Science Encyclopedia is filled with information about basic science concepts, tools, and discoveries as well as the world around us. Entries on people who have made important contributions to science are included, too. All entries are written in a way that makes them easy to understand.

Finding entries is easy, too. They are arranged in alphabetical order. There is also an index in each volume. The index lists all the entries, as well as topics that are covered in the volume but that are not themselves entries.

Science experiments and activities are also included in this volume. These and the many other features of *World Book Discovery Science Encyclopedia* make it an encyclopedia that you can use for research as well as reading just for fun.

Easy alphabetical access
Each letter of the alphabet is highlighted to help you locate entries alphabetically.

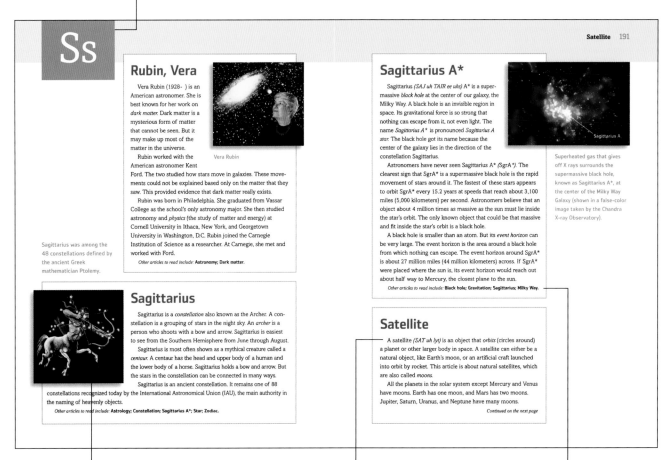

Ss

Rubin, Vera

Vera Rubin (1928-) is an American astronomer. She is best known for her work on *dark matter*. Dark matter is a mysterious form of matter that cannot be seen. But it may make up most of the matter in the universe.

Vera Rubin

Rubin worked with the American astronomer Kent Ford. The two studied how stars move in galaxies. These movements could not be explained based only on the matter that they saw. This provided evidence that dark matter really exists.

Rubin was born in Philadelphia. She graduated from Vassar College as the school's only astronomy major. She then studied astronomy and *physics* (the study of matter and energy) at Cornell University in Ithaca, New York, and Georgetown University in Washington, D.C. Rubin joined the Carnegie Institution of Science as a researcher. At Carnegie, she met and worked with Ford.

Other articles to read include: **Astronomy; Dark matter.**

Sagittarius was among the 48 constellations defined by the ancient Greek mathematician Ptolemy.

Sagittarius

Sagittarius is a *constellation* also known as the Archer. A constellation is a grouping of stars in the night sky. An *archer* is a person who shoots with a bow and arrow. Sagittarius is easiest to see from the Southern Hemisphere from June through August.

Sagittarius is most often shown as a mythical creature called a *centaur*. A centaur has the head and upper body of a human and the lower body of a horse. Sagittarius holds a bow and arrow. But the stars in the constellation can be connected in many ways.

Sagittarius is an ancient constellation. It remains one of 88 constellations recognized today by the International Astronomical Union (IAU), the main authority in the naming of heavenly objects.

Other articles to read include: **Astrology; Constellation; Sagittarius A*; Star; Zodiac.**

Sagittarius A*

Sagittarius *(SAJ uh TAIR ee uhs)* A* is a super-massive *black hole* at the center of our galaxy, the Milky Way. A black hole is an invisible region in space. Its gravitational force is so strong that nothing can escape from it, not even light. The name *Sagittarius A** is pronounced *Sagittarius A star.* The black hole got its name because the center of the galaxy lies in the direction of the constellation Sagittarius.

Astronomers have never seen Sagittarius A* *(SgrA*).* The clearest sign that SgrA* is a supermassive black hole is the rapid movement of stars around it. The fastest of these stars appears to orbit SgrA* every 15.2 years at speeds that reach about 3,100 miles (5,000 kilometers) per second. Astronomers believe that an object about 4 million times as massive as the sun must lie inside the star's orbit. The only known object that could be that massive and fit inside the star's orbit is a black hole.

A black hole is smaller than an atom. But its *event horizon* can be very large. The event horizon is the area around a black hole from which nothing can escape. The event horizon around SgrA* is about 27 million miles (44 million kilometers) across. If SgrA* were placed where the sun is, its event horizon would reach out about half way to Mercury, the closest plane to the sun.

Other articles to read include: **Black hole; Gravitation; Sagittarius; Milky Way.**

Superheated gas that gives off X rays surrounds the supermassive black hole, known as Sagittarius A*, at the center of the Milky Way Galaxy (shown in a false-color image taken by the Chandra X-ray Observatory).

Sagittarius A

Satellite

A satellite *(SAT uh lyt)* is an object that *orbits* (circles around) a planet or other larger body in space. A satellite can either be a natural object, like Earth's moon, or an artificial craft launched into orbit by rocket. This article is about natural satellites, which are also called *moons.*

All the planets in the solar system except Mercury and Venus have moons. Earth has one moon, and Mars has two moons. Jupiter, Saturn, Uranus, and Neptune have many moons.

Continued on the next page

Illustrations
Each volume of *Discovery Science Encyclopedia* contains hundreds of photographs, drawings, maps, and other illustrations. Each illustration is labeled or explained in a caption.

Pronunciations
The phonetic spelling for unusual or unfamiliar words is given. A key to the pronunciation is in the front of each volume.

Related references
The references listed at the bottom of many articles tell you which other articles to read to find out more or related information.

Experiments
Many experiments are found in *Discovery Science Encyclopedia*. These experiments extend or enrich the subject of the article they accompany and are suitable for use at home or in the classroom.

Guide words
Guide words at the top of a page help you quickly find the entry you are seeking.

Activities
Many activities are found in *Discovery Science Encyclopedia*. These simple activities, which can be done at home or in the classroom, extend or enrich the subject of the article they accompany.

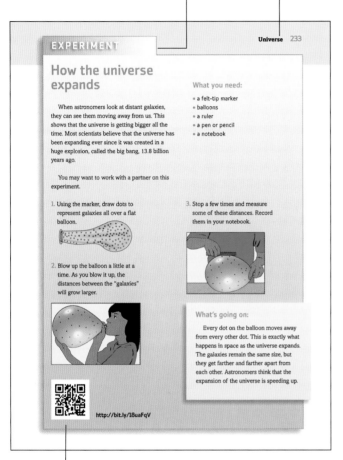

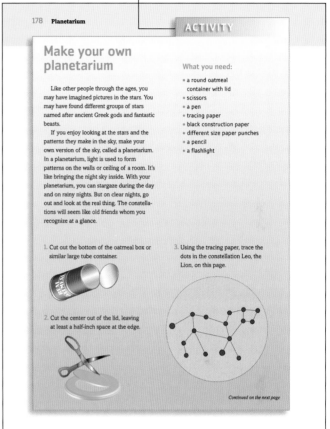

QR codes
This symbol is a QR code. You can find QR codes on all the pages with experiments and activities in the *World Book Discovery Science Encyclopedia*. Simply scan a code with your smartphone or tablet to see a video about the experiment or activity or related information about the subject of the project. (You will need to download a QR code reader to your device if you have not already done so.) If you do not have a mobile device, you can still access the videos linked to experiments and activities by keying in the URL beneath each QR code into a browser on your computer.

You can also find a QR code on the opposite page. This code links to a video explaining how to use the *World Book Discovery Science Encyclopedia*.

A library of all the videos and related information included in the *World Book Discovery Science Encyclopedia* can be found at
http://www.worldbook.com/all/item/1876.

Key to pronunciation

World Book Discovery Science Encyclopedia provides the pronunciations for many unusual or unfamiliar words. In the pronunciation, the words are divided into syllables and respelled according to the way each syllable sounds. The syllables appear in *italic letters*. For example, here are an article title and the respelled pronunciation for it:

Absorption *(ab SAWRP shuhn)*

The syllable or syllables that get the greatest emphasis when the word is spoken are in capital letters *(SAWRP)*.

Aerospace medicine

Aerospace medicine is the study and treatment of health problems caused by flying. Doctors and scientists in *aviation medicine* care for aircraft pilots, crews, and passengers. There are many common stresses of air travel. They include motion sickness, noise, vibration, and changes in oxygen levels. Rapid changes in speed and atmospheric pressure may also affect air travelers. Doctors who specialize in aviation medicine are called *flight surgeons.*

Aerospace medicine also includes *space medicine.* Space medicine deals with astronauts and others who work in space. In space, astronauts are often *weightless* (feeling no pull of gravity). This can cause many health problems. One problem is motion sickness. Astronauts may also lose their sense of direction. People who work in space for weeks or months may suffer a weakening of their bones and muscles. Another danger of space flight is radiation from the sun and other objects in space. People who are in space for long periods may also become homesick and develop a dislike for their co-workers.

Other articles to read include: **Astronaut; Bondar, Roberta; Space exploration.**

United States astronaut Leroy Chiao (right) uses an ultrasound device linked to space doctors on Earth to examine the eye of Russian cosmonaut Salizhan Sharipov on the International Space Station.

Allen Telescope Array

The Allen Telescope Array is a telescope designed to look for signs of intelligent life beyond Earth. The telescope collects and measures radio waves from nearby star systems. It is in Hat Creek, California, in the Cascade Mountains. The Allen Telescope Array is a project between the SETI Institute and the University of California at Berkeley. SETI stands for the *S*earch for *E*xtra *T*errestrial *I*ntelligence.

The Allen Telescope Array is a group of many small radio antennas, called *dish* antennas. Scientists decided to build the telescope as an array because it was less expensive than building

Continued on the next page

Dish antennas from the Allen Telescope Array collect and measure radio waves from space that may be signs of intelligent life beyond Earth.

Allen Telescope Array   *Continued from the previous page*

one large dish. In addition, the array can be used to make detailed maps of the sky by combining the signals from all the antennas. Each dish measures about 20 feet (6 meters) in diameter. The Allen Telescope Array began operating in October 2007 with 42 antennas.

Researchers from the SETI Institute use the telescope to search for signals broadcast by intelligent beings. Radio waves are one of our most important ways to communicate on Earth. If intelligent beings exist elsewhere in the universe, they might also use radio signals to communicate with others. Berkeley scientists use the telescope to study the natural radio waves coming from galaxies, gas clouds, and other objects in space.

Other articles to read include: **Extraterrestrial intelligence; SETI Institute; Telescope.**

X-ray images of Alpha Centauri taken in 2003 and 2005 by the XMM-Newton satellite observatory show a mysterious, never-before-seen dimming of Alpha Centauri A. Some scientists have suggested that the star may brighten and dim in cycles, as the sun does. Alpha Centauri B is hidden behind Alpha Centauri A in the 2005 image.

Alpha Centauri

Alpha Centauri *(AL fuh sehn TAWR eye)* is star system in the *constellation* Centaurus. A constellation is a grouping of stars in a particular part of the night sky. Alpha Centauri consists of two sunlike stars named Alpha Centauri A and Alpha Centauri B. They form a *binary system* (two closely spaced stars that orbit each other). Alpha Centauri can be seen from Earth only in the Southern Hemisphere. Alpha Centuri A is brighter than Alpha Centauri B. In 2012, scientists found evidence of a planet *orbiting* (circling) Alpha Centauri B. The planet is roughly the size of Earth but orbits much closer to its star than Earth orbits the sun.

A third star, called Proxima Centauri, may orbit Alpha Centauri A and B, about once every 1 million years. This orbit would make Alpha Centauri a triple star system. Proxima Centuri is the closest star to Earth besides the sun. It is about 4.2 *light-years* from Earth. A light-year equals the distance light travels in a vacuum in a year, about 5.88 trillion miles (9.46 trillion kilometers).

Other articles to read include: **Extrasolar planet; Proxima Centauri; Star.**

Andromeda

Andromeda is a *constellation* best seen from the Northern Hemisphere. A constellation is a grouping of stars that appear together in the night sky. Andromeda extends from the constellation Perseus to the northeast corner of the great square of the constellation Pegasus. The brightest star of Andromeda, called Alpheratz, is often drawn to complete the square of Pegasus.

The constellation Andromeda represents the wife of the hero Perseus in Greek mythology. She was the daughter of Cassiopeia and Cepheus, the rulers of Ethiopia. Cassiopeia dared to compare Andromeda's beauty to that of certain servants of Poseidon, the god of the sea. In anger, Poseidon sent a sea serpent to attack Ethiopia. A priest said Andromeda should be sacrificed to the serpent to save the land.

Perseus saw Andromeda chained to a rock, fell in love with her, and killed the serpent. They then married. The hero Hercules was one of their descendants. Andromeda became a constellation after her death.

Other articles to read include: **Andromeda Galaxy; Constellation; Pegasus; Star.**

The Andromeda constellation represents a beautiful princess who was rescued from a sea monster.

Andromeda Galaxy

The Andromeda *(an DROM uh duh)* Galaxy is the closest large *galaxy* to our home galaxy, the Milky Way. A galaxy is a vast system of stars, gas, dust, and other matter held together in space by gravity. Andromeda lies about 2.5 million *light-years* from Earth. A light-year is the distance that light travels in a vacuum in a year, about 5.88 trillion miles (9.46 trillion kilometers). The Andromeda Galaxy is one of the farthest objects visible to the unaided eye. It appears on fall and winter nights in the Northern Hemisphere, northwest of the Great Square of Pegasus in the constellation Andromeda. Andromeda looks like a thin disk tilted to our line of sight. You cannot see

Continued on the next page

The Andromeda Galaxy is the closest spiral galaxy to our own galaxy, the Milky Way.

Andromeda Galaxy *Continued from the previous page*

Andromeda's individual stars without a powerful telescope.

Like the Milky Way, the Andromeda Galaxy is a *spiral galaxy.* It has sweeping arms of stars wrapped around a bulging center. The Andromeda Galaxy has about the same *mass* (amount of matter) as the Milky Way. But the Andromeda Galaxy is larger and gives off more light. Gravity is causing the Andromeda Galaxy and the Milky Way to move toward each other. In a few billion years, they will collide and form a single larger galaxy.

Other articles to read include: **Andromeda; Galaxy; Milky Way.**

Aquarius the Water Bearer is one of the oldest sky patterns named by ancient people.

Aquarius

Aquarius *(uh KWAIR ee uhs)* is a *constellation* known as the Water Bearer. A constellation is a grouping of stars in a particular part of the night sky. Aquarius is said to represent a man holding a water pitcher. The constellation can be drawn in several ways.

Aquarius sits in the southern sky between the constellations Pisces and Capricornus. It is best viewed around September through November.

Aquarius contains the Helix Nebula, one of the closest *planetary nebulae* to Earth. A planetary nebula (plural *nebulae*) is a cloud of dust and gas thrown out by a star, about the size of the sun, as it dies. The Helix Nebula lies about 700 *light-years* away. A light-year is the distance light travels in a vacuum in a year, about 5.88 trillion miles (9.46 trillion kilometers).

Aquarius was one of the 48 constellations defined by the ancient Greek mathematician Ptolemy. Today, it is one of 88 constellations recognized by the International Astronomical Union (IAU). The IAU is the leading authority in the naming of heavenly objects. Aquarius is also one of the 12 signs of the zodiac used in *astrology.*

Other articles to read include: **Astrology; Constellation; Nebula; Ptolemy; Star; Zodiac.**

Arecibo Observatory

The Arecibo Observatory is an astronomical observatory with the world's most powerful *radio* telescope. A radio telescope collects and measures radio waves given off by objects in space. The Arecibo Observatory is 50 miles (80 kilometers) west of San Juan, the capital of Puerto Rico. The observatory opened in 1963.

Arecibo's radio telescope has the world's largest *dish* (bowl-shaped reflector). The dish was built into a bowl-shaped valley. It is 1,000 feet (305 meters) across and consists of 38,778 aluminum panels. The size of the Arecibo telescope allows astronomers to observe objects that other telescopes cannot detect. For example, astronomers at the observatory discovered planets beyond the solar system and ice at the poles of Mercury.

In 1996, special mirrors were added to sharpen the telescope's focus. Astronomers can track an object for several hours by continually repositioning the mirrors. The telescope is also used as a giant radar system to map the surfaces of planets, comets, and asteroids as well as electrically charged regions of Earth's *atmosphere* (blanket of gases).

Other articles to read include: **Observatory; Telescope.**

The Arecibo Observatory in Puerto Rico uses the largest dish in the world. It measures 1,000 feet (305 meters) across. The telescope was built in a bowl-shaped valley.

Aries the Ram represents a sheep that was sent by the god Zeus to rescue the son and daughter of a king in Greek mythology. It can be drawn in many ways, using different stars.

Aries

Aries is a *constellation* that is also known as the Ram. A constellation is a grouping of stars in a particular part of the night sky. Aries is easiest to see from the Northern Hemisphere. It is best viewed in October and November. Aries was among the 48 constellations defined by the ancient Greek mathematician Ptolemy. Today, it is one of 88 constellations recognized by the International Astronomical Union (IAU). The IAU is the leading authority in the naming of heavenly objects. Aries is also one of the 12 signs of the zodiac.

Aries is often drawn as a simple constellation that includes only four main stars. The stars are arranged in a line that is slightly hooked on one end.

The story of Aries comes from Greek mythology. Aries was a winged ram with golden *fleece* (wool). He was sent to Earth by the god Zeus to save the daughter and son of a king. The king had been told by a priest to sacrifice the children. But the ram took the children on its back, flying to safety. The son lived, but the daughter was lost at sea. The son then sacrificed the ram to the god Zeus and hung its fleece in a grove of trees. The Greek hero Jason later captured the Golden Fleece and brought it back to Greece.

Other articles to read include: **Astrology; Constellation; Ptolemy; Star; Zodiac.**

Aristarchus

Aristarchus *(AR ih STAHR kuhs)* of Samos was a Greek astronomer. He lived from about 310 B.C. to about 230 B.C. He was the first to guess that Earth *revolves* (moves in a circle) around the sun. Samos is a Greek island in the Aegean Sea.

No one knows how Aristarchus developed his theory about Earth's motion. His surviving writings, *On the Magnitudes and Distances of the Sun and Moon,* do not mention his theory. But his idea was quoted by Archimedes *(AHR kuh MEE deez),* the most important mathematician of ancient times.

Other articles to read include: **Astronomy; Orbit; Sun.**

Armstrong, Neil Alden

Neil Alden Armstrong (1930-2012) was a United States astronaut. He was the first person to set foot on the moon.

Armstrong was born on Aug. 5, 1930, on his grand-parents' farm in Auglaize County, Ohio. He was a Navy pilot from 1949 to 1952. Later, he tested new aircraft. He became an astronaut in 1962.

After one space flight in 1966, Armstrong joined the Apollo 11 mission as mission commander. On July 20, 1969, Armstrong and Edwin "Buzz" Aldrin, Jr., landed the lunar module Eagle on the moon's surface. When Armstrong stepped onto the moon, he said, "That's one small step for a man, one giant leap for mankind."

Neil Alden Armstrong

Armstrong received the Presidential Medal of Freedom in 1969. From 1971 to 1979, Armstrong was a professor of engineering at the University of Cincinnati. In 1986, he served on the commission investigating the space shuttle Challenger disaster. Armstrong died on August 25, 2012.

Other articles to read include: **Astronaut; Challeger disaster; Moon; Space exploration.**

Aryabhatta

Aryabhatta (A.D. 476-550) was an Indian scientist, mathemati-cian, and poet. He may have been born near what is now the South Gujarat-North Maharashtra region of central India. He probably studied in Kusumapura, now called Patna, in the Indian state of Bihar. India's first Earth-orbiting satellite, launched in 1975, was named after Aryabhatta.

Aryabhatta stated that Earth is a sphere. He also suggested that Earth *rotates* (spins) on its *axis* and *revolves* (moves in a circle) around the sun. The axis is an imaginary line that passes through Earth's center and ends at either the North Pole or South Pole.

Aryabhatta advanced a theory of how an *eclipse* (darkening of an object in space) takes place. He also calculated the value of *pi* to be 3.1416. Pi is the ratio of a circle's *circumference* (boundary) to its *diameter* (distance across the middle).

Other articles to read include: **Eclipse; Orbit.**

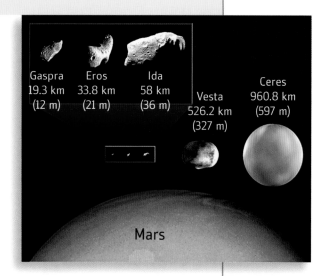

Ceres (shown in an image taken by the Hubble Space Telescope) is the largest asteroid in the Main Belt. Ceres is also considered a *dwarf planet,* a round object that orbits the sun but is much smaller than even a small planet like Mars.

Asteroid

An asteroid *(AS tuh royd)* is a rocky or metallic object smaller than a planet that *orbits* (travels around) the sun. Most asteroids are found between the planets Mars and Jupiter. This area is called the Main Belt, commonly called the asteroid belt. Most Main Belt asteroids orbit the sun at distances between roughly 2 and 3 *astronomical* units. An astronomical unit (AU) equals about 93 million miles (150 million kilometers). It is the same as the average distance between Earth and the sun.

Astronomers think there are hundreds of thousands of asteroids in the Main Belt. An astronomer is a scientist who studies the universe and the objects in it.

Asteroids come in many sizes. The largest asteroid is *Ceres (SEER eez).* It is about 600 miles (970 kilometers) across. Astronomers also consider Ceres a *dwarf planet.* One of the smallest asteroids, 1991 BA, was discovered in 1991. It is only about 20 feet (6 meters) across. There may be asteroids as small as a pebble. These asteroids would be too small to see from Earth, even with a powerful telescope. Only about 1,000 asteroids in the Main Belt are more than 18 miles (30 kilometers) across.

Asteroids also have a variety of shapes. Gravity tends to pull large objects in space into a ball. The largest asteroids appear roughly ball-shaped. But the gravitational pull of smaller asteroids is too weak to greatly change their shapes. These asteroids tend to take on irregular, *elongated* (long and thin) forms. Scientists think some oddly shaped asteroids may be piles of *rubble* (broken pieces) only loosely held together by gravity.

Astronomers think the asteroids formed much like the planets. Both came from tiny pieces of rock orbiting the sun. The pieces crashed and stuck together to form bigger objects. Many of these objects came together to make planets. But the enormous pull of Jupiter's gravity may have stopped some of these objects from sticking together to form a planet.

Astronomers divide asteroids into three main groups. One group is mostly made of carbon. Carbon is a soft, black substance that is plentiful on Earth. Asteroids in the second group

Continued on the next page

are rich in minerals and also contain some metals. The third group is made of such metals as iron and nickel.

Some asteroids called *near-Earth asteroids* follow orbits that can bring them close to our planet. Astronomers put these asteroids into three groups, according to their orbit—*Amors, Apollos,* and *Atens.* The orbits of Amors lie between those of Earth and Mars. Apollos have orbits that cross Earth's orbit. Atens follow orbits that lie mostly between Earth's orbit and the sun. Astronomers have discovered more than 800 near-Earth asteroids larger than 0.6 mile (1 kilometer) in diameter. They estimate that about 1,000 such asteroids may exist.

Earth's *atmosphere* (blanket of gases) protects us from most asteroid strikes. Asteroids smaller than about 160 feet (50 meters) in diameter usually burn up before they can reach the surface. The impact of larger asteroids on land could kick large amounts of dust into the atmosphere. The dust could block sunlight and cool the air for many months. It might even cause widespread loss of crops and starvation. Even larger impacts may trigger mass *extinctions* (sudden die-offs of many kinds of animals). Asteroids large enough to cause worldwide damage strike Earth only about once every million years. Several teams of astronomers are working to identify potentially harmful near-Earth asteroids.

Other articles to read include: **Ceres; Dwarf planet; Main Belt; Near-Earth Asteroid Tracking Program; Solar system.**

The scoop on NASA's Mars Science Laboratory rover, also known as Curiosity, holds soil dug from the Martian surface for inspection by a camera.

Astrobiology

Astrobiology is the search for and study of life in the universe. Astrobiology combines parts of astronomy, biology, and other sciences. Scientists who specialize in astrobiology are called *astrobiologists.* Human beings know of no life besides that on Earth. But astrobiology is a scientific way to find out if such life might exist.

Astrobiologists study life on Earth to help them learn what makes life possible. For example, scientists have found that life as we

Continued on the next page

Astrobiology *Continued from the previous page*

know it cannot exist without liquid water. But they have also found that some *organisms* (living things) can survive in a surprising range of conditions. These organisms are known as *extremophiles (ehk stree muh fylz)*. For example, some organisms can live at high temperatures of about 250 °F (121 °C). Scientists have also realized that not all life needs light or food as a direct energy source. Some organisms get their energy from other sources, such as the chemical reactions between water and rock.

Many scientists think that the planet Mars and Europa, a moon of Jupiter, might be able to support life. Both of these bodies have or once had liquid water beneath their surface. Both also have sources of chemical energy. Life may also exist on planets that orbit stars other than the sun.

Other articles to read include: **Europa; Extrasolar planet; Extraterrestrial intelligence; Mars.**

Astrologers often use charts and tarot cards to try to determine a person's future.

Astrology

Astrology *(uh STRAHL uh jee)* is the study of how the sun, moon, stars, and planets supposedly affect people's lives. Many people throughout the world believe in astrology. Other people think that astrology is only a form of entertainment. Most scientists would say that there is no scientific reason for the belief that astrology gives real information about a person's character or future.

Astrology is based on the idea that the position of heavenly bodies can affect a person's life. Astrologers study these positions by *casting* (drawing) a circular chart called a *horoscope (HOHR uh skohp)* or *birth chart*. A horoscope is like a diagram, or picture, of the sky. It shows the position of the planets in relation to both Earth and the stars at a certain time. In most cases, it shows the position of these bodies at the time of a person's birth. In astrology, the moon, Pluto, and the sun are called planets along with Mercury, Venus, Mars, Jupiter, Saturn, Uranus, and Neptune. Each planet represents a force that affects people in a certain way.

The *zodiac (ZOH dee ak)* has special meaning to people who

Continued on the next page

follow astrology. The zodiac is a band of stars that seems to encircle Earth. The zodiac is divided into 12 sections called the *signs* of the zodiac. Astrologers believe that each person comes under the special influence of a particular sign of the zodiac, depending on the date of the person's birth.

Other articles to read include: **Moon; Planets; Sun; Zodiac;** *and those on individual signs of the zodiac.*

Astronaut

An astronaut is a person who pilots a spacecraft or works aboard one. Astronaut is the name used in the United States. *Cosmonaut (KAHZ muh nawt)* is the name used in Russia. Chinese astronauts are often called *taikonauts*.

In the United States, most astronauts work for the National Aeronautics and Space Administration (NASA). NASA chooses two basic kinds of astronauts: pilots and mission specialists.

Astronaut Bruce McCandless II floats in space during a 1983 shuttle mission. He used a device called a Manned Maneuvering Unit to move around the shuttle.

Pilot astronauts must have more than 1,000 hours of experience flying jet airplanes before they begin training. They command and pilot the spacecraft.

Mission astronauts must have at least three years of experience in the work they will do on the spacecraft. They take care of the spacecraft, do experiments, launch satellites, and walk in space.

NASA sometimes also chooses astronauts called *payload specialists.* Payload specialists are scientists who do scientific experiments in space. Payload specialists do not go through full NASA astronaut training. Astronauts train at the Lyndon B. Johnson Space Center in Houston, Texas. They study science, spacecraft tracking, and other subjects. They also have flight training. Mission specialists are not normally pilots, but they learn how airplanes work and get some flying practice.

All astronauts learn survival skills. They need to know what to do if the spacecraft lands in the sea or in a hard-to-reach area on

Continued on the next page

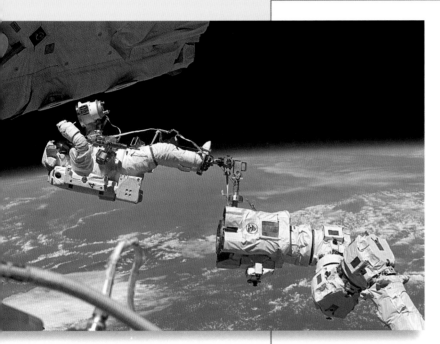

An astronaut spacewalks outside the International Space Station. The astronaut is aided by robotic instruments.

Astronaut *Continued from the previous page*

land. Astronauts also have mission training. They study the spacecraft and its equipment.

Astronauts are not always sent on space flights right away. While they are waiting, they work on engineering and other jobs. But once they are chosen for a crew, they begin training in machines called *simulators*. These machines are as much like a spacecraft as possible. The astronauts learn to solve problems that might come up in space. They also train in models of the spacecraft.

Sometimes astronauts get special training for a space flight. For example, they may practice working with jet-powered back-packs. During a mission, the packs are used to fly outside the spacecraft without a safety line.

Astronauts may also work on the ground. They give information and instructions to crews in space. They work with engineers and scientists. They also suggest changes to improve the space-craft and equipment.

On April 12, 1961, cosmonaut Yuri Gagarin of the Soviet Union (now Russia) became the first person to travel in space. He made one orbit, or trip around Earth. Twenty-three days later, on May 5, Alan B. Shepard, Jr., became the first U.S. space traveler, but he did not go into orbit.

John H. Glenn, Jr., was the first American to go into orbit. He circled Earth three times on February 20, 1962. The first woman in space was the Soviet cosmonaut Valentina Tereshkova. She was in space for three days in 1963. Astronauts from many other countries have flown on missions with the Russians and the Americans. On Oct. 15, 2003, Yang Liwei became the first astronaut sent into space by China. Only a few hundred people have ever gone into space.

Glenn himself flew again in space in October 1998, when he was 77 years old.

Other articles to read include: **Aerospace medicine; National Aeronautics and Space Administration; Space exploration;** *and those on individual astronauts.*

Astronomical unit

An astronomical *(AS truh NOM uh kuhl)* unit (AU) is used by astronomers to measure distances in the solar system. One astronomical unit is the average distance between Earth and the sun, about 93 million miles (150 million kilometers). For example, Jupiter averages about 5 AU's from the sun. Pluto's average distance from the sun is about 39 AU's. In 2012, the International Astronomical Union (IAU) set the astronomical unit at exactly 149,597,870,700 meters. The IAU is the leading authority in matters of astronomy.

Other articles to read include: **Solar system.**

Mars 1.52 AU's

Earth 1 AU

Venus 0.72 AU's

Mercury 0.38 AU

Sun

An astronomical unit is the average distance between Earth and the sun, or 149,597,870,700 meters.

Astronomy

Astronomy is the study of stars, planets, and everything else that makes up the *universe.* The universe is everything that exists in space and time. Scientists who study the universe are called *astronomers.*

Astronomers study objects in the *solar system,* such as the sun, planets, small, rocky objects called *asteroids,* and balls of dust and ice called *comets.* They also study objects that are far from the solar system. They examine stars other than the sun and *galaxies* (large groups of stars). They search for planets around other stars. Astronomers try to learn how big space objects are, how they move, what they are made of, how they were formed, and how they change. They also study the history of the universe and try to determine what might happen in the universe in the future.

Astronomers use special instruments, such as huge telescopes, to learn about the

Continued on the next page

Stars burst into life in the Pillars of Creation, a part of the Eagle Nebula imaged by the Hubble Space Telescope in 1995. Images made by another space telescope in 2007 suggest that the pillars had been destroyed by a high-energy cloud of hot dust or gas.

The Cassini spacecraft releases the Huygens probe above Saturn's largest moon, Titan, in 2004, in an artist's illustration. As the probe descended, it collected information about the moon's atmosphere and took photographs of its surface.

An astronomer studies an image produced by the Expanded Very Large Array of radio telescopes. The colors in the "painting" represent different amounts of radio energy sent out by objects in the sky.

Astronomy *Continued from the previous page*

universe. Some telescopes collect and measure *visible light* (the light we can see with our eyes). Other telescopes collect and measure invisible forms of energy, such as radio waves or X rays.

Most telescopes are based on Earth, but astronomers also rely on telescopes that orbit Earth in artificial satellites. Astronomers also send out *probes* (spacecraft) to get a closer look at planets, moons, and other objects. These spacecraft often carry telescopes and cameras. They may also carry instruments that detect other things, including water, minerals, or heat. Space probes have landed on the the moon, Venus, Mars, Saturn's moon Titan, and an asteroid. Astronomers have also launched *rovers* to explore the moon and Mars. These remote-controlled vehicles enable scientists to examine these bodies at extremely close range, or even sample the rocks on their surface.

Computer modeling also plays a major role in astronomy. Such models help astronomers study processes that occur much too slowly for them to observe or processes that occurred over billions of years. Astronomers can also use computer models to study places that are impossible to reach, such as the interiors of stars.

Astronomy is one of the oldest sciences. It began thousands of years ago when people first looked up at the sky and

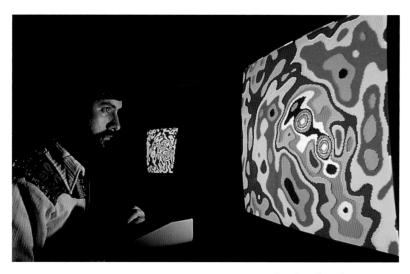

Continued on the next page

wondered about what they saw. The ancient Greeks, Chinese, and *Babylonians* (people in what is now the country of Iraq) all studied the sky. They wanted to know why the sun, moon, planets, and stars seemed to move across the sky.

For hundreds of years, most astronomers believed that the sun and planets orbit Earth. Then in the early 1500's, a Polish astronomer named *Nicolaus Copernicus (NIHK uh LAY uhs koh PUR nuh kuhs)* questioned this idea. Copernicus sug-

Astronomers use many instruments, including telescopes, to study objects far away in space.

gested that Earth and the other planets move around the sun. Some astronomers before Copernicus had suggested that Earth moved in space. In the 200's B.C., for example, the Greek astronomer Aristarchus had even suggested that Earth and the other planets moved around the sun. But by about the A.D. 100's, these theories had been rejected.

In the early 1600's, an Italian astronomer and physicist named Galileo *(GAL uh LAY oh)* Galilei built one of the first telescopes and used it to study the stars and planets. He found moons orbiting the planet Jupiter. He also studied how Jupiter and other planets move. What Galileo found agreed with Copernicus's idea that Earth and the other planets orbit the sun. After that, more and more people saw that Copernicus was right. Copernicus is known as the founder of modern astronomy.

Over the years, astronomers built bigger and better telescopes. They used those telescopes to discover new objects in space. They discovered all the planets orbiting the sun. They found rings and moons around some of the planets. They discovered aster-oids and comets moving around the solar system. In the 1900's, they discovered objects circling the sun beyond the orbit of the farthest planet, Neptune. One such object, Pluto, was once con-sidered a planet. The largest of these objects, including Pluto, are now called *dwarf planets*.

Although Copernicus was right about the sun being the center of the solar system, he thought that the sun was the center of the universe. We now know that the sun is only one of hundreds of billions of stars in a galaxy called the Milky Way. The Milky Way

Continued on the next page

Astronomy *Continued from the previous page*

is not the center of the universe, either. Astronomers have discovered many other galaxies far away from ours. They have even found planets orbiting stars beyond the sun.

Other articles to read include: **Galaxy; Solar system; Space; Space exploration; Universe;** *and those on individual astronomers.*

Maat Mons, one of many volcanoes on Venus, and what appear to be lava flows shown in a three-dimensional colorized image made by NASA's Magellan spacecraft.

Aurora

An aurora is a colorful glow in the night sky. Auroras usually appear in the far northern and southern parts of the world. Auroras in the Northern Hemisphere are called the *northern lights* or *aurora borealis*. Auroras in the Southern Hemisphere are called the *aurora australis*. The lights of an aurora appear as curved lines, clouds, and streaks. Some auroras move, grow brighter, or flicker suddenly. The most common color is green. But auroras that appear very high in the sky may be red or purple.

Auroras form when the *solar winds* reach Earth. The solar winds are a flow of *particles* (tiny bits of matter) from the sun. The particles contain electrical energy. When the particles strike other particles that surround Earth, energy is released. Some of this energy appears in the form of light. Auroras are most intense when violent eruptions on the surface of the sun release additional particles into the solar wind.

Other articles to read include: **Magnetic storm; Solar wind; Sun.**

The brilliant lights of an aurora color the night sky over Alaska.

Barnard, Edward Emerson

Edward Emerson Barnard (1857–1923) was an American *astronomer*. Astronomers study stars, planets, and other objects and forces that makes up the universe. Barnard became famous for his skill as an observer of astronomical objects. He discovered the fifth satellite of Jupiter, Amalthea, in 1892. He also photographed the Milky Way and comets.

Barnard is probably best known for his discovery of Barnard's Star in 1916, which is named in his honor. The star is the fourth-closest star to Earth. Barnard's Star lies about 6 *light-years* away. One light-year is the distance light travels in a vacuum in a year, about 5.88 trillion miles (9.46 trillion kilometers).

In 1895, Barnard joined the staff of the Yerkes Observatory in Wisconsin. His observations there led him to conclude that many starless areas in the Milky Way are *nebulae* (clouds of dust particles and gases). Barnard was born in Nashville, Tennessee.

Other articles to read include: **Astronomy; Milky Way; Nebula; Star; Yerkes Observatory.**

Edward Emerson Barnard

Betelgeuse

Betelgeuse *(BEE tuhl jooz)* is one of the brightest stars in the constellation Orion, the Hunter. Betelgeuse is also called *Alpha Orionis.* It gives off at least 100,000 times as much light as the sun does. Since people first began observing the star, Betelgeuse has changed in brightness and size.

Betelgeuse is at least 495 *light-years* from Earth and may be as far as 640 light-years. One light-year equals about 5.88 trillion miles (9.46 trillion kilometers).

Astronomers classify Betelgeuse as a *red supergiant* (a massive star that has burned up nearly all of its fuel). The star has a deep red color. That is because its surface temperature is so low for a star—only half that of the sun. But Betelgeuse is about 600 to 800 times as wide as the sun. Stars of this size eventually explode

Continued on the next page

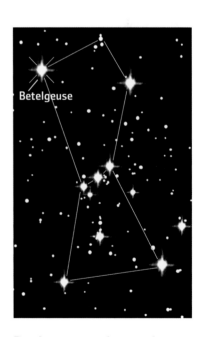

Betelgeuse, a red supergiant (above left), forms a shoulder in one version of the constellation Orion, the Hunter (above).

Betelgeuse   *Continued from the previous page*

in an event called a *supernova*. When it becomes a supernova, Betelgeuse will appear millions of times brighter than it appears now. It will temporarily outshine even the moon.

In 2009, scientists found a cloud of gas surrounding Betelgeuse. This cloud is so large that, if it were in our solar system, it would stretch from the sun to Neptune. This finding provided more evidence that Betelgeuse is in the last stages of its life before becoming a supernova.

Other articles to read include: **Orion; Star; Sun; Supernova.**

The Big Dipper and the Little Dipper both have seven stars. Polaris, or the North Star, is the very bright star at the end of the Little Dipper's handle.

Big and Little Dippers

The Big Dipper and Little Dipper are two of the most famous groups of stars in the night sky. The groups are shaped like two *dippers,* one larger and the other smaller. Dippers are cups with long handles.

Both the Big Dipper and the Little Dipper have seven stars. The Big Dipper is part of a larger group of stars called *Ursa Major,* or the Big Bear. The Little Dipper includes almost all of the stars in *Ursa Minor,* or the Little Bear. Long ago, people thought that these groups of stars looked like bears with a tail. The Dippers appear to move in the sky during the year. The Big Dipper's handle curves down and the Little Dipper's handle curves up, compared with each of their cups.

The stars in the Little Dipper include one of the most famous stars in the sky—Polaris, or the North Star. The North Star is the very bright star at the end of the Little Dipper's handle. If you walk toward the North Star, you will always be heading north.

Other articles to read include: **Constellation; North Star; Star.**

Big bang

The big bang is the name of an event that marked the beginning of our universe. At the moment of the big bang, the universe was unimaginably hot and *dense* (closely packed together). It was thousands of times smaller than the head of a pin.

After the tiniest fraction of a second, the universe began to expand very quickly. You can imagine the universe as a balloon. Suppose you attached the balloon to a tank of gas and opened the nozzle all the way. The balloon would *inflate* (grow larger) rapidly. Most scientists believe that the universe inflated like a balloon. They think it grew to the size of a galaxy in just a fraction of a second. As the universe expanded, it grew cooler and less dense.

Scientists have no way to observe events that may have taken place before the big bang. One theory is that nothing existed before the big bang. Another theory is that more than one universe exists, and the big bang happened when two universes touched. A third theory suggests that a universe like ours existed before the big bang. Eventually, it shrank to a point smaller than an atom and exploded into the current universe.

Other articles to read include: **Cosmology; Galaxy; Space; Star; Universe.**

Binary star

A binary *(BY nuhr ee)* star is a pair of stars that orbit each other. The stars are held together by the force of gravity. From Earth, binaries often look like single stars, even through most telescopes. In some cases, more than two stars are orbiting one another.

The stars in some binaries are so close that they almost touch. In these binaries, the gravity of each star *distorts* (twists) its companion. This causes enormous tides to form on the surfaces of both stars. One star may become an *X-ray pulsar,* a star that radiates X rays in precisely timed bursts. Other close pairs give off powerful radio waves. In still other close pairs, one of the stars pulls matter upon itself from the other star. This matter may explode, causing the star to flare brightly. Some stars in a binary system appear to orbit another, invisible object. The invisible object may be a *black hole.* A black hole is an object whose gravity is so strong that not even light can escape it.

Other articles to read include: **Black hole; Gravitation; Pulsar; Star.**

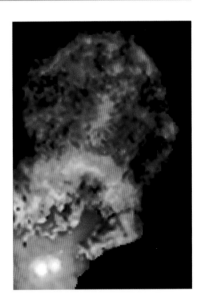

A young binary star system called XZ Tauri ejects a massive amount of hot gas, as shown in an image taken by the Hubble Space Telescope. The gas extends nearly 60 billion miles (96 billion kilometers) into space.

Black hole

A black hole shoots twin jets of matter and energy out into space, in an artist's illustration. Astronomers believe supermassive black holes reside at the center of almost every galaxy, including our Milky Way.

A black hole is an invisible region in outer space. Its gravitational force is so strong that any objects that get too close are trapped forever. A black hole is invisible because not even light can get away from its gravitational pull.

The surface of a black hole is known as the *event horizon*. This is not a normal surface that you could see or touch. At the event horizon, the pull of gravity becomes infinitely strong. An object can exist there for only an instant as it plunges inward at the speed of light.

Astronomers cannot see black holes directly. However, they can see how black holes affect stars and other nearby objects. For example, a black hole may attract gas from a star and heat it up. The heated gas gives off rays of energy called *X rays*. Scientists can use special telescopes to see these X rays. If scientists know where the X rays are, they can locate the black hole.

Astronomers believe that black holes form from large stars that run out of fuel. Then the star shrinks as it is crushed by its own gravitational weight. After a time, the star explodes and throws off its outer layers. It shrinks more and more—down to a tiny point. That point is a black hole.

Scientists think that some very large stars simply collapse into black holes without exploding. The biggest black holes are billions of times more massive than the sun. These black holes were probably created very early in the history of the universe. Scientists think that such black holes lie at the center of almost all galaxies.

There is strong evidence that a supermassive black hole lies at the center of our Milky Way Galaxy. This black hole is known as Sagittarius A* (SgrA*). The clearest sign that SgrA* is a supermassive black hole is the rapid movement of stars around it. The fastest of these stars appears to orbit SgrA* every 15.2 years at speeds that reach about 3,100 miles (5,000 kilometers) per second. Astronomers believe that an object about 4 million times as massive as the sun must lie inside the star's orbit. The only known object that could be that massive and fit inside the star's orbit is a black hole.

Other articles to read include: **Galaxy; Gravitation; Milky Way; Sagittarius A*; Star; Universe.**

Blue giant

A blue giant is a large, bright star that glows with a bluish-white light. A blue giant may be many thousands of times as bright as the sun. The largest blue giants are called *blue supergiants.*

A blue giant's color comes from its high surface temperatures. These tend to be greater than 27,000 °F (15,000 °C). The part of the sun that we see has a temperature of about 10,000 °F (5500 °C).

Few stars in our galaxy are blue giants. But they shine so brightly that they can be seen from far away. For this reason, we can see many blue giants in the night sky. Spica is perhaps the most famous blue giant. It is the brightest star in the *constellation* Virgo. A constellation is a grouping of stars in a particular area of the night sky.

A blue giant star may be 20,000 to 50,000 times as bright, 10 to 50 times as heavy, and 25 times as large as the sun.

Blue giants burn up their fuel more quickly than other stars do. A blue giant may use up all its fuel in tens of millions or hundreds of millions of years. In contrast, the sun will likely burn for about 10 billion years. When a blue giant runs out of fuel, it turns into another kind of star called a *red supergiant.*

Because blue giants burn out so quickly, all the blue giants we can see must be fairly young. In fact, astronomers look for blue giants to find places where new stars are forming.

Other articles to read include: **Red giant; Star.**

Blue moon

Blue moon is a term that has many definitions. According to one modern definition, a blue moon is the second full moon in a month that has two full moons. According to an older definition, a blue moon is the third full moon in a season that has four full moons. In the early 1900's, the *Maine Farmers' Almanac* published dates on which blue moons would appear, using the older definition. The newer definition—the second full moon in a month—originated in *Sky & Telescope* magazine in 1946. Other publications adopted the definition, and many people accepted it. In 1999, *Sky & Telescope* published an article explaining that the 1946 definition originated from a misreading of the *Maine Farmers' Almanac.*

As early as 1528, the term *blue moon* was used to describe a silly belief. Later, people described uncommon events as occurring "once in a blue moon."

Other articles to read include: **Moon.**

A blue moon shines over Cincinnati, Ohio, on August 31, 2012.

Guion Stewart Bluford, Jr.

Bluford, Guion Stewart, Jr.

Guion Stewart Bluford *(GY uhn STOO urt BLOO furd),* Jr., (1942-   ) was the first African American to travel in space. On August 30, 1983, Bluford and four other astronauts began a six-day flight aboard the space shuttle Challenger. During the flight, Bluford launched a satellite for India. He also helped test the shuttle's robotic arm. The astronauts used the arm to move a heavy weight from the cargo area into space and back again.

Bluford was born on November 22, 1942, in Philadelphia. He received a Ph.D. degree in aerospace engineering from the Air Force Institute of Technology in 1978.

Bluford entered the Air Force in 1964. He began training to become an astronaut in 1978. Bluford continued to serve on space shuttle flights until 1993. In that year, he resigned as an astronaut and retired from the Air Force. He then held executive positions at a variety of computer, engineering, and aerospace companies.

Other articles to read include: **Astronaut; Space exploration.**

Charles Frank Bolden, Jr.

Bolden, Charles Frank, Jr.

Charles Frank Bolden, Jr. (1946-   ), became the administrator of NASA, the United States space agency, in 2009. Bolden, a pilot and astronaut, was appointed by President Barack Obama. He became the first African American to head the agency.

Bolden was born in Columbia, South Carolina, on August 19, 1946. He studied at the U.S. Naval Academy in Annapolis. A Marine Corps fighter pilot, Bolden served in the Vietnam War (1957-1975) from 1972 to 1973. He also served as a commander in the Persian Gulf War of 1991.

Bolden joined the NASA Astronaut Corps in 1980. He flew on four space shuttle flights and served as mission commander on two of the flights. After his final space shuttle flight in 1994, he left NASA to return to active duty in the Marine Corps as the Deputy Commandant of Midshipmen at the Naval Academy. He retired from the Marines in 2003.

Other articles to read include: **Astronaut; National Aeronautics and Space Administration; Space exploration.**

Bondar, Roberta

Roberta Bondar *(BAHN dahr)* (1945-   ) was the first Canadian woman to travel into space. She is a doctor of medicine. In January 1992, she and six other astronauts took an eight-day flight aboard the space shuttle Discovery. During the mission, Bondar studied how space flight affects human beings. She also examined how gravity affects and helps shape other living things and certain materials. Bondar worked on tools and methods for doing research in the weightless state of space flight.

Roberta Lynn Bondar was born in Sault Sainte Marie, Ontario. She earned a medical degree from McMaster University in Hamilton in 1977. Her medical specialty is *neurology (nu ROL uh jee),* the study of the nervous system and its diseases. Bondar served as an astronaut from 1983 to 1992. After leaving the astronaut program, Bondar used her experience to educate people about science. From 2003 to 2009, she served as the chancellor of Trent University in Peterborough, Ontario.

Other articles to read include: **Aerospace medicine; Astronaut; Space exploration.**

Roberta Bondar

Brahe, Tycho

Tycho Brahe *(TEE koh BRAH hee)* (1546-1601) was a Danish *astronomer.* An astronomer is a scientist who studies objects in the universe beyond Earth. He was known by just his first name. Tycho felt that it was important to observe the planets and stars on a regular basis. The telescope had not yet been invented. Instead, Tycho used his eyes and simple instruments to figure the positions of objects in the sky. His observations were far more precise than those of any earlier astronomer.

Tycho's observations of the planets showed that the tables that were being used to predict their motions were not correct. In 1572, Tycho observed a *supernova* (type of exploding star). This observation helped show that there were changes in the sky beyond the moon's orbit. At the time, many people thought that the distant sky never changed.

Tycho Brahe

Continued on the next page

Brahe, Tycho *Continued from the previous page*

Like many astronomers of his time, Tycho did not believe that Earth and the other planets move around the sun. He believed that if Earth moved in this way, he would see changes in the positions of the stars. He did not realize that such changes were too small for his instruments to detect. But his observations later helped his one-time assistant, the German astronomer and mathematician Johannes Kepler, to confirm that Earth *revolves* (travels) around the sun.

Tycho was born in Knudstrup (then a Danish city but now in Sweden), near Malmo.

Other articles to read include: **Astronomy; Kepler, Johannes; Orbit; Planet; Supernova.**

A brown dwarf passes close to a much larger star, in an artist's illustration.

Brown dwarf

A brown dwarf is a dim heavenly body that has more *mass* than a planet but less mass than a star. Mass is the amount of matter in an object. Brown dwarfs are about the same size as the planet Jupiter. But they have from 13 to 75 times as much mass as Jupiter. Brown dwarfs are difficult to detect because they are so dim.

Stars and brown dwarfs form in the same way. A cloud of dust and gas shrinks under the force of gravity. A ball of gas forms at the cloud's center. As the cloud continues to shrink, the ball heats up. When the core of the ball becomes hot enough, simple hydrogen atoms begin to *fuse* (join together).

If the ball has enough mass—more than about 75 times the mass of Jupiter—fusion will continue. The object then becomes a star. If the ball has less mass, little fusion occurs. The object then becomes a brown dwarf.

The brown dwarf continues to shrink. *Electrons* (tiny particles that orbit the center of an atom) in the core of the brown dwarf push against each other more and more strongly. This pushing creates pressure that works against the force of gravity. Eventually, the pressure equals the force of gravity. The brown

Continued on the next page

dwarf stops shrinking and begins to cool. As it cools, fusion stops. The brown dwarf's temperature continues to drop, and its glow slowly fades.

Since the 1970's, astronomers had predicted that a large number of brown dwarfs exist. But astronomers were not certain that they had discovered any until 1995. Some scientists believe the number of brown dwarfs in the universe may be similar to the number of stars.

Other articles to read include: **Gravitation; Jupiter; Red dwarf; Star.**

Callisto

Callisto *(kuh LIHS toh)* is a large moon of Jupiter. Callisto is almost as large as the planet Mercury. It is Jupiter's second-largest moon behind Ganymede. It is also the third-largest moon in the solar system behind Ganymede and Titan, Saturn's largest moon. Callisto is 2,996 miles (4,821 kilometers) in diameter. It *orbits* (travels around) Jupiter every 16.7 Earth days at a distance of 1,170,000 miles (1,883,000 kilometers).

NASA's Voyager 2 space probe captured this image of Callisto while passing by Jupiter in 1979.

Comets and *asteroids (AS tuh royds)* have been crashing into Callisto for more than 4 billion years. As a result, the moon has more *craters* than almost any other body in the solar system. Craters are bowl-shaped holes in the ground. A comet is a big chunk of ice and dust in space. An asteroid is a large chunk of rock in space. Because of this bombardment, large parts of Callisto's icy surface are covered by dark dirt. The dirt comes from crumbled crater rims and cliffs. However, Callisto is still twice as bright as Earth's moon.

Some scientists think there may be an ocean of salty water beneath Callisto's surface. Measurements taken by spacecraft show that Callisto acts as if it is covered by a shell that is *conducting* (carrying) electric current. Scientists suspect that the "shell" is actually an ocean of salty liquid water beneath the surface. Scientists are trying to determine how such an ocean could have formed and why it would not have frozen by now.

Callisto was named after a follower of Artemis, the Greek goddess of wild animals and hunting. Callisto and three other moons of Jupiter are known as the *Galilean satellites.* They were discovered by Italian astronomer Galileo Galilei in 1610.

Other articles to read include: **Asteroid; Comet; Galileo** (scientist); **Ganymede; Impact crater; Jupiter; Satellite.**

Canadian astronaut Chris Hadfield (foreground) poses in one of the laboratories of the International Space Station with American astronaut Tom Marshburn.

Canadian Space Agency

The Canadian Space Agency (CSA) is the government agency that is responsible for Canada's space program. The agency was created in 1989. Its headquarters are in St.-Hubert, Quebec, southeast of Montreal.

The CSA has five major areas: (1) Space Science, (2) Space Technologies, (3) Satellite Communications, (4) Earth and Environment, and (5) Human Presence in Space. Space Science researchers investigate such subjects as climate change and air pollution. They also study the development of living things and the growth of crystals in space. Space Technologies workers develop new technologies for use in space. They may later use these technologies to create products for use on Earth. Other activities include assembling and testing satellites and other spacecraft. This work takes place at the CSA's David Florida Laboratory in Ottawa, Ontario. Satellite Communications researchers help to develop new communications technologies. They also monitor the demand for satellite communications.

Scientists working in the Earth and Environment division study Earth's surface. They *monitor* (keep track of) the condition of natural resources and conduct research on the *atmosphere* (blanket

Continued on the next page

of air around Earth). They use equipment such as RADARSAT, Canada's Earth-observing satellite. RADARSAT, launched in 1995, scans the surface of Earth to help create maps. In 1997, RADARSAT became the first satellite to scan and map all of Antarctica. The mapping project has provided much valuable data, including information on *ice streams* (currents of ice that flow like rivers through the surrounding ice sheet). RADARSAT images showed, for example, that ice streams travel great distances at speeds up to 3,000 feet (900 meters) per year. This information has helped scientists who are studying global warming.

The Human Presence in Space division includes Canada's astronaut program and the country's projects for the International Space Station (ISS). Canada selected its first astronauts in 1983. In 1984, Marc Garneau became the first Canadian to fly in space. In 1992, Roberta Bondar became the first Canadian woman in space. In 1999, Julie Payette became the first Canadian to board the ISS.

In 1981, Canada developed a robotic arm called the *Remote Manipulator System,* also known as the *Canadarm.* This device became an important part of the space shuttle program of the United States. The arm was mounted in the shuttle's payload bay. It was used to release, capture, and move satellites. Astronauts also used the Canadarm as a mobile work platform. In the late 1990's, Canada designed a new, more advanced arm for use on the ISS.

Other articles to read include: **Astronaut; Bondar, Roberta; Garneau, Marc; Space exploration.**

Cancer

Cancer is a *constellation* (grouping of stars) in the night sky. It is also known as the Crab. The word *cancer* means *crab* in the Latin language. Cancer can be seen from much of the Northern Hemisphere. It is best viewed from January to April.

Cancer is often drawn with five stars. Lines can be drawn from a central star to three other stars. One of these lines passes through a fifth star. The stars in Cancer are all fairly dim. Bright city lights can make Cancer difficult to see.

Other articles to read include: **Astrology; Constellation; Zodiac.**

Cancer, the Crab, is a constellation of the Northern Hemisphere. But it is difficult to see in brightly lit cities.

Annie Jump Cannon

Cannon, Annie Jump

Annie Jump Cannon (1863–1941) was one of the leading American *astronomers* of her time. An astronomer is a scientist who studies the sky and objects beyond Earth.

In 1896, she joined the staff of the Harvard College Observatory. With other astronomers there, she developed a way to classify stars by the color of the light they give off. She used it to classify over 350,000 stars. Cannon's classification system is still in use today. Cannon also discovered 300 *variable stars* (stars that change in brightness), five *novae* (types of exploding stars), and a *binary star.* A binary star is a pair of stars that orbit each other. They are held close together by gravity.

In 1925, Cannon became the first woman to receive an honorary doctorate degree in science from Oxford University in the United Kingdom. She was born in Dover, Delaware.

Other articles to read include: **Astronomy; Binary star; Star.**

Canopus (right) is the third brightest star as seen from Earth. Only the sun and Sirius are brighter.

Canopus

Canopus *(kah NOH pus)* ranks as the third-brightest star in Earth's night sky. Only the sun and Sirius appear brighter. Canopus is the brightest star in the constellation Carina, the Keel. Canopus is also known as Alpha Carinae. Historians do not know the origin of the name *Canopus.* Canopus lies in the southern sky but can be seen from as far north as the southern United States and the northern coast of Africa.

Canopus is an extremely large type of star called a *yellow-white supergiant.* Its yellow-white appearance results from a high surface temperature of nearly 14,500 °F (8,000 °C). Because of its large size, Canopus gives off nearly 15,000 times as much light as the sun.

Astronomers do not fully understand how yellow-white supergiants form, but the stars seem to be related to large, relatively cool stars called *red giants.* Canopus may once have been a red giant, or it may be in the process of becoming a red giant.

Other articles to read include: **Red giant; Sirius; Star.**

Capricornus

Capricornus is a *constellation* (grouping of stars) in Earth's night sky. It represents a mythical creature that has the head of a goat and the tail of a fish. Capricornus can be seen from much of the Southern Hemisphere. It is best viewed from July through September.

Capricornus can be drawn in several ways. In many of these drawings, the stars form a triangle. The triangle represents the creature's body.

Capricornus was among the 48 constellations defined by the ancient Greek mathematician Ptolemy. Today, it is one of 88 constellations recognized by the International Astronomical Union (IAU). The IAU is the leading authority in the naming of heavenly objects.

The Tropic of Capricorn is named for Capricornus. The tropic is an imaginary line that traces the southern boundary of Earth's Tropical Zone. The constellation is found almost directly above the Tropic of Capricorn.

Capricornus is also known as Capricorn. Capricorn is a sign of the *zodiac.* The zodiac is a set of constellations used in a kind of fortunetelling called *astrology.*

Other articles to read include: **Astrology; Constellation; Ptolemy; Zodiac.**

Capricornus is a constellation seen from much of the Southern Hemisphere. It represents a mythical beast that is half goat and half fish.

Cassini

Cassini is a spacecraft sent to Saturn to study the planet and its rings and satellites. Since going into orbit around Saturn in 2004, Cassini has provided us with the most spectacular images as well as the most detailed information ever collected about Saturn. Cassini has also studied Saturn's *magnetosphere,* a zone of strong *magnetic fields* originating in the planet. A magnetic field is the influence that a magnet—in this case, the planet—creates in the region around it. NASA, the United States space agency, launched Cassini on October 15, 1997.

Engineers and scientists at NASA's Jet Propulsion Laboratory built Cassini. The Italian Space Agency provided a large antenna

Continued on the next page

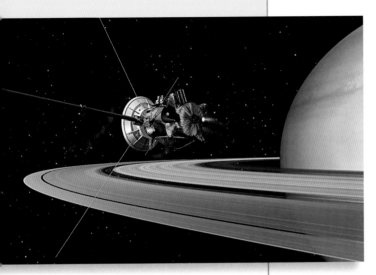

The Cassini probe began orbiting Saturn in 2004.

Cassini *Continued from the previous page*

and several other elements of the spacecraft. The craft was named for the Italian-born French astronomer Giovanni Domenico Cassini, who made major discoveries about Saturn in the late 1600's.

Cassini carried a probe called Huygens *(HOY gehns)*. The European Space Agency designed and built Huygens to drop into the atmosphere of Titan, Saturn's largest satellite. The probe was equipped to study Titan's atmosphere and surface. The probe was named for the Dutch physicist, astronomer, and mathematician Christiaan Huygens, who discovered Titan in 1655.

Some of Cassini's studies have focused on Saturn's *atmosphere* (blanket of gases) and interior. Other observations have revealed lakes on Titan and erupting geysers on another moon, Enceladus. Cassini has also investigated the rings and smaller moons to help scientists understand the origin and evolution of the satellite and ring system. In 2006, Cassini found evidence of tiny "moonlets" orbiting inside the rings.

Cassini and Huygens have studied Titan closely for two reasons: (1) it is one of the largest satellites in the solar system, and (2) it has the thickest atmosphere of any moon. Titan's atmosphere consists mostly of nitrogen and has a thick, smoglike haze. Visible light cannot pass through the haze, so Cassini carries a radar that can penetrate the atmosphere. The spacecraft

Continued on the next page

A dark red area (right), in a false-color image of Saturn taken by Cassini, marks the eye of a monster storm that covers the planet's north pole. Framing the eye, which is 1,250 miles (2,000 kilometers) across, is a *hexagonal* (six-sided) system of winds (yellow-green). Winds in the lower clouds of the storm (red, far right), shown in a closer view by Cassini, blow at more than 330 miles (150 meters) per hour.

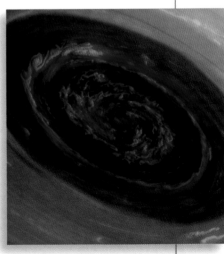

also has cameras equipped with special light filters that enable them to photograph Titan's surface.

On December 25, 2004, Cassini released Huygens. It arrived at Titan's atmosphere on January 14, 2005. For 2 ½ hours, the probe analyzed chemicals, recorded sounds, and measured winds as it parachuted toward the surface. Titan's haze cleared at an altitude of about 20 miles (30 kilometers). The probe's cameras were then able to photograph Titan's surface. The images revealed a landscape that appeared to have been carved by rains of liquid methane and ethane. On touching down, Huygens became the first craft to land on a satellite of a planet other than Earth.

Many scientists believe chemicals on the surface of Titan, called *organic chemicals* (chemicals with carbon), may be able to support life. Cassini also found evidence of an ocean of liquid water beneath Titan's surface. Liquid water is used by all living things on Earth to survive. The water raises the possibility of life evolving in this underground ocean.

After Cassini completed its primary mission in 2008, NASA granted it two mission extensions. The first extension allowed the spacecraft to continue collecting data until 2010. The second and final extension will fund the Cassini mission until 2017. Cassini's final duty will be a controlled "crash" into Saturn's surface.

Other articles to read include: **Cassini, Giovanni Domenico; European Space Agency; National Aeronautics and Space Administration; Ring; Satellite; Saturn; Space exploration; Titan.**

Saturn's rings glow against the blackness of space in a false-color image (above left) taken in ultraviolet light by Cassini. The red areas represent thinner rings that likely have more particles of dust and rock than the icier rings colored in turquoise. Saturn and its rings appear in their natural color (above) in a composite photograph made from 45 images taken by Cassini. The shadow cast by the giant planet covers the rings on the side turned away from the sun.

Titan seems to be strung like a gem on Saturn's rings in an image showing the rings edge-on. The colored bands below Titan are shadows cast by the ring system.

Giovanni Cassini

Cassini, Giovanni Domenico

Giovanni Domenico Cassini (1625–1712) was an Italian-born French *astronomer.* Astronomers study the sky and objects beyond Earth. Cassini discovered four moons of the planet Saturn. He also discovered a large gap in Saturn's rings that is now known as the *Cassini division.* A United States space probe was named after Cassini. The probe has helped scientists understand the origin and history of Saturn's satellite and ring system.

Cassini also became known for creating tables of the sun's movement through the sky. Later, he calculated the distance between Earth and the sun. Cassini's observations of Jupiter were so precise that he could tell the difference between shadows cast by moons of Jupiter and fixed shadows on Jupiter's surface. Cassini used the fixed shadows to determine the length of Jupiter's day.

Cassini was born in Perinaldo, in what is now northern Italy. In 1650, he became a professor of astronomy at the University of Bologna. He went to Paris in 1669 and became the first director of the Paris Observatory. He became a French citizen in 1673. Cassini is also known by the French name Jean Dominique Cassini.

Other articles to read include: **Astronomy; Cassini; Jupiter; Ring; Satellite; Saturn.**

The five brightest stars in the constellation Cassiopeia form the letter W.

Cassiopeia

Cassiopeia *(KAS ee uh PEE uh)* is a *constellation* (grouping of stars) in Earth's night sky. It can be seen easily from the Northern Hemisphere. Cassiopeia is on the side of the North Star opposite the Big Dipper. It is about the same distance from the North Star as that constellation. Five of the brightest stars in Cassiopeia form a large letter W.

Cassiopeia lies directly north of the constellation of Andromeda. In Greek mythology, Cassiopeia was the mother of Andromeda, who was rescued from a sea monster by the hero Perseus.

Other articles to read include: **Andromeda; Constellation; North Star.**

Ceres

Ceres is the largest *asteroid (AS tuh royd)* in the Main Belt. An asteroid is a rocky or metallic object smaller than a planet that orbits a star. The Main Belt is an area with many asteroids between the orbits of Mars and Jupiter. There are probably hundreds of thousands of asteroids there.

Ceres accounts for more than one-fourth of the total *mass* (amount of matter) of the Main Belt asteroids. In fact, Ceres has enough mass to be considered a *dwarf planet*. Ceres probably formed early in the history of the solar system from many smaller bodies that collided and stuck together. But scientists think the gravitational influence of Jupiter prevented Ceres from growing to the size of a planet.

Ceres's shape resembles a slightly squashed sphere. It has a fairly smooth, rocky surface. It orbits the sun about every 4 Earth years. Ceres's average distance from the sun is about 257 million miles (414 million kilometers).

Ceres is named for the Roman goddess of agriculture. It was the first asteroid discovered. The Italian astronomer Giuseppe Piazzi found it by chance in 1801.

In 2007, NASA, the United States space agency, launched the Dawn spacecraft to study Ceres and another asteroid named Vesta. The craft orbited Vesta in 2011 and 2012. Dawn was expected to reach Ceres in 2015.

Other articles to read include: **Asteroid; Dawn; Dwarf planet; Main Belt.**

Studies of the asteroid Ceres (shown in an image taken by the Hubble Space Telescope) will help astronomers learn more about the history of the solar system.

Challenger disaster

The Challenger disaster was a deadly space shuttle accident. It was one of the worst accidents in the history of space flight.

On January 28, 1986, the space shuttle Challenger launched from the Kennedy Space Center in Florida. The trouble began about four minutes into the flight. A problem in one of the rocket engines led the shuttle to break apart in midair. The pieces landed in the Atlantic Ocean.

Continued on the next page

Challenger disaster *Continued from the previous page*

The 1986 Challenger disaster took the lives of seven astronauts, including school teacher Christa McAuliffe (top row, second from the left).

None of the seven crew members survived the accident. The crew included the first schoolteacher to fly on a shuttle, Christa McAuliffe, and the first Asian-American astronaut, Ellison Onizuka. The other crew members were Francis R. (Dick) Scobee, Michael J. Smith, Judith A. Resnik, Ronald E. McNair, and Gregory B. Jarvis.

Investigators traced the cause of the accident to a problem with a seal called an O ring. Investigators also determined that launch officials had ignored warnings that the seals had not been tested at low temperatures. The accident prompted a long investigation into possible flaws in the shuttle. Space shuttles did not start flying again until September 29, 1988.

Other articles to read include: **Columbia disaster; McAuliffe, Christa; Onizuka, Ellison Shoji; Space exploration.**

Chandra X-ray Observatory

The Chandra *(SHAHN druh)* X-ray Observatory is an *artificial satellite.* An artificial satellite is a human-made object that *orbits* (circles) another body, in this case, Earth. Chandra carries an X-ray telescope and two cameras. The observatory was built to study and collect X rays given off by gas that has been heated to millions of degrees. Sources of these X rays include *supernovae* (exploding stars), colliding galaxies, and matter swirling around *black holes.* A black hole is an object whose gravitational pull is so strong nothing can escape it. In December 1999, Chandra produced evidence that tens of millions of galaxies have huge black holes at their centers. Chandra has also helped scientists learn more about how stars and galaxies form.

Continued on the next page

The Chandra X-ray Observatory was named for the Indian-born American *astrophysicist (AS troh FIHZ uh sihst)* Subrahmanyan Chandrasekhar *(SU brah MAN yuhn SHAHN druh SAY kahr)*. An astrophysicist studies stars and other objects in space. NASA, the United States space agency, launched Chandra from the space shuttle Columbia on July 23, 1999.

Other articles to read include: **Black hole; Chandrasekhar, Subrahmanyan; Observatory; Space exploration; Supernova; Telescope.**

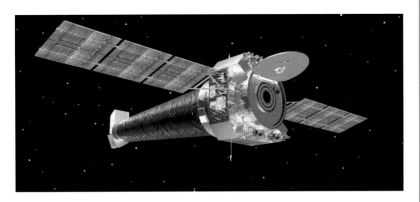

The Chandra X-ray Observatory was launched by space shuttle Columbia in 1999. Chandra was designed to detect X rays from high-energy areas of the universe.

Chandrasekhar, Subrahmanyan

Subrahmanyan Chandrasekhar *(SU brah MAN yuhn SHAHN druh SAY kahr)* (1910–1995) was an American *astrophysicist (as troh FIHZ uh sihst)*. An astrophysicist is a scientist who studies objects in space. Chandrasekhar shared the 1983 Nobel Prize in physics with William A. Fowler. They won for their research on how stars change and eventually die.

Chandrasekhar is best known for his work on *white dwarf stars.* White dwarfs are slowly cooling stars at the end of their life. They are very heavy, shrunken stars.

Many white dwarf stars are part of a *binary star.* A binary star is two stars that closely orbit each other. Sometimes, a white dwarf in a binary will pull matter from its companion star. Chandrasekhar discovered that white dwarfs that steal enough matter to become larger than 1.4 times the size of our sun collapse from their own gravitation. After they collapse, they

Continued on the next page

Subrahmanyan Chandrasekhar

Chandrasekhar, Subrahmanyan *Continued from the previous page*

explode in an event called a *supernova*. Eventually, they become *neutron (NOO tron) stars*. A neutron star is the smallest and densest type of star known.

Chandrasekhar went by the nickname Chandra *(SHAHN druh)*. He was born in Lahore, in what is now Pakistan. The Chandra X-ray Observatory was named in his honor. NASA, the United States space agency, launched the Chandra X-ray Observatory on July 23, 1999.

Other articles to read include: **Binary star; Chandra X-ray Observatory; Neutron star; Supernova; White dwarf.**

Chang-Díaz, Franklin

Franklin Chang-Díaz (1950-) was a United States astronaut. He became the first Hispanic-American to travel in space. He flew on seven NASA space shuttle missions between 1986 and 2002.

Ever since he was a young child, he knew he wanted to become an astronaut. In 1968, he moved to the United States to follow his dream. Chang-Díaz lived with relatives in Hartford, Connecticut. In 1973, he received a bachelor's degree in mechanical engineering from the University of Connecticut. Chang-Díaz earned a doctor's degree in applied plasma physics from the Massachusetts Institute of Technology (MIT) in 1977, the same year he became a U.S. citizen. Chiang-Díaz joined the astronaut program in 1980. From 1993 to 2005, he was director of the Advanced Space Propulsion Laboratory at the Johnson Space Center in Houston. He then retired from NASA and started his own rocket engine company.

Other articles to read include: **Astronaut; Space exploration.**

Franklin Chang-Díaz

China National Space Administration

The China National Space Administration is a government agency that is in charge of space flight for the People's Republic of China. The agency oversees the development and use of space technology. It has launched many missions. Astronauts in the Chinese space program are sometimes called *taikonauts*.

The agency was created in 1993. However, China has had a space program since the 1950's. In April 1970, China sent its first satellite into space aboard a CZ-1 launcher. In the 1980's, China developed impressive space technology that included liquid-hydrogen engines, powerful Long March rockets, and recoverable satellites. China has three satellite launch sites.

In the 1990's, China began developing the Shenzhou, a spacecraft designed to carry astronauts. The Shenzhou resembles Russia's Soyuz capsule. In October 2003, China became the third nation to launch a person into space. Chinese astronaut Yang Liwei orbited Earth aboard a Shenzhou craft for 21 hours before landing safely. Another Shenzhou craft carried two astronauts into orbit on a five-day mission in October 2005. On the third piloted Shenzhou flight in September 2008, two astronauts performed the country's first spacewalk.

China took a big step in its plan to place a new space station in orbit by around 2020 with the first piloted docking of two Chinese spacecraft. The Shenzhou 9 capsule docked with the Tiangong-1 mini-station on June 18, 2012, for a 10-day mission. Its three-member crew included China's first woman taikonaut, 34-year-old Yang Liu. A veteran military-transport pilot, Liu conducted life-science experiments and practiced tai chi, an ancient Chinese form of exercise, during her stay in orbit.

Other articles to read include: **Astronaut; Space exploration; Yang Liwei.**

Chinese astronauts Wang Liu, Yang Liu, and Haipeng Jing (right to left in photo) speak to a television audience from the orbiting Tiangong-1 space module on June 18, 2012. The module is a small orbiting space station.

Arthur C. Clarke

Clarke, Arthur C.

Arthur C. Clarke (1917-2008) was a British-born author of science fiction and related nonfiction. Clarke's novels are noted for their scientific accuracy and advanced technology, including space elevators and ships designed for space voyages that last for generations. He described communications satellites years before people could reach space. Clarke's book *The Exploration of Space* (1951) helped make the idea of space travel popular in the 1950's.

Clarke's novels include *Childhood's End* (1953), his finest single work; *The City and the Stars* (1956); *Rendezvous with Rama* (1973); and *The Fountains of Paradise* (1979). His nonfiction works include *Interplanetary Flight* (1950), *The Challenge of the Sea* (1960), *Profiles of the Future* (1962), *The View from Serendip* (1977), and *Astounding Days: A Science Fiction Autobiography* (1990).

With film director Stanley Kubrick, Clarke wrote the screenplay for the motion picture *2001: A Space Odyssey* (1968). He continued the series with the novels *2010: Odyssey Two* (1982), *2061: Odyssey Three* (1988), and *3001: The Final Odyssey* (1997). His short fiction was published in *Collected Stories* (2001).

Arthur Charles Clarke was born in Somerset County, England. He became a science fiction fan as a teenager. In the mid-1950's, he settled in Ceylon (now Sri Lanka), to pursue his love of scuba diving. In 1998, he was knighted by Queen Elizabeth II and thus became known as Sir Arthur Clarke.

Other articles to read include: **Communications satellite; Space exploration.**

Collins, Eileen Marie

Collins, Eileen Marie (1956-), is the first woman to command a United States space shuttle. She commanded the shuttle Columbia on a flight from July 23 to 28, 1999. During the flight, the shuttle launched the Chandra X-ray Observatory, an orbiting telescope. Collins also commanded the shuttle Discovery from July 26 to August 9, 2005, the program's first flight following the 2003 Columbia disaster.

Continued on the next page

Collins was born in Elmira, New York. She earned a bachelor's degree in mathematics and economics from Syracuse University in 1978. She also earned two master's degrees, one in operations research from Stanford University in 1986 and one in space systems management from Webster University in 1989.

Collins enlisted in the U.S. Air Force in 1978. Before becoming an astronaut in 1991, she worked as a test pilot and as a math instructor at the Air Force Academy. She retired from the Air Force in 2005, having reached the rank of colonel, and retired from the astronaut program in 2006.

Other articles to read include: **Astronaut; Columbia disaster; Space exploration.**

Eileen Collins

Collins, Michael

Michael Collins (1930-) is an American astronaut who is best known as a member of the Apollo 11 mission. That mission was the first to put people on the surface of the moon. Collins piloted the command module, *Columbia,* as it orbited the moon. His fellow astronauts, Neil A. Armstrong and Buzz Aldrin, landed on the moon on July 20, 1969.

Collins was born in Rome, Italy. He graduated from the United States Military Academy in West Point, New York, in 1952 and became an Air Force officer. He became an astronaut in 1963. Collins piloted the Gemini 10 space flight in 1966. He resigned from the astronaut program in 1969. From 1971 to 1978, Collins was director of the Smithsonian Institution's National Air and Space Museum. Collins has written several books about space travel. *Carrying the Fire: An Astronaut's Journeys* (1974) is a memoir of his experiences as an astronaut.

Other articles to read include: **Armstrong, Neil Alden; Astronaut; Moon; Space exploration.**

Michael Collins

Seven astronauts died during the Columbia disaster, including the first Israeli astronaut, Ilan Ramon (far right in photo).

Columbia disaster

The Columbia disaster was a major space shuttle accident take took place on February 1, 2003. It was the second shuttle accident to end in death. The first was the Challenger accident in 1986.

The space shuttle Columbia broke apart over Texas while returning to Earth from a 16-day mission. All seven crew members died. The crew included Ilan Ramon, the first Israeli astronaut; Rick D. Husband; William C. McCool; Michael P. Anderson; Kalpana Chawla; David M. Brown; and Laurel Blair Salton Clark.

The accident led to a long investigation. Investigators found that a wing of the shuttle had been hit by a chunk of foam during take-off. The foam fell off the shuttle's *external* (outside) fuel tank and made a small hole in the wing. As the shuttle returned to Earth, the hole got worse. The wing failed, leading the shuttle to tumble out of control and break apart.

Officials halted shuttle launches until July 26, 2005. They developed procedures and tools that could reduce such accidents in the future and ways to repair the shuttle while it was in space.

Other articles to read include: **Challenger disaster; Space exploration.**

Comet

A comet is an icy object in space that releases gas or dust. Comets move around the sun in a long, *elliptical* (oval) path.

A comet has a solid *nucleus* (core) made of ice and rocky dust particles. It is like a dirty snowball. The nucleus is surrounded by a cloudy atmosphere called the *coma*. A comet also has one or two tails that appear when it gets near the sun. The sun's heat turns some of the ice into gas. The gas and bits of rock stuck in the ice form the comet's tail.

The nucleus of most comets is around 10 miles (16 kilometers) in diameter. Some comas can be nearly 1 million miles (1.6

Continued on the next page

million kilometers) across. Some comet tails extend to distances of over 300 million miles (480 million kilometers).

Astronomers (scientists who study outer space) believe that comets are leftover *debris (duh BREE)* (rock and dust) from the formation of the planets of the solar system about 4.6 billion years ago. Some scientists believe that comets originally brought to Earth some of the water and compounds that make up living things.

Astronomers classify comets according to how long they take to orbit the sun. Short-period comets need less than 200 years to complete one orbit. Long-period comets take 200 years or longer. Scientists think that short-period comets come from a band of objects called the *Kuiper belt.* The belt lies beyond the orbit of Neptune. The gravitational pull of the outer planets can nudge objects out of the Kuiper belt and into the inner solar system. There, they become active comets.

Long-period comets come from the *Oort cloud.* The Oort cloud is a ball-like collection of icy bodies about 5,000 times farther away from the sun than Earth's orbit. The gravity of passing stars can cause icy bodies in the Oort cloud to enter the inner solar system and become active comets.

Comets lose ice and dust each time they return to the inner solar system. They leave behind trails of debris. When Earth passes through one of these trails, the debris becomes meteors that burn up in the *atmosphere* (blanket of air around Earth). Eventually, some comets lose all their ice. They break up and scatter into clouds of dust. Or they turn into fragile objects similar to asteroids.

You need a telescope to see most comets. Some comets can be seen from Earth without a telescope when they come close to the sun. At that point, the sunlight makes the dust in the comet shine.

Halley's Comet, the most famous comet, passes by Earth about every 76 years. In 1986, the last time it was near Earth, five spacecraft flew past the comet. They collected a great deal of information to help scientists learn more about comets.

Comet McNaught spreads its dazzling tail across the night sky in an image made by the European Southern Observatory in Chile in 2007. McNaught was the brightest comet visible from Earth in 40 years.

Continued on the next page

Comet *Continued from the previous page*

In 2004, the European Space Agency launched the Rosetta spacecraft. It was to go into orbit around Comet Churyumov-Gerasimenko in 2014. Rosetta carried a small probe designed to land on the comet's nucleus.

In 2005, the United States launched the Deep Impact spacecraft to Comet Tempel 1 as it neared the sun. The craft consisted of two smaller probes: an impactor and a flyby craft. In July, the impactor intentionally slammed into the nucleus. Moments before the collision, the probe took never-before-seen, close-up photos of the nucleus's rough, cratered surface. The flyby craft recorded the crash. The collision *vaporized* (turned to gas) the impactor and produced a brilliant plume of dust. The appearance of the plume suggested that the nucleus's surface consists of dry, powdery dust grains loosely held together by gravity.

Other articles to read include: **Halley's Comet; Kuiper belt; Oort cloud; Solar system.**

Communications satellite

A communications satellite is a spacecraft that orbits Earth. It receives radio, television, and other signals. It then relays the signals back to Earth.

From high above Earth, a satellite can direct the signals over a large area. Without satellites, most radio transmissions could not reach far beyond the horizon. Satellites can direct radio waves to such *remote* (hard-to-reach) areas as the middle of a desert or an ocean. A satellite can also send a message to many places at once.

Early communications satellites carried long-distance telephone calls. Satellites still perform this task. They provide service to places that have no access to telephone wires or cell phone service.

Communications satellites play a major role in television broadcasting. Satellites deliver programs to local cable TV companies. They also send signals directly to homes through satellite TV services. Satellites can also send and receive Internet signals. Many stores and gas stations use satellites to approve credit card sales.

Continued on the next page

There are two main types of communications satellites, based on their orbits—geostationary *(JEE oh STAY shuh NEHR ee)* orbit satellites, called GEOSAT's and low-Earth-orbit satellites, called LEOSAT's. A GEOSAT orbits about 22,300 miles (35,900 kilometers) above the *equator* (imaginary line around Earth's middle). GEOSAT's circle Earth in a *geostationary orbit.* Such an orbit matches the rate at which Earth spins. A station on Earth can communicate with a satellite only while it is overhead. A GEOSAT stays over the same point. So it remains within range of its station and does not need to be tracked.

A LEOSAT flies lower and faster than a GEOSAT. LEOSAT's may be only 200 to 500 miles (320 to 800 kilometers) above the ground. They may orbit Earth about every two or three hours and must be tracked by stations. LEOSAT's can be smaller, cheaper, less powerful, and easier to launch than GEOSAT's because they are closer to the ground. But a LEOSAT may be in tracking range of a station for only a short time. Once a tracking station loses contact, the signal is interrupted. Some services, such as electronic mail, can operate with interruptions. Other services, such as TV and telephones, cannot. To provide uninterrupted service, a LEOSAT system must have a number of satellites. The satellites pass the signal to one another as they move out of range of a tracking station.

Communications satellites fire small rockets occasionally to stay in the correct orbit. This process is called *station keeping.* A satellite's lifetime is limited by the amount of rocket fuel it can carry. Most satellites last from 7 to 15 years.

Arthur C. Clarke, a British science-fiction writer, is credited with inventing the idea of communications satellites. In a 1945 article, he described a satellite in geostationary orbit that could serve as a relay station in the sky. The first communications satellite, Score, was launched on December 18, 1958. It broadcast a taped greeting from United States President Dwight D. Eisenhower. Echo 1 was the first satellite to relay voice messages from one place to another. It was launched on August 12, 1960. The American Telephone and Telegraph Company (now part of AT&T Inc.) launched Telstar 1 on July 10, 1962. Satellite TV and radio services became popular in the 1990's and 2000's.

Other articles to read include: **Clarke, Arthur C.; Satellite, Artificial.**

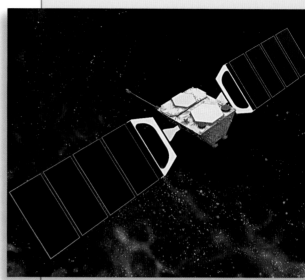

Communications satellites, such as the LEO satellite seen here, enable instant worldwide communication.

Compton Gamma Ray Observatory

The Compton Gamma Ray Observatory is released into orbit from the space shuttle Atlantis in 1991.

Compton Gamma Ray Observatory was an artificial satellite used to study *gamma rays* from space. Gamma rays are an invisible, powerful form of light. They are given off by a wide variety of heavenly bodies, including the sun and *quasars* (the extremely bright cores of some galaxies). The Compton Gamma Ray Observatory discovered many new sources of gamma rays in the sky. But astronomers have not learned what kind of heavenly body these rays came from.

Astronomers (scientists who study outer space) use Earth-orbiting telescopes to study gamma rays from space because Earth's atmosphere *absorbs* (takes in) most of these rays. Telescopes built to detect *visible light* (light we can see) use lenses or mirrors. But gamma rays are so powerful that they pass right through most materials. A gamma-ray telescope uses a special detector.

NASA, the United States space agency, launched the Compton telescope from the space shuttle Atlantis in 1991. The observatory was named for American physicist Arthur H. Compton, who shared the 1927 Nobel Prize for physics. He received the award for his work with X rays, which are smiliar to gamma rays.

In June 2000, NASA deliberately destroyed the Compton telescope by directing it back to Earth. As the satellite descended, much of it burned in the atmosphere (blanket of air around Earth). The remaining parts splashed down in the Pacific Ocean. Officials at NASA decided to end the observatory's mission after the ability to control the telescope became threatened. Engineers had determined that the satellite could go out of control and crash into a populated area.

The Compton Gamma Ray Observatory was the second of NASA's four "Great Observatories" to go into orbit. The others are the Hubble Space Telescope, which was launched in 1990; the Chandra X-ray Observatory, launched in 1999; and the Spitzer Space Telescope Facility, launched in 2003.

Other articles to read include: **Gamma rays; Hubble Space Telescope; Observatory; Satellite, Artificial; Telescope.**

Constellation

A constellation is a grouping of stars in a particular part of the night sky. The word *constellation* can also mean the part of the sky around a group of stars. The ancient Greek mathematician Ptolemy grouped the stars into 48 constellations. Modern *astronomers* (scientists who study outer space) have divided the sky into 88 constellations.

Stars that make up constellations appear to be the same distance from Earth, but they are not. For example, the stars in the Big Dipper range from about 60 to 120 *light-years* from Earth. A light-year is the distance light can travel in a vacuum in one year. It is equal to about 5.88 trillion miles (9.46 trillion kilometers). The stars in a constellation appear to be the same distance from Earth because they are so far away and appear in the same area of the sky.

Down through history, many groups of people throughout the world have named patterns in the sky. These groups include the ancient Chinese, Native Americans, and the Aborigines of Australia. The ancient Greeks, Romans, and people of various other early civilizations observed groups of stars in the northern two-thirds of the sky. They named the star-groups after animals, gods, and characters in stories. For example, the constellation Leo was named for a lion. The constellation Andromeda was named after a heroine in an ancient Greek story.

Between the 1400's and 1700's, Europeans explored the southern part of the world. Mapmakers and explorers named the star groups they could see in the southernmost third of the sky. For example, the constellation Telescopium was named for the telescope. Tucana was named for the toucan, a large-billed bird of Central and South America.

Some constellations can be seen only during certain seasons. That is because of changes in the tilt of Earth's *axis* during the year. The

Continued on the next page

The stars in the Big Dipper range from about 60 to 120 light-years from Earth. They only appear to be the same distance from us.

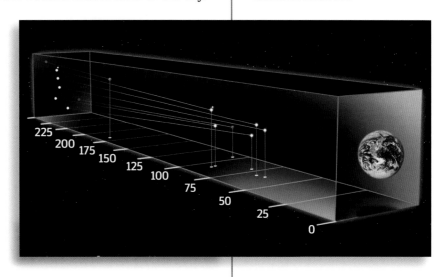

Constellation *Continued from the previous page*

axis is an imaginary line that passes through Earth from the North Pole to the South Pole. People in different parts of the world also see different parts of the sky. Their view depends on their distance north or south of the *equator* (imaginary line around the middle of Earth). People at the equator can see all the constellations during the course of a year.

Other articles to read include: **Star; Zodiac;** *and those on individual constellations.*

Copernicus, Nicolaus

Nicolaus Copernicus *(NIHK uh LAY uhs koh PUR nuh kuhs)* (1473–1543), was a Polish *astronomer.* An astronomer is a scientist who studies the stars, planets, and other parts of the universe. Copernicus became famous for explaining that Earth is a spinning planet that travels around the sun. These motions make the sun, the other planets, and the stars appear to move in the sky. Copernicus changed the way people think about the universe and their place in it. He is considered the founder of modern astronomy.

In Copernicus's time, most astronomers thought that Earth was the center of the universe. They also thought our planet remained motionless in space. The Greek astronomer *Ptolemy (TOL uh mee)* had developed this idea in the A.D. 100's. According to Ptolemy, the other heavenly bodies moved around Earth. But he could not really explain certain unusual motions of the planets across the sky. Ptolemy explained these motions using a complicated system of circles. However, Copernicus realized that this explanation was not accurate.

Nicolaus Copernicus

Continued on the next page

Some astronomers before Ptolemy had suggested that Earth did in fact move. In the 200's B.C., the Greek astronomer Aristarchus *(AR ih STAHR kuhs)* had even suggested that Earth and the other planets moved around the sun. By Ptolemy's time, these theories had been rejected. But Copernicus knew about some of them.

In 1543, Copernicus explained his ideas in a book, *On the Revolutions of the Heavenly Spheres.* This book explained that Earth travels around the sun once a year and that Earth spins around once a day. Copernicus died on May 24, 1543, about two months after his book was printed. Later, scientists proved that Copernicus's explanation about Earth's motions was correct.

Other articles to read include: **Aristarchus; Astronomy; Galileo; Orbit; Planet; Ptolemy; Solar system.**

Corona

The corona *(kuh ROH nuh)* is the outer layer of the sun's atmosphere *(AT muh sfihr)*. It is also the hottest layer of the solar atmosphere. Temperatures there may reach 4,000,000 °F (2,200,000 °C).

The corona is visible without a telescope or other light-gathering device only during a total *solar eclipse* of the sun. An eclipse of the sun happens when the moon blocks our view of the sun. Then, the corona looks like a circle of light shining from behind the moon. A person should never look directly at a total eclipse without protection for the eyes. The light can damage the eyes.

The corona and other layers of the sun's atmosphere consist of gaslike substance called *plasma*. Plasma is made of electrically charged atoms called *ions* and electrically charged particles called *electrons* that form at extremely high temperatures. The corona continually expands into space, forming a flow of ionized particles called the *solar wind*.

The corona is extremely violent. Streaks of plasma known as *solar plumes* spread outward from the sun's poles. Long, gaseous rays called *coronal streamers* spread out from areas closer to the

The corona is visible only during a total solar eclipse of the sun. This image is a combination of an eclipse image and an image of the unblocked sun.

Continued on the next page

Corona   *Continued from the previous page*

equator (imaginary line around the sun's middle). About once every day, the sun throws off a huge ball of plasma known as a *coronal mass ejection.*

Astronomers (scientists who study stars and other objects in the universe) study the corona with special instruments from the ground and from space. One of these instruments is a type of telescope that blocks some of the sun's bright light. Other instruments can take pictures of the corona. The Japanese-led Hinode space mission began studying the corona in detail in 2006.

Other articles to read include: **Coronal mass ejection; Eclipse; Hinode; Solar wind; Sun.**

Coronal mass ejection

Coronal mass ejections (CME's) are gigantic eruptions of electrically charged material from the sun. A CME might release enough energy to supply Earth's commercial energy needs for more than 12,000 years. CME's are so large that when the front of the eruption reaches Earth, Mercury and Venus are still covered by its tail. A typical ejection leaves the sun at a speed of about 500 miles (800 kilometers) per second.

CME's are related to the *magnetic field* around the sun. A magnetic field is the space affected by the attraction power of a magnet. CME's occur when a large bubble or tube of magnetism erupts from below the surface of the sun. The magnetism sweeps a large amount of material into the atmosphere around the sun, called the *corona*, and out into space. These eruptions also increase the level of X rays being given off by the sun and create bursts of radio energy. The ejections create what scientists call *space weather*. If this material strikes Earth, it can damage satellites around the planet. If the ejection is large enough, it can damage electronic equipment on the ground. A CME that struck Earth in 1859 caused fires in telegraph transmission lines in the United States and Europe.

Continued on the next page

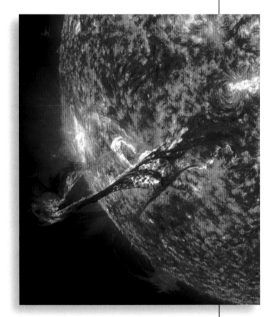

A coronal mass ejection can hurtle massive amounts of matter out into space. These bursts of matter pose a threat to electronic devices in space and on Earth.

Another ejection in 1989 shut down power in Quebec, Canada.

In 1997, scientists observed what looked like a circular wave on the sun's surface moving away from the spot where a CME had been produced. In 2007, astronomers confirmed the existence of these waves, sometimes called *solar tsunamis*. Scientists believe that the process responsible for producing CME's is also responsible for producing these huge waves. A solar tsunami observed in 2009 measured about 60,000 miles (100,000 kilometers) high and moved at a speed of about 560,000 miles (900,000 kilometers) per hour.

Other articles to read include: **Corona; Magnetic storm; Sun.**

COROT

COROT, *(kaw ROH),* is a space telescope. It is used to study the *interior* (insides) of distant stars and to search for planets outside the solar system. COROT was developed by France, the European Space Agency, and several other countries. It was launched in December 2006 and took its first images in January 2007. Mission planners intended COROT to operate for about 2 ½ years but the mission was extended.

COROT stands for *COnvection, ROtation,* and *planetary Transits.* Astronomers can learn about a star's interior by studying vibrations that begin within the star. The scientists use the information in much the same way that geologists use vibrations from earthquakes to learn about Earth's interior. In the case of a star, the vibrations produce tiny changes in brightness. Astronomers measure these variations to *model* (map) the interior of the star.

COROT also searches for planets outside the solar system, called *extrasolar planets* or *exoplanets.* The telescope does this by detecting the drop in brightness that occurs when an orbiting planet passes between its star and Earth. This event is known as a *transit.*

The COROT satellite, launched by the European Space Agency in 2006, is used to search for planets circling distant stars.

Continued on the next page

COROT *Continued from the previous page*

Astronomers have used transits to discover and study exoplanets with telescopes on Earth. But Earth's atmosphere changes the light that reaches the surface. This limits astronomers' ability to see small changes in brightness. Because COROT observes above Earth's atmosphere, it can detect the small drops in brightness. In 2009, the COROT team announced the discovery of the first exoplanet with a rocky surface. The team named the planet COROT 7b. In March 2010, the COROT team announced the discovery of a planet with a temperature and chemical makeup similar to those of some planets in our solar system.

Other articles to read include: **European Space Agency; Extrasolar planet; Telescope; Satellite; Star; Transit.**

Cosmic microwave background radiation

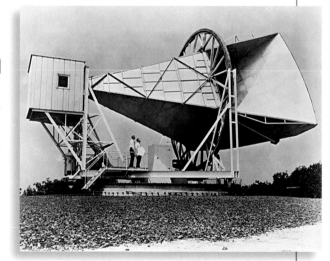

The cosmic microwave background (CMB) radiation is energy left over from the early universe. Scientists think the energy formed soon after the *big bang,* the event that marked the beginning of our universe about 13.8 billion years ago. The CMB is made up of *microwaves,* a type of invisible energy.

The American physicists Arno Penzias and Robert Wilson discovered the CMB radiation in the 1960's. They were using a type of telescope that can detect microwaves. They noticed a weak signal coming from every direction in the sky. After discussing the signal with other scientists, Penzias and Wilson concluded that they were detecting energy left over from the early universe. They shared the 1978 Nobel Prize in physics for the discovery.

The Horn Antenna radio telescope in Holmdel Township, New Jersey, used by Arno Penzias and Robert W. Wilson in their discovery of the cosmic microwave background radiation, is now a National Historic Landmark.

Several space telescopes have studied the CMB radiation. One of these probes, called Planck, has made a detailed map of this energy. Scientists use this map to help understand how the universe grew and changed over time.

Other articles to read include: **Big bang; Planck; Telescope; Universe.**

Cosmic rays

Cosmic rays are tiny particles that move through space at high speeds. Cosmic rays are *subatomic particles* (bits of matter smaller than an atom). Cosmic rays travel across our galaxy, the Milky Way, and probably other galaxies. They may even cross the wide empty distances between galaxies. By studying cosmic rays, scientists can learn more about distant parts of space.

Primary cosmic rays come mostly from outside the solar system. Most of these particles are *atomic nuclei* (the cores of atoms). Primary rays move through space at almost the speed of light. The speed of light is 186,282 miles (299,792 kilometers) per second, the fastest anything can travel.

Secondary cosmic rays form when primary rays strike atoms in Earth's atmosphere (blanket of air). The primary ray and the atom turn into a shower of secondary rays. Secondary rays include all types of subatomic particles. Secondary rays can continue split into even more secondary rays. Some secondary rays reach Earth's surface. Primaries almost never reach the surface.

Cosmic rays do not harm living things on Earth's surface. But above the atmosphere, they can reach harmful levels. Some cosmic rays have caused problems with electronic circuits on spacecraft.

Scientists have used balloons and spacecraft to study primary cosmic rays. They use large instruments on the ground to detect and study secondary rays.

Other articles to read include: **Redshift; Van Allen belts.**

Cosmic rays split into and create many different particles when they strike Earth's atmosphere.

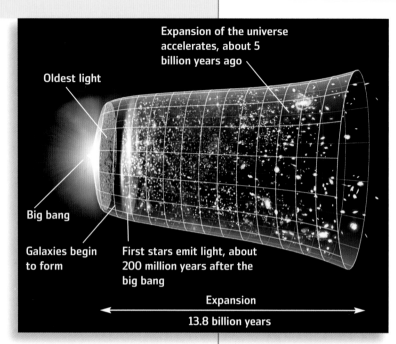

Oldest light

Expansion of the universe accelerates, about 5 billion years ago

Big bang

Galaxies begin to form

First stars emit light, about 200 million years after the big bang

Expansion

13.8 billion years

A timeline of the history of the universe shows a rapid expansion in the earliest moments after the big bang (far left). The expansion slowed quickly and evened out for several billion years. Then, for unknown reasons, it began to increase about 5 billion years ago.

Cosmology

Cosmology *(kahz MAHL uh jee)* is the study of the organization of the universe and the forces that shape it. Scientists who study cosmology are called *cosmologists.* Cosmologists try to explain how the universe formed, what has happened to it since, and what might happen to it in the future.

Several of the most important discoveries in cosmology were made by American astronomer Edwin Hubble in 1929. In the early 1900's, many astronomers believed that all stars and other celestial objects were part of the Milky Way, the galaxy that contains our solar system. In the 1920's, Hubble studied a hazy patch of sky called the Andromeda Nebula. Hubble noticed that it contained stars like those in the Milky Way. But these stars were much fainter. He concluded that the stars in the nebula must be much farther from Earth than stars in our own galaxy. His work proved that the Andromeda Nebula was actually a galaxy separate from our own.

Hubble later studied the speed at which galaxies move away from one another. He realized that the farther apart galaxies are from each other, the faster they move away. Hubble concluded that the universe is expanding at an even rate.

Perhaps the biggest event in cosmology since Hubble was the discovery in the late 1990's that the expansion of the universe is speeding up. Many scientists had thought that the expansion was slowing down due to the *gravitation* (force of gravity) of all the objects in the universe. But studies of distant *supernovae* (exploding stars) showed that they are fainter than expected. This is a sign that the stars are farther away than predicted. An unknown force makes the universe expand more rapidly. Scientists have named this force *dark energy.* They are trying to determine its nature. At least two-thirds of the energy in the universe is dark energy.

Other articles to read include: **Andromeda Galaxy; Big bang; Galaxy; Gravitation; Hubble, Edwin Powell; Milky Way; Nebula; Supernova; Universe.**

Crab Nebula

The Crab Nebula *(NEHB yuh luh)* is a huge cloud of gas and dust in space. It appears in a *constellation* (group of stars) named Taurus. The Crab Nebula formed from a *supernova* (star explosion) seen in 1054. The nebula is the remains of the star's outer layers.

The supernova threw hot gases and dust into space. The gases of the Crab Nebula are still very hot. The Crab Nebula is also still *expanding* (getting bigger). It is now about 10 *light-years* across. A light-year is the distance light can travel in a vacuum in one year. It equals about 5.88 trillion miles (9.46 trillion kilometers).

The Crab Nebula got its name from a scientist's drawing made in the 1840's. In the drawing, the nebula looked like a crab. When seen through a small telescope, the Crab Nebula looks like a dim blob of light.

Near the center of the Crab Nebula is a dim star. Scientists think it is a small object called a *pulsar* that is left over from the supernova. Pulsars give off regular bursts of radiation.

Other articles to read include: **Nebula; Supernova; Taurus.**

The Crab Nebula is a cloud of gas and dust left over after a supernova in 1054. A supernova is the violent explosion at the end of certain stars' lives.

Cygnus

Cygnus, *(SIHG nuhs),* the Swan, is a *constellation* in the Northern Hemisphere. A constellation is a grouping of stars in the night sky. The name *Cygnus* means *swan* in the Latin language.

Cygnus's most noticeable feature is the Northern Cross. It is formed by the constellation's five brightest stars. The brightest of these stars, Deneb, marks the tail of the Swan. Several other stars extend the Swan's "wings."

Other articles to read include: **Constellation; Deneb; Star.**

Cygnus is a constellation that represents a swan. It can be drawn in several ways.

Dd

Dark matter

Dark matter is an invisible substance that makes up most of the matter in the universe. Dark matter is invisible because it does not give off, *reflect* (turn back), or *absorb* (take in) light rays.

Astronomers (scientists who study the universe) cannot see dark matter directly. Instead, they detect the *gravitation* (force of gravity) given off by dark matter. This evidence of dark matter comes from studies of *galaxies* (groups of billions of stars) and *radiation* (energy and particles given off by a substance). These studies show that the *mass* (amount of matter) of the invisible parts of the universe is many times larger than the mass of its visible parts. All matter has a force of gravity. The amount of matter in an object or area can be determined by measuring this force. The more gravitation there is around an object or area, the more matter is there.

Astronomers do not know for sure what makes up dark matter. Some believe it could be made up of dust, dead stars, cold gas, and *black holes*. A black hole is a region of space with extremely strong gravity. Others believe that it is made of particles that astronomers have not discovered and identified yet.

The Swiss scientist Fritz Zwicky first argued for the existence of dark matter in 1933. Zwicky was studying a cluster of galaxies called the Coma Cluster. The galaxies moved around one another too quickly to be held together by the gravitation of their visible matter alone. Zwicky concluded that gravitation from invisible matter must help hold the cluster together. More evidence for the existence of dark matter later came from other scientists.

Other articles to read include: **Black hole; Galaxy; Gravitation; Universe.**

Clusters of dark matter (colorized in blue) surround hot gas (pink) from two galaxies that collided, in an image made with information from the Hubble Space Telescope and the Chandra X-ray Observatory. As the galaxies collided, the regular matter in them slowed down, but the dark matter did not. In the process, the two types of matter separated.

Dawn

Dawn is a space probe designed to study Ceres and Vesta, two of the largest asteroids *(AS tuh royds)* in the solar system. An asteroid is a rocky or metallic object smaller than a planet that *orbits* (travels around) the sun. These two bodies formed early in the history of the solar system. They have changed very little since that time. By studying information gathered by Dawn, scientists hope to learn more about the early solar system. The Dawn Mission, which was launched in 2007, is a project of NASA, the United States space agency.

Ceres and Vesta orbit the sun between the orbits of Mars and Jupiter. This region is known as the Main Belt. Ceres, the largest asteroid in the Main Belt, is also classified as a *dwarf planet.*

Dawn carries scientific instruments for mapping the surfaces of the asteroids. Its instruments can also measure the gravitational pull of each asteroid to determine its *mass* (amount of matter).

Dawn reached orbit around Vesta for a one-year study in 2011. During the mission, Dawn revealed that Vesta is the solar system's only surviving *planetesimal (PLAN uh TEHS uh muhl).* Planetesimals are also known as *protoplanets.* They were asteroid-sized objects that collided and stuck together to form the planets, moons, and other solid or mostly solid objects of the solar system.

Asteroids are much like the common rocks and minerals found on Earth. They are usually made of the same materials throughout. However, measurements made by Dawn indicated that Vesta has three layers—an inner core, a middle layer called the *mantle,* and an outer crust. In this way, Vesta is more like the inner planets of the solar system than the asteroids. The inner planets, also called the *terrestrial planets,* are Mercury, Venus, Earth, and Mars.

After studying Vesta, Dawn began its three-year journey to Ceres. The probe was scheduled to begin orbiting Ceres in 2015.

Other articles to read include: **Asteroid; Ceres; Dwarf planet; Main Belt; Planet; Space exploration; Vesta.**

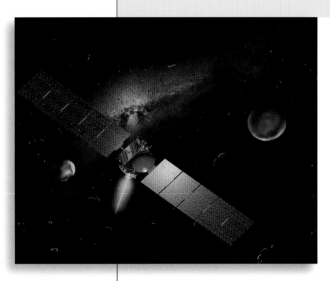

Dawn was designed to orbit and observe the asteroids Vesta, beginning in 2011, and Ceres, beginning in 2015.

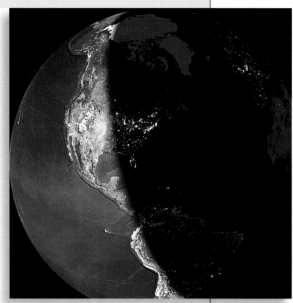

Darkness covers the eastern portion of the United States, much of Canada, and most of South America as night moves from east to west across the planet.

Day and night

Day and night are lengths of time caused by Earth's *rotation* (spinning motion). We usually say "day" for the time when the sun is shining on our part of Earth. We say "night" for the time when our part of Earth is dark, or turned away from the sun. But the night is really a part of the whole day. A *solar day* is the length of time that it takes Earth to rotate once on its *axis* with respect to the sun. The axis is an imaginary line that passes through Earth's center and exits at the poles. Each day begins at midnight.

In most countries, the day is divided into two parts of 12 hours each. The hours from midnight to noon are the a.m. hours. The hours from noon to midnight are the p.m. hours. The letters *a.m.* stand for *ante meridian,* which means *before noon.* The letters *p.m.* stand for *post meridian,* which means *after noon.*

In addition to rotating, Earth *orbits* (revolves around) the sun once a year. This journey gives us the seasons. The lengths of days and nights are different in each season because of the tilt of Earth's axis. When the North Pole tilts toward the sun, the Northern Hemisphere has summer, with long days and short nights. After six months, Earth moves to the other side of the sun. The North Pole now tilts away from the sun. The Northern Hemisphere has short days and long nights. The seasons are reversed in the Southern Hemisphere.

Other articles to read include: **Planet; Sun.**

Deimos

Deimos *(DY mos)* is one of the two tiny moons *orbiting* (traveling around) the planet Mars. Deimos is smaller than the other moon, named Phobos. Deimos whirls around Mars every 30 hours.

Neither Deimos nor Phobos is perfectly round. They are shaped more like a common rock on Earth. The largest diameter of

Continued on the next page

Deimos is about 9 miles (15 kilometers). Phobos is about 17 miles (27 kilometers) across. The two satellites have many *impact craters* that formed when *meteoroids* (space rocks) crashed into them.

Scientists do not know where Deimos and Phobos formed. They may have formed at the same time as Mars. Or they may have been *asteroids (AS tuh royds)* pulled into orbit by Mars's *gravitation* (force of gravity). An asteroid is a rocky or metallic object smaller than a planet that orbits the sun. The color of both satellites is a dark gray that is similar to the color of some kinds of asteroids.

The American astronomer Asaph Hall discovered Deimos and Phobos in 1877. He named them for the twin sons of Ares *(AYR eez)*, a Greek god of war. Ares was known by the ancient Romans as Mars. The name *Deimos* comes from a Greek word that means *fear* or *terror.*

Other articles to read include: **Gravitation; Mars; Phobos; Satellite.**

Impact craters mark the surface of Deimos, shown in two views in a photograph taken by the Mars Reconnaisance Orbiter.

Deneb

Deneb, *(DEHN ehb),* is the brightest star in the constellation Cygnus, the Swan. Deneb is also called *Alpha Cygni.* It is one of the most brilliant stars visible to the unaided eye. Deneb appears faint only because it is far away.

Scientists are not sure of Deneb's exact distance from Earth, but many think it is about 2,600 *light-years* away. A light-year is the distance light can travel in a vacuum in one year, about 5.88 trillion miles (9.46 trillion kilometers). Scientists have calculated that if Deneb is that far away, the star must be about 160,000 times as bright as the sun. Deneb is about 200 times as wide as the sun.

Deneb appears bluish-white because of its extremely high surface temperature, nearly 15,000 °F (8300 °C). Deneb is often classified as a *blue-white supergiant.* Stars in this class burn much hotter and brighter than the sun.

Other articles to read include: **Cygnus; Light-year; Star.**

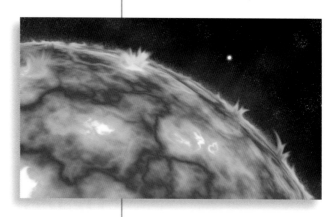

Deneb, also known as Alpha Cygni, is about 200 times as wide as the sun.

Dione

Dione shines against the rings of its home planet, in an image taken by the Cassini space probe.

Dione, *(dy OH nee),* is the fourth-largest moon of Saturn. It is about 696 miles (1,120 kilometers) wide. The moon *orbits* (travels around) Saturn every 2.74 days. Dione circles Saturn at an average distance of around 234,500 miles (377,400 kilometers).

Dione's surface consists mainly of water ice. Bright, heavily cratered *terrain* (landscape) covers one-half of the moon's surface. The other half also has many craters. It appears darker but has light streaks often known as "wispy terrain." The streaks are actually large cracks in the ice with bright, clifflike walls. Parts of Dione are also covered by smooth plains. Scientists believe that floes of ice evened out the surface there.

The Italian-born French astronomer Giovanni Domenico Cassini discovered Dione using a telescope in 1684. In the early 1980's, the United States space probes Voyager 1 and Voyager 2 flew by Dione. The probes took photographs of the wispy terrain. However, scientists could not clearly see the bright streaks. The U.S. spacecraft Cassini, sent to explore Saturn, photographed Dione in 2004 and again in 2005. Cassini showed that the wispy terrain consisted of ice cliffs.

Other articles to read include: **Cassini; Cassini, Giovanni Domenico; Enceladus; Iapetus; Mimas; Rhea; Satellite; Saturn; Titan; Voyager.**

Draco

Draco is a *constellation* also known as the Dragon. A constellation is a grouping of stars in a particular region of the night sky. Draco sits close to the North Star. It can be seen from the Northern Hemisphere for most of the year. Draco was among the 48 constellations defined by the ancient Greek mathematician Ptolemy.

As commonly drawn, Draco includes 16 or 17 main stars. Four stars form the head of the dragon, between the constellations Hercules and Cygnus. The body of Draco is a trail of stars that

Continued on the next page

winds among the constellations Cepheus, Ursa Minor, Boötes, and Ursa Major.

Thuban, a star in the body of Draco, was once Earth's northern *polestar* or North Star, about 5,000 years ago. A polestar is an easily seen star that lines up with one of Earth's poles. Over time, the motion of Earth caused the pole to drift and point to the current North Star, Polaris.

Other articles to read include: **Constellation; North Star; Ptolemy; Star.**

Because Draco the Dragon is so close to the North Star, it can be seen in the Northern Hemisphere for most of the year. But it can never been seen in the Southern Hemisphere.

Dwarf planet

A dwarf planet is an object in space that is smaller than a planet and larger than a comet or *meteoroid* (rocky object in space). Dwarf planets *orbit* (travel around) the sun. They are not *satellites* (moons) of another body. The *mass* (amount of matter) of a dwarf planet is large enough for its *gravitation* (force of gravity) to shape it into a nearly *spherical* (round) body. But a dwarf planet is not massive enough for its gravitational pull to sweep the region of its orbit relatively free of other objects.

All but one of the dwarf planets known to astronomers are in the Kuiper *(KY puhr)* belt. The Kuiper belt is a band of objects in the outer regions of the solar system, just beyond Neptune, the farthest planet from the sun. Ceres, the largest asteroid, is also considered a dwarf planet. It orbits the sun in an area between the orbits of Mars and Jupiter called the Main Belt.

The first dwarf planet discovered in the Kuiper belt was Pluto.

Continued on the next page

In an artist's representation, the dwarf planet Eris is shown with its moon Dysnomia. The sun is the brightest star in the distance.

Dwarf planet *Continued from the previous page*

When Pluto was found in 1930, it was called the ninth planet. Beginning in the 1990's, however, astronomers found many more objects in the Kuiper belt. One of these objects, later named Eris, was about the same size as Pluto. Many people believed the new object should be called the 10th planet. But scientists soon discovered more objects that were about the same size as Eris and Pluto. Adding several new planets to the solar system—with the possibility of many more in the Kuiper belt—led astronomers to consider a new way to classify these objects.

The group in charge of classifying objects in space is the International Astronomical Union (IAU). In 2006, the IAU put Pluto, Eris, and Ceres into a new category called dwarf planets. The IAU currently recognizes five dwarfs. The other bodies in this class are Haumea and Makemake.

Dwarf planets in the Kuiper belt appear small and faint when viewed from Earth. Even with the best telescopes, astronomers have difficulty measuring the exact size and shape of possible dwarfs. For this reason, it is difficult to tell whether an object is large enough to be called a dwarf planet.

Other articles to read include: **Ceres; Eris; Haumea; Kuiper belt; Makemake; Planet; Pluto.**

Eclipse

An eclipse is the darkening of a planet, moon, or star. This darkening takes place when the shadow of one planet or moon falls on another planet or moon. Eclipses occur on Earth because Earth and the moon always cast shadows into space as they block the light of the sun.

A *lunar eclipse* takes place when Earth's shadow covers the moon. Most times the shadow does not cover the moon entirely. And the moon does not become completely dark. Instead, part or all of the moon becomes reddish in color.

A *solar eclipse* takes place when the moon passes between the sun and Earth. The moon may darken all or part of the sun.

A person should never watch a solar eclipse with unprotected eyes. The light from the sun is very strong and will hurt the eyes. Only glasses with special filters are safe. Sunglasses do not provide enough protection.

Astronomers can predict eclipses with great accuracy. At least two solar eclipses and as many as three lunar eclipses may be seen each year from various places on Earth.

Heavenly bodies other than Earth and the moon also can eclipse each other. The planet Jupiter sometimes blocks sunlight from its moons. Likewise, Jupiter's moons sometimes cast shadows on the planet.

Other articles to read include: **Corona; Jupiter; Moon; Planet; Satellite; Sun.**

A solar eclipse occurs only during a new moon, when the moon is directly between Earth and the sun. The area on Earth that is fully shadowed by the moon is called the path of totality. People who are outside this area but still nearby may see a partial eclipse.

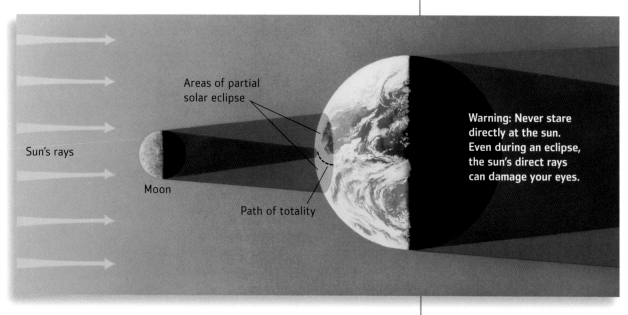

Sun's rays

Moon

Areas of partial solar eclipse

Path of totality

Warning: Never stare directly at the sun. Even during an eclipse, the sun's direct rays can damage your eyes.

Electromagnetic waves

Electromagnetic waves are related patterns of electric and magnetic energy. They are composed of particles called *photons*. There are many different kinds of electromagnetic waves. The different types of waves are separated by the amount of energy they carry. The more energy the waves have, the closer the waves are to one another. The distance or length between two waves in a row is called the *wavelength*.

The *electromagnetic spectrum* is made up of all the wavelengths of electromagnetic waves. People can see only the part called the visible spectrum or visible light. The electromagnetic spectrum ranges from gamma rays, which have the shortest wavelength, to X rays, ultraviolet radiation, visible light, infrared radiation, and radio waves, which have the longest wavelength. Microwaves are generally considered short radio waves.

Astronomers (scientists who study objects beyond Earth) use telescopes that can "see" all of the different types of electromagnetic waves. With the information collected from the different telescopes, they can better understand the different types of energy *emitted* (given off) by the many different objects in space.

In 1864, the Scottish scientist James Clerk Maxwell predicted the existence of electromagnetic waves. In the late 1880's, the German physicist Heinrich R. Hertz supplied proof that the waves existed. In 1905, the German physicist Albert Einstein proposed that electromagnetic waves are made of particles that were later called photons. In 1923, the American physicist Arthur Compton described some of the properties of a photon.

Other articles to read include: **Cosmic microwave background radiation; Gamma rays; Light.**

The electromagnetic spectrum is the entire range of the different types of electromagnetic waves. At one end of the spectrum are gamma rays, which have the shortest wavelength. At the other end of the spectrum are radio waves, which have the longest wavelength.

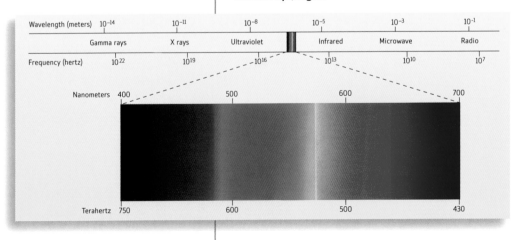

Wavelength (meters)	10^{-14}	10^{-11}	10^{-8}	10^{-5}	10^{-3}	10^{-1}
	Gamma rays	X rays	Ultraviolet	Infrared	Microwave	Radio
Frequency (hertz)	10^{22}	10^{19}	10^{16}	10^{13}	10^{10}	10^{7}

Nanometers	400	500	600	700

Terahertz	750	600	500	430

Ellipse

An ellipse *(ih LIHPS)* is a figure with a shape like a flattened hoop. It can be drawn using a loop of string. The string is attached to two points, called *foci (FOH sy)* (the plural of focus). Each focus lies toward one end of the ellipse. The loop of string must be larger than the distance between the foci. A pencil is then held inside the loop. The pencil is pulled all the way around the foci, keeping the string tight. The result is an ellipse. A line passing through the foci is called the *major axis*. A line passing through the middle of the *major axis* is called the *minor axis*.

In the 1600's, a German astronomer, Johannes Kepler, discovered that the planets travel in elliptical orbits. The sun is at one focus of a planet's orbit.

Other articles to read include: **Kepler, Johannes; Orbit; Planet.**

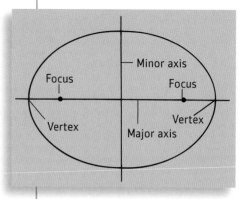

An ellipse, in geometry, is an oval figure that resembles a flattened hoop.

Enceladus

Enceladus *(ehn SEHL uh duhs)* is the sixth-largest moon of Saturn. Enceladus *reflects* (bounces back) nearly 100 percent of the light that hits its smooth, icy surface.

Much of what we know about Enceladus comes from information gathered by the Cassini spacecraft. Cassini showed a plume of particles erupting from Enceladus's south polar region. The plume is fed by jets shooting out from the surface. The jets release mostly water vapor and grains of water ice. But they also release some *organic* (carbon-containing) molecules. Some of the water from these jets becomes part of one of Saturn's rings. Many scientists think the jets are evidence of liquid water below the surface. If Enceladus has liquid water, it may be possible to find life there.

Enceladus has a variety of surface features. Cracks and ridges cross broad plains. Some areas show impact craters that formed when a comet or other solid body struck the surface. Other areas do not have craters. Scientists think that ice flows or particles from Enceladus's jets buried any craters that were once there.

Other articles to read include: **Cassini; Dione; Iapetus; Mimas; Rhea; Satellite; Saturn; Titan.**

Deep cracks mark the icy surface of Enceladus, as seen in a photograph taken by the Cassini space probe.

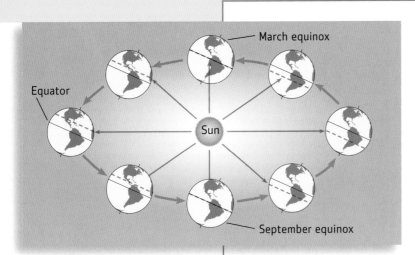

Equator

March equinox

Sun

September equinox

Equinox

Equinox *(EE kwuh nahks)* is one of two special days of the year. On these two days, day and night are almost the same length everywhere on Earth. One equinox happens on March 19, 20, or 21. The other happens on September 22 or 23.

The length of day and night changes throughout the year

The equinoxes happen when the sun's rays shine directly on the equator. The dotted lines show where the sun's rays hit Earth directly at different times of the year.

because of the way Earth moves around the sun. In winter, days are short and nights are long. In summer, days are long and nights are short. In between, at the start of spring, there comes a time when day and night have the same length. This time is the spring equinox. The other equinox happens on the first day of autumn. It is the autumnal equinox.

Other articles to read include: **Day and night; Orbit; Sun.**

Eratosthenes

Eratosthenes *(ehr uh TOS thuh neez)* (276?–195? B.C.) was a Greek mathematician. He found a way to measure Earth's *circumference* (distance around the middle). He did this without leaving northern Africa, where he lived. Instead, he made a calculation based on *geometry* (the study of shapes, angles, and other figures).

Like other Greek scientists of his time, Eratosthenes knew that Earth is round. He observed that at noon on a certain day, a post in one town would cast no shadow. But in another town, the post would cast a shadow. Eratosthenes measured the angle of this shadow. He used this to figure out the angle between the two towns, as measured from Earth's center.

Eratosthenes then measured the distance between the towns. Finally, he multiplied this distance by the number of times that the angle went into 360°, the measure of a complete circle. The result was the distance around the entire Earth. Eratosthenes's distance was not exactly right. But, it was surprisingly close for his time. His measurement of Earth's circumference was between 28,000 and 29,000 miles (45,000 and 47,000 kilometers). The actual value is 24,860 miles (40,008 kilometers).

Other articles to read include: **Planet; Sun.**

Eris

Eris is a planet-sized object that orbits the sun at the outer edges of the solar system. This region is called the Kuiper *(KY pur)* belt. Astronomers classify Eris as a *dwarf planet*. A dwarf planet is smaller than a planet and larger than a comet or *meteoroid* (rocky object in space). Eris is about 1,450 miles (2,350 kilometers) in diameter. It is about the size of Pluto, another dwarf planet.

Eris has a shiny, icy surface that reflects almost all starlight back into space. The orbit of Eris ranges from 3.5 billion to 9 billion miles (5.6 billion to 14.5 billion kilometers) from the sun. One complete orbit takes about 557 Earth years.

The dwarf planet Eris with its moon Dysnomia as seen by the Hubble Space Telescope.

Scientists announced the discovery of Eris on July 29, 2005. In 2006, the dwarf planet was named Eris for the Greek goddess of *chaos* (confusion) and *strife* (conflict). Eris and the other dwarf planets that orbit beyond Neptune are also called *plutoids*.

Other articles to read include: **Dwarf planet; Kuiper belt; Pluto; Solar system.**

Europa

Europa *(yu ROH puh)* is a large moon of the planet Jupiter. Europa is 1,940 miles (3,122 kilometers) across. It is just a bit smaller than Earth's moon.

Europa is made mostly of rock. But its surface is covered in water ice. The surface is very smooth. But there are shallow cracks, ridges, and other features in places. Deep beneath Europa's ice, there may be an ocean of liquid water. If it exists, this ocean might hold living things.

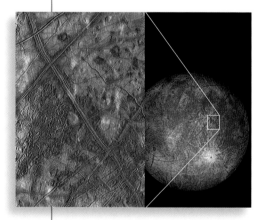

Many cracks cut across the thick sheet of ice covering the surface of Europa.

Several *probes* (small spacecraft) have visited Europa. They used special equipment to learn more about the moon. The United States launched another such probe in 2011. Named Juno, the craft will reach Jupiter in 2016.

The Italian astronomer Galileo Galilei discovered Europa in 1610. One of the probes that visited Europa, in 1995, was named for Galileo. He discovered Europa along with the three other large moons of Jupiter, Callisto, Ganymede, and Io. Together, these four moons are called the Galilean satellites.

Other articles to read include: **Callisto; Galileo; Ganymede; Io; Jupiter; Satellite.**

A European Space Agency
Ariane rocket launches from
French Guiana in 2012.

European Space Agency (ESA)

The European Space Agency (ESA) is a space program run by the nations of Western Europe. It was created in 1975. Members of the ESA are Austria, Belgium, the Czech Republic, Denmark, Finland, France, Germany, Greece, Ireland, Italy, Luxembourg, the Netherlands, Norway, Portugal, Romania, Spain, Sweden, Switzerland, and the United Kingdom. In 1980, the ESA formed a private organization, Arianespace. This company launches satellites aboard Ariane rockets from a launch site in French Guiana.

The ESA directed the building of the orbiting laboratory Spacelab. United States space shuttles carried Spacelab on missions from 1983 to 1998. The ESA then began constructing Columbus, a permanent laboratory module for the International Space Station (ISS). A space shuttle delivered Columbus to the ISS in 2008.

In 1985, the ESA launched the space probe Giotto. It took photographs and collected information as it passed within 370 miles (600 kilometers) of Halley's Comet. In 1990, the ESA and the United States launched the probe Ulysses. The probe made observations over the sun's poles in 1994 and 1995.

The ESA launched the Mars Express probe in 2003, the SMART-1 probe to the moon in 2004, and the Venus Express probe in 2005. The ESA also built the Huygens probe, which was carried to a position near Saturn's moon Titan by the U.S. Cassini spacecraft. Huygens descended through Titan's atmosphere in 2005. It became the first craft to land on a satellite of a planet other than Earth. The ESA and NASA, the United States space agency, have partnered on many space missions, including the Hubble Space Telescope.

In 2009, the ESA launched two telescopes. The Herschel Space Observatory studies light from some of the first galaxies and the formation of planets around distant stars. The Planck mission maps the cosmic microwave background (CMB) radiation, energy left over from the beginning of the universe.

Other articles to read include: **Cassini; Herschel Space Observitory; International Space Station; Planck; Space exploration.**

Evening star

An evening star is a planet that can be seen after sunset. The planets Venus and Mercury are often seen as evening stars. They move in orbits that are closer to the sun than Earth's orbit. For this reason, they appear to move from one side of the sun to the other. Venus and Mercury can be seen only in the western sky after sunset or in the eastern sky before sunrise. When either of these planets is seen at sunrise, it is called a *morning star.*

Planets are not really stars. They are solid, liquid, or gaseous bodies. Planets do not give off their own light as stars do. They shine by reflecting sunlight. Ancient people thought planets were wandering stars. By Roman times, they recognized that the morning and evening stars were the same. In 1543, the Polish astronomer Nicolaus Copernicus identified the positions of these "stars" in the solar system.

Other articles to read include: **Mercury; Venus; Planet; Star.**

Evening star

Venus appears close to the horizon during sunset and is sometimes called the evening star.

Extrasolar planet

Extrasolar planets are planets found outside the *solar system.* The solar system includes the sun and all of the objects that orbit the sun, including Earth and the other planets. Extrasolar planets are also called *exoplanets.* The first known exoplanet was discovered in 1992.

Astronomers have found hundreds of extrasolar planets. Many of these planets are *gas giants* (large planets formed mostly of

Continued on the next page

Extrasolar planet *Continued from the previous page*

Extrasolar planets called hot Neptunes are about twice the size of Earth with about 20 times the *mass* (amount of matter). Astronomers are unsure whether they are rocky planets like Earth or gaseous planets like Jupiter.

gases with no solid surface). Scientists were suprised to find gas giants orbiting closer to their home star than Mercury orbits the sun. In the solar system, Saturn and the other gas giants orbit far from the sun. Such close orbits would make their surfaces too hot to support life as we know it.

Scientists hope to find planets like Earth. Most scientists consider liquid water necessary for life as we know it. So they look for planets in the *habitable zone* of their star. Planets in this zone are cool enough that liquid water can form and warm enough to prevent water from freezing. Earth is in the habitable zone of the sun.

Scientists search for exoplanets in several ways. They look for tiny changes in the amount of light coming from a star. If the light grows dimmer, it may mean that a planet is passing in front of the star and blocking the light. Astronomers also look for tiny changes in stars' movements. These changes may be caused by the slight pull of a planet's gravity on its home star. Scientists can also study a star's light. If the light from the star changes color, scientists know that the star is being pushed and pulled by an orbiting planet.

In 2007, astronomers announced the discovery of two small planets orbiting the star Gliese 581, about 20 *light-years* away. A light-year is the distance light can travel in a vacuum in one year, about 5.88 trillion miles (9.46 trillion kilometers). Although these planets are much bigger than Earth, they are most likely rocky worlds. One of the planets may orbit in the star's habitable zone.

Some exoplanets may not orbit a star. Instead, they float alone through space. These planets may have been knocked out of their orbit around their home star by another star or large object. The lone planets may have also been flung away from their home star soon after they were formed.

Other articles to read include: **COROT; Extraterrestrial intelligence; Habitable zone; Kepler; Light-year; Planet; Solar system; Star.**

Extraterrestrial intelligence

Extraterrestrial *(EHKS truh tuh REHS tree uhl)* intelligence is life living somewhere other than Earth that has the ability to think and learn. No life has been found anywhere except Earth. But many scientists think that there may be intelligent life on planets around other stars. Beings that originate beyond Earth are often referred to as *extraterrestrials* or simply *aliens.*

Scientists think that intelligent life may exist on other worlds because the universe contains such a huge number of stars and planets. Our own galaxy, the Milky Way, has hundreds of billions of stars. It alone could contain more than a trillion planets. Furthermore, the universe has more than 100 billion galaxies. Scientists expect that many planets do not have the conditions—such as liquid water—necessary to support life as we know it. But if even a tiny fraction of planets have the right conditions, the Milky Way still might contain millions of worlds with life. Some of these worlds may have intelligent life.

One effort to find extraterrestrial intelligence is called SETI, which stands for *Search for Extraterrestrial Intelligence.* SETI research involves looking near other stars for signals sent by extraterrestrials in the form of light or radio waves. In 1960, the American astronomer Frank Drake conducted the first SETI experiment. He used a radio telescope to try to detect signals coming from two relatively nearby stars. During the 1990's and early 2000's, scientists used radio telescopes to hunt for signals coming from many hundreds of stars. The Allen Telescope Array in California is a group of radio telescopes designed to conduct SETI studies of about 1 million stars.

In the late 1990's, astronomers also began searching for brief, bright flashes of *visible light* (light we can see). Scientists think that extraterrestrials might produce such flashes with powerful lasers. No natural objects in space are known to produce such flashes.

Scientists have no evidence that Earth has ever been visited by extraterrestrials. Each year, many people report seeing *unidentified flying objects* (UFO's). Some people believe that such objects could be spacecraft from other worlds. But scientists who study UFO reports have found that most sightings can be explained as ordinary things.

Other articles to read include: **Allen Telescope Array; Extrasolar planet; SETI Institute; Unidentified flying object.**

Ff

Fermi Gamma-ray Space Telescope

Gamma rays (shown in purple) surround the remnant of a *supernova* (exploding star), in an image made by the Fermi Gamma-ray Space Telescope.

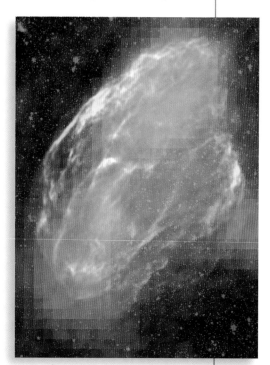

The Fermi Gamma-ray telescope is a telescope in orbit around Earth. It is used to study *gamma rays* from space. Gamma rays are a high-energy form of light rays invisible to humans. The United States space agency NASA launched Fermi on June 11, 2008. NASA named the telescope in honor of the Italian-born American physicist Enrico Fermi. The Fermi telescope is a joint project of NASA and the U.S. Department of Energy, with help from scientific institutions in France, Germany, Italy, Japan, and Sweden.

Gamma rays originate in extreme environments. For example, some come from *pulsars*. These rapidly spinning objects are the remains of stars that exploded. Gamma rays may also come from *black holes*. These objects have a gravitational pull so strong that nothing can escape from them, not even light. Some gamma rays come in flashes known as *gamma-ray bursts*. One of Fermi's major goals is to investigate the cause of such bursts.

The telescope has also detected gamma rays coming from Earth. These rays are created by lightning.

Other articles to read include: **Black hole; Compton Gamma Ray Observatory; Electromagnetic waves; Gamma-ray burst; Gamma rays; Pulsar; Satellite, Artificial.**

Fourth dimension

The fourth dimension, in math and physics, is a way of thinking about time. We think of space as having three dimensions. For example, a box has length, width, and depth. These three dimensions describe the box's *position* in space. But to describe something's *movement* through space, we need a fourth dimension: time.

In the early 1900's, the German-born American physicist Albert Einstein developed a new way of thinking about space and time. His ideas are known as *relativity*. According to relativity, space and time are part of a single structure, called space-time. Hermann Minkowski, a German mathematician, showed that Einstein's ideas described a universe with four dimensions.

Other articles to read include: **Space; Space-time; Universe.**

Gagarin, Yuri Alekseyevich

Yuri Alekseyevich Gagarin *(YOOR ee ah leh KSEH yuh vihch gah GAHR ihn)* (1934-1968) was the first human being to reach space. He was a pilot in the air force of the Soviet Union (now Russia). Gagarin circled Earth once on April 12, 1961. He was in orbit for 89 minutes. The entire trip lasted 1 hour and 48 minutes. During this mission, Gagarin traveled at a speed of more than 17,000 miles (27,000 kilometers) per hour. At one point, he was about 203 miles (327 kilometers) above the ground. Gagarin's spacecraft was named Vostok 1.

Gagarin was born on March 9, 1934, in Gzhatsk, near Moscow. He entered the Soviet air force in 1955. In 1959, he began training to become an astronaut. He was killed in a plane crash on March 27, 1968.

Other articles to read include: **Astronaut; Orbit; Space exploration.**

Yuri Alekseyevich Gagarin

Galaxy

A galaxy is a huge collection of stars, gas, dust, and other matter held together by gravity. The sun, Earth, and all the other planets in the solar system are located in the Milky Way Galaxy. Our galaxy takes its name from its appearance as a "milky" band stretching across the night sky. In fact, the word *galaxy* comes from the Greek word for *milk*.

In the 1920's, the American astronomer Edwin P. Hubble discovered that the universe contains many other galaxies beyond our own. Each galaxy consists of from hundreds of thousands to trillions of stars. Most astronomers think that galaxies also contain vast amounts of an invisible form of matter called *dark matter*. Dark matter is invisible because it does not *emit* (give off),

Continued on the next page

Five galaxies make up a grouping called called Stephan's Quintet. Four of the galaxies are colliding. One galaxy (lower left) is much closer to Earth than the other four.

The spiral arms of the Whirlpool Galaxy may owe their unusual appearance to streams of stars and dust pulled from a smaller nearby galaxy (right in image).

Galaxy *Continued from the previous page*

reflect (turn back), or *absorb* (take in) light rays. Astronomers can detect dark matter only by its gravitational pull on visible matter.

Galaxies range in size from a few thousand *light-years* in diameter to millions of light-years across. A light-year is the distance that light travels in a vacuum in one year—about 5.88 trillion miles (9.46 trillion kilometers). Each galaxy contains a total *mass* (amount of matter) ranging from roughly millions to trillions of times that of the sun.

The light from numerous stars enables astronomers to see galaxies at great distances. The light from the farthest and oldest-known galaxies took over 13 billion years to reach Earth. Astronomers therefore observe these galaxies as they appeared long ago, during the universe's early history. Hundreds of billions of galaxies are visible from Earth with a telescope.

There are three main types of galaxies: (1) *spiral galaxies,* (2) *elliptical (ih LIHP tuh kuhl) galaxies,* and (3) *irregular galaxies.*

Spiral galaxies are shaped like pinwheels with a bulge in the center. They have bright, curved arms that curl out from the central bulge. The Milky Way is a spiral galaxy.

Elliptical galaxies have an *oval* (flattened circle) shape. Many elliptical galaxies look like flattened globes. However, others are almost perfectly round. Elliptical galaxies are brightest at the center and get fainter toward the edges. They are the largest galaxies.

Irregular galaxies are galaxies that do not have a simple shape. They are made up of most every galaxy smaller than spiral galaxies.

Not all galaxies fall into one of these groups. *Peculiar galaxies* feature unusual shapes. These systems may result from the collision of two or more galaxies or other dramatic event. *Starburst galaxies* appear in a variety of shapes. They produce new stars at unusually high rates. *Active galaxies* give off vast amounts of *radiation* (energy) from their core.

Continued on the next page

Most galaxies, including our own, inhabit *groups* with dozens of galaxies, or *clusters* with hundreds to thousands of members. Groups and clusters, in turn, make up large *superclusters.*

Only three galaxies can be seen from Earth without a telescope. People who live north of the *equator* (imaginary line around Earth's middle) can see a spiral galaxy called the Andromeda *(an DROM uh duh)* Galaxy. People who live south of the equator can see two irregular galaxies—the Large Magellanic *(MAJ uh LAN ihk)* Cloud and the Small Magellanic Cloud.

Astronomers usually study galaxies by the light they *emit* (give off). But galaxies also emit other types of energy. Scientists can use special instruments to capture these types of energy for study.

Astronomers have learned that galaxies in the early universe and galaxies that exist today differ in important ways. The early universe had a greater number of small and active galaxies. It had fewer large spiral and elliptical galaxies than the present-day universe.

Astronomers have also learned that galaxies can collide and *merge* (come together) to form new galaxies of different sizes and types. In fact, they believe that over billions of years, many smaller galaxies may have merged to produce the galaxies, groups, and clusters we observe today.

The evolution of galaxies continues. In a few billion years, for example, the Milky Way and Andromeda galaxies will merge into a larger galaxy.

Other articles to read include: **Andromeda Galaxy; Dark matter; Hubble, Edwin Powell; Light-year; Local Group; Magellanic Clouds; Milky Way; Star; Universe.**

The night sky of a planet in one of the first galaxies would have seemed crowded, compared with Earth's night sky, as shown in an artist's illustration. When the first galaxies formed, they packed billions of newborn stars into relatively small spaces.

Three galaxies have collided to form an unusual object that astronomers have nicknamed "the Bird." The Bird is more than 1 billion times as bright as the sun.

Galileo Galilei

Galileo

Galileo *(GAL uh LAY oh* or *GAL uh LEE oh)* (1564–1642), an Italian astronomer, was one of the greatest scientists of all time. He was one of the first people to use a telescope to learn more about the *solar system* (the sun and all the planets and other bodies that travel around the sun). He also discovered basic laws about how objects fall to Earth due to the force of gravity. Galileo pioneered the idea that ordinary people should enjoy reading about scientific discoveries. He wrote in clear, witty Italian rather than Latin, the scholarly language of his time.

Galileo was born in Pisa, Italy. His full name was Galileo Galilei. Galileo studied medicine at the University of Pisa. But he was more interested in mathematics. He later taught mathematics at the University of Pisa and at the University of Padua.

At the University of Padua, he developed the *laws of falling bodies.* He stated that all objects fall at the same speed, no matter how much *mass* (amount of matter) they have. At that time, people believed that if two bodies with different masses were dropped from the same height at the same time, the heavier one would hit the ground first.

Galileo also discovered that all objects fall to the ground with the same *acceleration* (rate of increase in speed), unless air or some other force acts on the objects to slow them down. More than 400 years later, United States astronaut David Scott confirmed Galileo's theory while on the moon. Scott held out a hammer and a feather and dropped them at the same time. Without air to slow it down, the feather fell as fast as the hammer.

While he was in Padua, Galileo also began studying astronomy. He built a telescope and used it to look at the moon and planets. He saw that the moon is covered with mountains and craters. Earlier scientists had believed that the surface of the moon was smooth.

Galileo also discovered the four largest moons of Jupiter. The moons—Callisto, Europa, Ganymede, and Io—are sometimes called the Galilean moons in his honor.

Galileo also became interested in the motion of Earth in

Continued on the next page

space. Nearly everyone at that time believed that the sun and other planets moved around Earth and that Earth stood still. But Galileo agreed with the ideas of a Polish astronomer, Nicolaus Copernicus. Copernicus said—correctly—that all the planets, including Earth, move around the sun.

In 1632, Galileo finished his most complete work on the structure of the heavens. It was called the *Dialogue Concerning the Two Chief World Systems*. In this work, he supported Copernicus's theory. At that time, the Roman Catholic Church taught that Earth was the center of the universe. In 1633, the church condemned Galileo for going against its teachings. The church punished him by not allowing him to leave his house for the rest of his life. In 1992, however, the church admitted that it had made a mistake in condemning Galileo.

Other articles to read include: **Astronomy; Copernicus, Nicolaus; Gravitation; Jupiter; Planet; Solar system; Telescope.**

Galileo

Galileo was a spacecraft sent to observe Jupiter, its moons, and rings. NASA, the United States space agency, launched Galileo on October 18, 1989. The craft orbited Jupiter from December 7, 1995, to September 21, 2003. It was named after the Italian astronomer and physicist Galileo, who discovered Jupiter's four largest moons in 1610.

On the way to Jupiter, Galileo visited the asteroids *(AS tuh royds)* Gaspra and Ida. An asteroid is a rocky or metallic object smaller than a planet that *orbits* (travels around) the sun.

Five months before arriving at Jupiter, Galileo released a smaller probe. On the day Galileo arrived at Jupiter, this probe plunged into Jupiter's atmosphere. The probe was able to study the atmosphere for 61.4 minutes before the intense heat there shut down its instruments. Eventually, the entire probe melted and *evaporated* (turned to gas).

Continued on the next page

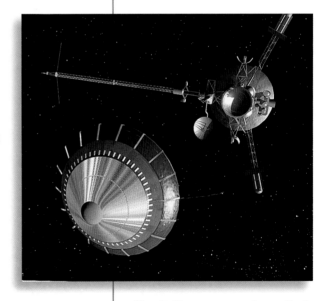

The Galileo spacecraft studied the planet Jupiter for eight years. The satellite released a small probe (left) that plunged into the planet's atmosphere to gather data about the chemical makeup of the planet.

Galileo *Continued from the previous page*

One of the probe's major discoveries was that Jupiter's chemical makeup is similar to the original makeup of the sun. This finding provided evidence that Jupiter formed closer to the sun and then moved farther away over time. The finding also provided evidence that Jupiter is a "failed star." Such bodies do not have enough *mass* (amount of matter) to become a star.

Galileo's observations of Jupiter's four largest moons produced many surprises. For example, Galileo found that Io's volcanoes are hotter than Earth's. A blanket of dark, smooth material covers the surface of Callisto. Ganymede has a dense core and a *magnetic field* (a region in which magnetism can be detected). Grooves and ridges crisscross the icy surface of Europa. In places, the ice on Europa seems to have broken into blocks. This suggests that there may be an ocean of water underneath.

NASA designed Galileo to orbit Jupiter for only two years. But the craft continued to provide valuable information for almost eight years. Eventually, Galileo ran low on fuel. NASA intentionally crashed Galileo into Jupiter's atmosphere on September 21, 2003. NASA scientists did this to avoid any risk that the craft would crash into and *contaminate* (pollute) Europa. Many scientists believe that if water exists below the surface of Europa, it may be capable of supporting life as we know it.

Other articles to read include: **Callisto; Europa; Galileo** (scientist); **Ganymede; Io; Jupiter; Space exploration.**

Gamma-ray burst (GRB)

A gamma-ray burst (GRB) is a very powerful series of flashes of light. GRB's have been observed originating in distant galaxies. A GRB consists mostly of X rays and *gamma rays.* A gamma ray is a form of light. No two GRB's are identical—each burst gives off a unique series of flashes. Gamma rays carry more energy than any other form of light.

Space telescopes detect about one GRB per day, but there are probably many more. These bursts originate in all directions of

Continued on the next page

the sky. Astronomers have detected the light from GRB's that took place in some of the first galaxies in the universe. This light traveled for over 13 billion years before reaching Earth.

Scientists think that some GRB's are produced by exploding stars. When a star with at least 8 to 11 times the *mass* (amount of matter) of the sun reaches the end of its life, the star explodes in an event called a *supernova.* Scientists think some of these explosions are powerful enough to produce a GRB. Scientists also believe that some GRB's occur when the remains of two exploded stars collide.

United States military satellites detected the first GRB's in the late 1960's. These satellites were designed to watch for gamma rays released during nuclear weapons tests. The discovery of GRB's remained a secret while scientists on the project studied them. In 1973, the American scientists Ray Klebesadel, Ian Strong, and Roy Olson reported the discovery.

Other articles to read include: **Compton Gamma Ray Observatory; Fermi Gamma-ray Space Telescope; Galaxy; Gamma rays.**

Gamma-ray bursts are some of the most energetic events in the universe.

Gamma rays

Gamma rays are a form of energy. They are one type of *electromagnetic waves* (the different forms of light rays). The rays are made of particles called *photons.* Gamma rays are the most powerful of these rays. Gamma rays are so strong that they can pass through a concrete wall. Only a thick layer of lead can stop a gamma ray. You cannot see gamma rays because they are invisible to the human eye.

Scientists have found gamma rays in space. They usually come from objects called *pulsars* (dense, rapidly spinning stars), *supernovae* (exploding stars), galaxies, and the sun. Sometimes gamma rays come from *radioactive material* in rocks or soil on Earth. Radioactive materials give off forms of light energy and tiny fast-moving particles. Gamma rays are also produced in lightning strikes. The rays can kill living cells, so doctors sometimes use them to treat people who have cancer.

A French scientist named Paul Villard discovered gamma rays in 1900.

Other articles to read include: **Electromagnetic waves; Gamma-ray burst; Pulsar; Supernova.**

Beneath Ganymede's varied surface are a thick layer of ice, a rocky layer, and a metal core. A thin ocean of salty water may lay about 105 miles (170 kilometers) beneath the surface.

Ganymede

Ganymede *(GAN uh meed)* is the largest moon of the planet Jupiter. It is also the largest moon in the solar system. It is even larger than the planet Mercury. Ganymede orbits Jupiter every 7.15 Earth days at a distance of 664,900 miles (1,070,000 kilometers). Ganymede is one of the four moons of Jupiter discovered by the Italian astronomer Galileo Galilei in 1610.

Ganymede's surface is made up of almost equal amounts of dark and bright *terrain* (land). The dark areas are made mostly of ice mixed with pieces of dark rock. These areas have many *impact craters* and large cracks. The craters were made by asteroids and comets crashing into the surface. Forces released by the biggest impacts produced many of the cracks. Other cracks formed when changes in the structure and temperature of the moon caused it to expand.

The bright terrain is has many fewer craters. It formed as the surface expanded and cracked. Water, ice, or both flooded low-lying areas and craters. The cracking and stretching of the new terrain created parallel sets of ridges and valleys.

Other articles to read include: **Galileo** (scientist); **Impact crater; Jupiter; Satellite.**

Marc Garneau

Garneau, Marc

Marc Garneau *(gahr NO)* (1949 -) was the first Canadian to travel in space. He is a captain in the Royal Canadian Navy. Garneau flew with six American astronauts aboard the United States space shuttle Challenger from October 5 to 13, 1984. Garneau also made shuttle flights in 1996 and 2000.

Garneau was born in Quebec City. He earned a doctoral degree in electrical engineering from the Imperial College of Science and Technology in London. Garneau joined the Royal Canadian Navy in 1965. He became an expert on communications and weapon systems. In 1983, Garneau was chosen to be one of Canada's first six astronauts. He served as president of the Canadian Space Agency (CSA) from November 2001 to

Continued on the next page

November 2005. Garneau became the *chancellor* (head) of Carleton University in Ottawa in 2003. Garneau was elected to the Canadian Parliament in 2008.

Other articles to read include: **Astronaut; Canadian Space Agency; Space exploration.**

Gas giant

A gas giant is a type of planet made of mostly gases with little or no rock. The solar system has four such planets—Jupiter, Neptune, Saturn, and Uranus. The two most common gases that make up gas giants are hydrogen and helium. These chemical elements are the two most abundant substances in the universe.

Gas giants have also been found outside the solar system. Planets outside the solar system are called *extrasolar planets* or *exoplanets*. These extrasolar gas giants do not get much larger in size than Jupiter, but they can have much more *mass* (amount of matter).

Because of their large size, extrasolar gas giants are easier to spot *orbiting* (traveling around) faraway stars. Many of the exoplanets first discovered were gas giants orbiting very close to their home star. These gas giants are very hot and are sometimes called "hot Jupiters."

Other articles to read include: **Extrasolar planet; Jupiter; Neptune; Planet; Saturn; Uranus.**

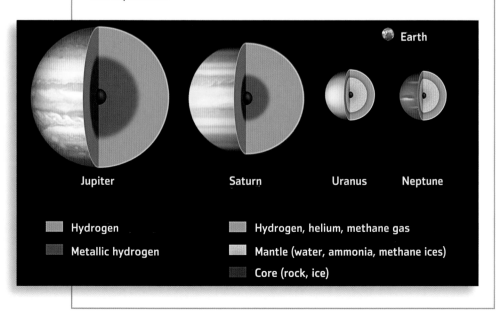

Earth

Jupiter

Saturn

Uranus

Neptune

Hydrogen

Metallic hydrogen

Hydrogen, helium, methane gas

Mantle (water, ammonia, methane ices)

Core (rock, ice)

The four outer planets of the solar system are often called the "gas giants." However, the two largest planets, Jupiter and Saturn, have a slightly different combination of materials than the two smaller gas giants, Neptune and Uranus do.

The constellation Gemini represents the twin brothers Castor and Pollux.

Gemini

Gemini *(JEHM ihn y)* is a *constellation* also known as the Twins. A constellation is a grouping of stars in a particular part of the night sky. Gemini is named for twin brothers in Greek mythology—Castor and Pollux. Castor and Pollux were good companions. As gods, they became the patrons of athletes and protectors of sailors at sea. They had power over winds and waves.

Gemini appears in the northern sky and is best viewed around January through March. As commonly drawn, Gemini includes about 17 stars. When connected, the stars form two conventional stick figures holding hands. Two bright stars, also named Castor and Pollux, represent the heads of the two brothers.

Gemini was among the 48 constellations defined by the ancient Greek mathematician Ptolemy. Today, it is one of 88 constellations recognized by the International Astronomical Union, the leading authority in the naming of heavenly objects.

Other articles to read include: **Astrology; Constellation; Ptolemy; Star; Zodiac.**

John Glenn

Glenn, John Herschel, Jr.

John Herschel Glenn, Jr., (1921-) was the first American to orbit Earth. On February 20, 1962, he circled Earth three times. The trip lasted less than five hours. Glenn's spacecraft was named Friendship 7.

Glenn was born in Cambridge, Ohio. He entered the United States Marine Corps in 1942. He served as a pilot in World War II (1939-1945) and the Korean War (1950-1953). He later became a *test pilot.* A test pilot is someone who flies new aircraft to aid in their development. In 1959, Glenn was selected to become an astronaut. He resigned as an astronaut in 1964. From 1974 to 1999, Glenn served as a U.S. senator from Ohio.

Glenn returned to space in 1998. In that year, he traveled aboard the space shuttle Discovery. He became the oldest person to travel in space.

Other articles to read include: **Astronaut; Space exploration.**

Gran Telescopio Canarias

The Gran Telescopio Canarias (GTC) is one of the largest telescopes in the world. The GTC sits atop a 7,900-foot (2,400-meter) mountain on the island of La Palma in Spain's Canary Islands.

The GTC is a *reflecting telescope,* a telescope that uses mirrors to collect and focus light. The GTC's large mirror, also called the *primary,* measures 34 feet (10.4 meters) in diameter. The primary mirror is made up of 36 smaller mirrors. They are fitted together to form a single curved surface. Two smaller mirrors direct light collected by the primary mirror to one of several different cameras. The GTC collects both visible and *infrared* (heat) light.

Construction of the GTC began in 2000. The telescope was first used on July 13, 2007. A partnership of Spain, Mexico, and the University of Florida built the telescope and operates it.

Other articles to read include: **Observatory; Telescope.**

The Gran Telescopio Canarias sits atop a mountain in the Canary Islands, just off the coast of southern Morocco in the Atlantic Ocean.

Gravitation

Gravitation is the force that causes objects to be pulled toward one another. Gravitation keeps the planets in orbit around the sun. It also keeps your feet firmly on the ground. Gravitation causes things to fall when they are dropped. Another name for gravitation is the *force of gravity.*

Gravitation acts between objects because of their *mass* (amount of matter). Every object has its own gravitational pull. But objects with a greater mass have a stronger gravitational pull than objects with less mass. Earth's gravitational pull keeps the moon in orbit around Earth. The moon's gravitational pull is not as strong as that of Earth because the moon has less mass. The moon's weaker gravitational pull is why astronauts visiting there can carry equipment that would be too heavy to carry on Earth.

In the late 1600's, the English scientist Sir Isaac Newton developed several important laws of gravitation. He explained that the force of gravity between two objects is directly related to their masses. Newton also explained that the force of gravity gets weaker as objects get farther apart. Newton explained that gravitation is the reason objects to fall to the ground and planets orbit the sun. However, Newton could not

Continued on the next page

Gravitation *Continued from the previous page*

explain what causes gravitation. Even so, scientists accepted Newton's ideas for more than 200 years.

In 1915, the German-born scientist Albert Einstein developed new ideas about gravitation that added to Newton's work. Einstein's ideas were called the *general theory of relativity.* Before Einstein, people had thought of space as being just emptiness. But Einstein said space is somewhat like a rubber sheet. His theory says that objects in space, such as the sun, actually change the shape of space. They cause space to curve, just as a bowling ball would make a rubber sheet bend downward. The curving of space causes objects to move toward one another. Many experiments have proved Einstein right. Though Einstein's work is widely accepted, the source of gravitation is still unknown.

Other articles to read include: **Moon; Orbit; Planet; Space.**

Gravitational lensing

Gravitational lensing can *magnify* (enlarge) such distant objects as this galaxy captured by the Hubble Space Telescope.

Gravitational lensing is a bending of light from a distant object. It is caused by the *gravitational field* of an object between the distant object and the viewer. A gravitational field is the area around an object that shows the effect of the object's gravity. The bending light is called lensing because the gravitational field acts much like a lens.

All objects with *mass* bend space because of their gravity. Mass is the amount of matter in an object. This warping is hard to see in small objects. However, huge objects can bend space enough to noticeably bend the light passing through it. For example, consider a distant bright star. Imagine that there is a massive object, such as a cluster of stars, between that distant star and an observer on Earth. The light from that distant star will be bent by the cluster of stars before reaching the observer. The German-born physicist Albert Einstein predicted this bending of light.

Gravitational lensing is often divided into three types. They are: (1) strong lensing, (2) weak lensing, and (3) microlensing. Strong lensing is easy to see. In some cases, strong lensing can make a distant object look larger. Astronomers can use this effect to see faint, distant objects.

Continued on the next page

In weak lensing, the bending is much smaller. Astronomers can see it only through small changes in the shape of the distant object.

In microlensing, the shape of a distant object does not change at all. However, the amount of light received from the object is slightly changed. Astronomers use microlensing to search for *extrasolar planets* (planets outside the solar system). Such a planet may be too faint to see. But as the planet crosses in front of its star, its gravitational field *focuses* the light from the star slightly. That is, the planet brings the rays of light together at one point. This focusing tells astronomers that the star may have a planet.

Other articles to read include: **Extrasolar planet; Gravitation; Light.**

The entire Earth could fit inside Jupiter's massive Great Red Spot. The storm's clouds have been darkened in this photo, taken by the Voyager 1 space probe in 1979, to show the clouds' movements more clearly. ▼

Great Red Spot

The Great Red Spot is a vast, reddish oval in the planet Jupiter's outer layer, or *atmosphere.* It is a huge mass of swirling gas that is wider than Earth. It extends about 7,450 miles (12,000 kilometers) from north to south. The spot's width from east to west is slowly shrinking. It measured about 10,500 miles (17,000 kilometers) in the early 2000's. The spot travels around Jupiter with the wind just south of the *equator* (imaginary line around Jupiter's middle). Astronomers do not know exactly what causes the spot's reddish color.

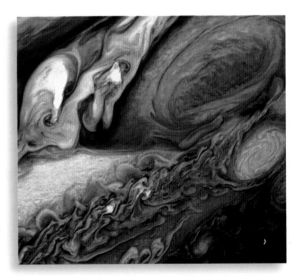

The English scientist Robert Hooke first observed a large spot in Jupiter's atmosphere in 1664. Astronomers first recorded the Great Red Spot's exact form and position in 1831. Since then, the spot has remained near the same position south of the equator.

Images taken by the two Voyager spacecraft in 1979 showed that the spot is a swirling cloud of gas that takes about seven days to *rotate* (spin around) once. Wind speeds at the outer edges of the spot reach up to 425 miles (685 kilometers) per hour.

Other oval features in Jupiter's atmosphere include *white ovals.* White ovals are much smaller and move around more than the Great Red Spot. In the late 1990's and early 2000's, three white ovals *merged* (joined) to form a larger oval. This oval later took on a reddish color. The new spot, often called the Little Red Spot, measures roughly half the size of the Great Red Spot.

Other articles to read include: **Jupiter; Voyager.**

Habitable zone

The habitable zone is an area around a star in which an orbiting planet or moon could have liquid water on its surface. Scientists believe liquid water must be present for life as we know it to exist. Scientists sometimes call the habitable zone the *Goldilocks Zone*. That is because the temperatures of planets or moons in this zone would be "just right." That is, the planets would be cool enough to keep all the liquid water from *evaporating* (turning to a gas) and warm enough to prevent all the water from freezing. Earth is in the habitable zone of the sun.

The location of a habitable zone depends on the size of the star. The hotter the star, the farther away a planet or moon needs to be to hold liquid water. Since the 1990's, many planets have been found circling other stars. Most of these *extrasolar planets* are very close to their star. They are much hotter than Mercury, the closest planet to the sun. They could not support life as we know it. Astronomers have found a few planets and moons that could be in the habitable zone of their star. However, they do not know if life exists on any of these bodies.

Other articles to read include: **Extrasolar planet; Orbit; Star.**

Planets that could possibly hold liquid water on the surface are said to reside in the habitable zone. Scientists believe liquid could be important for supporting life. Astronomers have discovered several planets orbiting other stars that sit within this zone.

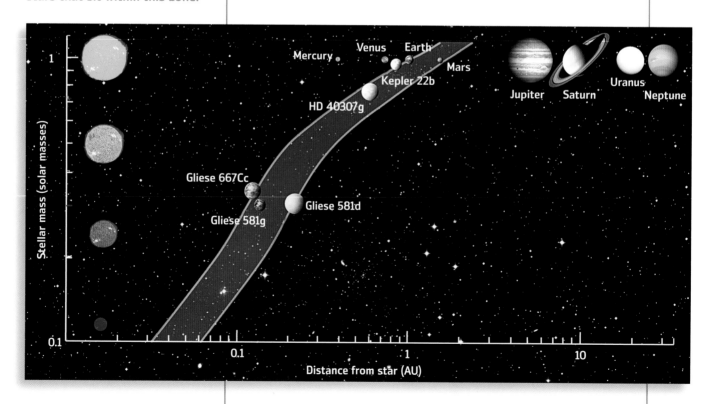

Hale, George Ellery

George Ellery Hale (1868-1938) was an American astronomer. He pioneered the development of scientific instruments for studying the sun. He also planned the construction of several giant telescopes. These telescopes include the Hale Reflecting Telescope at the Palomar Observatory near San Diego. This instrument has a diameter of 200 inches (508 centimeters).

Hale was born in Chicago and graduated from the Massachusetts Institute of Technology. In 1891, he introduced an instrument called the *spectroheliograph*. It allows scientists to see the type and amounts of the chemical elements on the surface of the sun. Hale also made important discoveries about sunspots. For example, he proved that these dark areas on the sun have strong *magnetic fields*. A magnetic field is the influence that a magnet or an electric current creates in the region around it.

In 1895, Hale founded the *Astrophysical Journal*, which became the leading journal for astronomers. He founded and became the first director of the Yerkes Observatory in Wisconsin and, later, the Mount Wilson Observatory in California.

Other articles to read include: **Astronomy; Palomar Observatory; Sun; Telescope.**

George Hale

Halley, Edmond

Edmond Halley *(HAL ee)* (1656-1742) was a British *astronomer* who studied *comets*. An astronomer is a scientist who studies stars, planets, and other objects in space. A comet is an icy body that moves around the sun in a long, oval path.

Halley became known for showing that comets move around the sun in a set path. He saw a comet in 1682 and proved that it was the same one that astronomers had seen in 1531 and 1607. He said that the comet would be seen again in 1758, and he was right. The comet is now called Halley's Comet. People can see it from Earth about every 76 years.

Edmond Halley

Continued on the next page

Halley, Edmond *Continued from the previous page*

Halley is also credited with figuring out how to measure the distance from Earth to the sun. On rare occasions, the planet Venus passes between the sun and Earth. Halley suggested measuring when the planet moves in front of the sun from two different locations on Earth. By comparing the different times from the two locations, a distance from Earth to the sun could be calculated using math. Halley died before Venus passed in front of the sun again. But his method was used by other scientists to find a fairly accurate measurement of the distance to the sun.

Halley was born in London. He went to school at Oxford University in England.

Other articles to read include: **Comet; Halley's Comet; Sun; Venus.**

Halley's Comet last passed by Earth in 1986. It returns, as it has for centuries, every 76 years.

Halley's Comet

Halley's *(HAL eez)* Comet is a very bright *comet* that can be seen from Earth about every 76 years. A comet is an icy body that moves around the sun in a long, oval path. The comet is named for Edmond Halley, an English *astronomer.* An astronomer is a scientist who studies stars, planets, comets, and other objects in space. Halley's Comet was last seen in 1986. Scientists believe it will reappear in 2061.

Before Halley, most people believed comets did not travel in regular paths. Halley demonstrated that comets, like planets, *orbit* (travel around) the sun. Halley observed that the paths of comets spotted in 1531 and 1607 matched the orbit of a comet seen in 1682. He concluded that the three comets were actually a single comet traveling around the sun. The comet becomes visible from Earth when its orbit takes it close to the sun. Halley predicted that the comet would reappear in 1758 and about every 76 years thereafter. When the comet returned as predicted in 1758, it became known as Halley's Comet. Unfortunately, Halley had died in 1742.

Chinese astronomers first saw the comet that was named for Halley more than 2,000 years ago.

Other articles to read include: **Comet; Halley, Edmond; Orbit.**

Harriot, Thomas

Thomas Harriot (1560-1621) was an English mathematician. He also studied astronomy, *navigation,* and mapmaking. Navigation is the practice of finding and guiding people or objects. Harriot is best known for his book on algebra, *Artis analyticae praxis* (1631). Harriot introduced the symbols for *greater than* (>), *less than* (<), and *square root* ($\sqrt{}$).

The Italian scientist Galileo is often credited with being the first person to study the moon with a telescope. However, Harriot may have beaten him by a few months. Between 1609 and 1613, Harriot used one of the earliest telescopes to study the sun, Earth's moon, and the moons of Jupiter. Harriot did not publish his studies. But he discussed them in letters to other astronomers.

Harriot was born in or near Oxford, England, in 1560. He graduated from Oxford University in 1580. Soon after, he began teaching mathematics and navigation to sailors.

In 1585, Harriot sailed on the second expedition to North America made by the English explorer Sir Walter Raleigh. Harriot's writings on the trip became the first book about the New World published in English. In 1595, Harriot returned to England. He went on to conduct research in astronomy, mathematics, and *optics.* Optics is the study of the characteristics of light. Harriot died in London on July 2, 1621.

Other articles to read include: **Galileo** (scientist); **Moon; Telescope.**

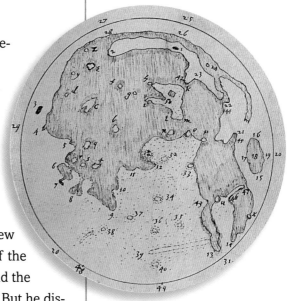

A map of the moon drawn by English astronomer Thomas Harriot on July 26, 1609, suggests that he was the first person to view the moon through a telescope. But Galileo published his drawings of the lunar surface before Harriot published his map.

Haumea

Haumea *(hah oo MAY ah)* is a rocky, ice-covered *dwarf planet.* A dwarf planet is a round object in space that is smaller than a planet and larger than a comet or *meteoroid* (rocky object). Haumea was named for the Hawaiian goddess of childbirth and *fertility* (the power to produce offspring).

Continued on the next page

Two tiny moons circle Haumea, a dwarf planet in the Kuiper belt, an area beyond orbit of Neptune.

Haumea *Continued from the previous page*

Haumea usually lies beyond the orbit of Neptune, the farthest planet from the sun. But at times, Haumea's *elliptical* (oval-shaped orbit) takes it closer to the sun than Pluto, another dwarf planet. Haumea orbits the sun in an area of the solar system called the *Kuiper (KY pur) belt*. The Kuiper belt begins beyond the orbit of Neptune. Astronomers think the belt is home to many dwarf planets and millions of other smaller objects.

Haumea is about one-third as large as Pluto. But it is more *oblong* (cigar-shaped) than Pluto and so is longer. It takes Haumea 282 Earth years to travel around the sun. Haumea *rotates* (spins) so quickly on its *axis* that it makes one complete turn every four hours. An axis is an imaginary line around which planets and other space bodies rotate. Because of Haumea's quick rotation, astronomers think the dwarf planet is made mostly of rock. But because it is so shiny, they think it must have a thin covering of ice.

Astronomers announced the discovery of Haumea in 2005. At that time, they also discovered two moons orbiting Haumea. The moons were named Hi'aka and Namaka, for the daughters of Haumea. Hi'aka is the patron goddess of the island of Hawaii and of hula dancers. Namaka is a water spirit in Hawaiian mythology.

Other articles to read include: **Dwarf planet; Eris; Kuiper belt; Makemake; Pluto.**

Heliosphere

The heliosphere is a vast, teardrop-shaped region of space containing electrically charged particles given off by the sun. The sun and the rest of the planets in the solar system are inside the heliosphere. Scientists estimate that the *nose* (blunt end) of the heliosphere is about 9 billion to 15 billion miles (15 billion to 24 billion kilometers) from the sun. This distance is two to three times the greatest distance from the sun to Pluto. The tail of the

Continued on the next page

heliosphere trails off at an even greater distance on the other side of the sun. The sun and the heliosphere are traveling together—nose first—through *interstellar space* (the space between the stars). This space contains a cloud of dust and gas called the *interstellar medium.* The heliosphere is traveling through the medium at about 16 miles (25 kilometers) per second.

The sun gives off a continuous flow of particles called the *solar wind.* The particles are mostly tiny electrically charged *protons* (particles with a positive charge) and *electrons* (particles with a negative charge). The wind creates the heliosphere bubble around the sun. The wind flows away from the sun at about 125 to 625 miles (200 to 1,000 kilometers) per second.

As the sun and heliosphere move through space, the interstellar cloud and the solar wind *resist* (push against) each other. The power of the solar wind decreases as the wind expands into space. As the wind approaches the edge of the heliosphere, the particles begin to encounter more resistance from the interstellar medium. Finally, the wind stops its outward flow. This is roughly the edge of the heliosphere.

The NASA Voyager space probes, launched in 1977, are the first spacecraft to explore the outer heliosphere. They were expected to exit the *heliosheath,* the outermost layer of the heliosphere, sometime after 2014. At that point, they will become the first *artificial* (human-made) objects to reach interstellar space. The NASA space probe IBEX, launched in 2008, is mapping the heliosphere. The NASA probe Cassini, launched in 1997, also mapped the heliosphere. Data from IBEX and Cassini have allowed scientists to create the first full sky map of the heliosphere.

Other articles to read include: **Cassini; Interstellar medium; Solar wind; Sun; Voyager.**

NASA's Voyager I and Voyager II are expected to become the first space probes to exit the *heliosheath* (the outer layer of the heliosphere) and reach the interstellar medium.

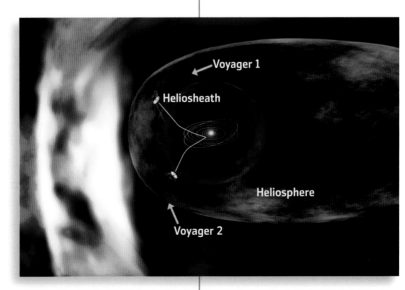

Voyager 1

Heliosheath

Heliosphere

Voyager 2

The constellation Hercules is most easily seen from the Northern Hemisphere.

Hercules

Hercules is a *constellation* easily seen from the Northern Hemisphere. A constellation is a grouping of stars in the night sky. Hercules is best seen high overhead in summer.

Four relatively bright stars form the body of Hercules. His head is a *red supergiant,* a reddish-colored star hundreds of times larger than the sun. This star is actually part of a *binary star* (a pair of stars that orbit each other). On one side of Hercules lies a *star cluster* numbering at least 100,000 stars. It is so far away that its light requires more than 30,000 years to reach Earth. Even under good conditions, the cluster is barely visible to the unaided eye.

In 1934, a star in Hercules exploded, throwing huge masses of gas and dust into space. As a result, the star suddenly became much brighter. Such an explosion is called a *nova.* The star has since faded to its normal brightness.

The constellation Hercules was named for one of the greatest heroes of Greek mythology. Hercules was among the 48 constellations defined by the ancient Greek mathematician Ptolemy. Today, it is one of 88 constellations recognized by the International Astronomical Union, the leading authority in the naming of heavenly objects.

Other articles to read include: **Binary star; Constellation; Nova; Ptolemy; Star; Star cluster.**

Sir William Herschel

Herschel family

The Herschel family included three related British *astronomers (uh STRON uh muhrz).* Astronomers are scientists who objects beyond Earth.

William Herschel (1738–1822) founded *stellar astronomy,* the study of objects beyond the *solar system.* The solar system is the sun and all the objects that *orbit* (travel around) it. In 1781, Herschel discovered the planet Uranus. He later found two satellites of Uranus and two satellites of Saturn. His other achievements include pioneering studies of the sun's motion through space, of the relative brightness of stars, and of *infrared* (heat)

Continued on the next page

rays. Herschel studied the sky with telescopes that he built himself. The mirror of one of these had a diameter of 4 feet (1.2 meters). It was the world's largest telescope until 1845.

Herschel's sister, Caroline Lucretia Herschel (1750–1848), was the first noted woman astronomer. She often assisted William Herschel in his work. In 1786, she independently discovered a comet. She later discovered seven more comets. Caroline Herschel also located a number of *nebulae (NEHB yuh lee)*. Nebulae are hazy clouds of gas and dust in space. In 1828, the Royal Astronomical Society presented her with a gold medal for her catalog of William Herschel's observations of nebulae and stellar systems.

William Herschel's son, John Frederick William Herschel (1792–1871), discovered thousands of stars, star clusters, and nebulae. From 1834 to 1838, he surveyed the southern skies as thoroughly as his father had studied the northern heavens. He also made contributions to mathematics and *optics*, the study of light.

Other articles to read include: **Astronomy; Nebula; Star; Telescope.**

Sir John Herschel

The Herschel telescope sits under construction in Cannes, France. ▼

Herschel Space Observatory

Herschel Space Observatory was a telescope in orbit around the sun. It made observations in *far-infrared light*. Infrared light is invisible to the human eye but can be felt on the skin as heat. Herschel was named after the British astronomer Sir William Herschel. The observatory was launched in 2009. Several European countries, Canada, China, Israel, Taiwan, and the United States contributed to the development and construction of Herschel.

The Herschel telescope gathered far-infrared light using the largest single mirror ever built for a space telescope. Astronomers used this information to study galaxies that formed early in the history of the solar system and areas where stars and their planets may be forming. The mission ended in 2013 after all the liquid helium used to cool the spacecraft's instruments evaporated.

Other articles to read include: **Galaxy; Herschel family; Observatory; Telescope.**

Victor Hess

Hess, Victor Franz

Victor Franz Hess (1883-1964) was an Austrian scientist. He won the 1936 Nobel Prize for physics for discovering *cosmic rays*. Cosmic rays are tiny particles that move through space at high speed. Hess shared the prize with Carl David Anderson, who discovered a particle called the *positron*.

Hess studied *ions* (electrically charged atoms) in Earth's atmosphere. Such ions are produced by *radiation* (energy in the form of waves or tiny particles of matter). Some of the radiation comes from materials inside Earth. Hess took instruments that detect radiation up mountains and carried them with him on balloon flights. He found that the number of particles increased dramatically at high altitudes. This was strong evidence that most of the radiation was arriving from space in the form of what became known as cosmic rays.

Hess was born in Steiermark, Austria. He was also known as Victor Francis Hess. Hess earned a doctoral degree from Graz University in 1906.

Other articles to read include: **Cosmic rays.**

The sun appears in an X-ray image taken by Hinode, launched by Japan's Aerospace Exploration Agency (JAXA).

Hinode

Hinode *(hih NOH day)* is a spacecraft designed to study the sun. It was launched on September 22, 2006, by the Japan Aerospace Exploration Agency (JAXA). *Hinode* is the Japanese word for *sunrise*.

One of Hinode's major goals is to observe the formation and motion of *magnetic fields* produced by the sun. A magnetic field is the influence that a magnet or an electric current creates in the region around it. Researchers have used Hinode to study how magnetic energy is generated in *solar flares*. Solar flares are energy bursts associated with the sun's magnetic field.

Hinode has found evidence that magnetic waves and rapid changes in the sun's magnetic field play important roles in heating the corona. The corona is the outermost layer of the sun's

Continued on the next page

atmosphere. Scientists have also used Hinode to study the relationship between the sun's magnetic field and the formation of the *solar wind*. The solar wind is the continuous stream of electrically charged particles that flows from the sun.

Hinode orbits Earth from pole to pole. As a result, the craft can see the sun continuously for months at a time. JAXA manages the mission from the Hinode Science Center at the National Astronomical Observatory of Japan in Tokyo.

Other articles to read include: **Corona; Satellite, Artificial; Solar wind; Space exploration; Sun.**

Hipparchus

Hipparchus *(hih PAHR kuhs)* (180 B.C.?-125 B.C.?) was a Greek *astronomer.* An astronomer is a scientist who studies the objects in the universe beyond Earth. Hipparchus is credited with discovering the *precession* (movement) of the *equinoxes.* Hipparchus was born in Nicaea, near what is now Istanbul, Turkey.

An *equinox (EE kwuh noks)* is either of two special points in the sky. At these points, the sun appears to cross the *celestial equator.* The celestial equator is an imaginary line across the middle of the sky.

The ancient Roman writer Pliny the Elder wrote that Hipparchus became excited about a new star. When he looked at earlier studies of stars, he noticed that the stars had shifted. He explained this shift by a slow precession of the equinoxes. This precession is caused by a slight change in the direction in which Earth's *axis* spins. The axis is an imaginary line through the center of Earth that exits at the poles. The change in direction results mainly from the gravitational pull of the moon and the sun on the bulge around Earth's equator.

The work of Hipparchus helped people to learn more about the motion of the sun and moon. It also improved the ability to predict *eclipses.* In an eclipse, the shadow of one object in space falls on another object, or one object moves in front of another to block its light.

Other articles to read include: **Astronomy; Eclipse; Equinox.**

Hipparchus

Hogg, Helen Sawyer

Helen Sawyer Hogg (1905–1993) was an American-born astronomer. She is best known for her research on *variable stars*. She discovered more than 250 of these stars, whose light changes brightness fairly often. Hogg chiefly studied variable stars in *globular star clusters* (ball-like groups of stars). Her work included measuring the *period* of many of these stars. A variable star's period is the time its light takes to change from bright to dim and back to bright. This information, in certain cases, helps astronomers determine the distance of the star from Earth.

Helen Battles Sawyer was born in Lowell, Massachusetts. She married Frank S. Hogg, a Canadian astronomer, in 1930. She studied astronomy at Radcliffe College in Cambridge, Massachusetts, in 1931. Her book, *Catalogue of Variable Stars in Globular Clusters,* was published in 1939. In 1935, Hogg joined the faculty of the University of Toronto, where she conducted most of her research. In 1957, Hogg became the first woman to serve as the president of the Royal Astronomical Society of Canada.

Other articles to read include: **Astronomy; Star; Star cluster.**

The American astronomer Edwin Hubble made numerous important discoveries about galaxies and the larger universe.

Hubble, Edwin Powell

Edwin Powell Hubble (1889-1953) was an American *astronomer.* An astronomer is a scientist who studies objects beyond Earth. Hubble's work changed the way astronomers think about the size and structure of the universe.

In the early 1900's, most astronomers thought that all visible objects in space were part of the Milky Way Galaxy. The Milky Way includes the sun, Earth, and the rest of the solar system. However, in the 1920's, Hubble studied a group of stars called the Andromeda Nebula. He realized that the stars he was looking at were much fainter than those in the Milky Way Galaxy. From this, he concluded that the Andromeda Nebula was actually a separate galaxy and not part of the Milky Way.

Continued on the next page

Hubble later studied the speed at which galaxies *recede* (move away) from one another. In 1929, he found that the farther a faraway galaxy was from the Milky Way, the more rapidly it appeared to be receding. Hubble concluded that distant galaxies recede at a rate directly related to their distance. This idea became known as Hubble's law.

Hubble was born in Marshfield, Missouri. He earned a Ph.D. degree from the University of Chicago in 1917. In 1919, he joined the staff of the Mount Wilson Observatory in California. He remained there until his death in 1953. The Hubble Space Telescope was named in his honor.

Other articles to read include: **Andromeda Galaxy; Galaxy; Hubble constant; Milky Way; Mount Wilson Observatory; Universe.**

Hubble constant

Hubble constant is a measure of how fast the universe is expanding. It serves as a key part of *Hubble's law.* This law is one of the most important observations in *cosmology* (the study of the universe's structure and development). Hubble's law describes the way distant galaxies *recede* (move farther away) as space expands. The Hubble constant and Hubble's law are named for their discoverer, American astronomer Edwin P. Hubble. Scientists can use the Hubble constant to estimate the universe's current age.

In 1929, Hubble discovered that the farther a galaxy was from our own Milky Way, the more rapidly it appeared to be receding. Hubble concluded that distant galaxies recede at a rate related to their distance. According to Hubble's law, two galaxies that are 20 million *light-years* apart are receding from each other twice as fast as two galaxies that are 10 million light-years apart. One light-year is the distance that light travels in a vacuum in a year.

In the late 1990's, astronomers studying information from the Hubble Space Telescope estimated a value for the Hubble constant—210 kilometers (130 miles) per second. Information from other spacecraft since then have confirmed this value with even greater certainty.

Other articles to read include: **Cosmology; Galaxy; Hubble, Edwin Powell; Light-year; Milky Way; Universe.**

Hubble Space Telescope

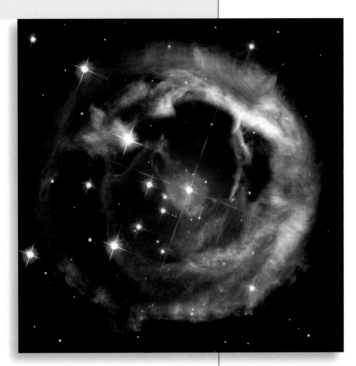

Light from a red giant that suddenly brightened then dimmed speeds through surrounding dust clouds, in a false-color image taken by the Hubble Space Telescope.

The Hubble Space Telescope is one of the most important scientific devices ever developed. Since entering orbit around Earth in 1990, Hubble has provided astronomers with images of celestial objects and phenomena in detail never seen before. The telescope is named for American astronomer Edwin P. Hubble. NASA, the United States space agency, operates Hubble in cooperation with the European Space Agency.

Hubble has taken pictures of stars surrounded by dusty disks that might someday become planetary systems and galaxies on the edge of the observable universe. It has captured images of galaxies colliding and tearing each other apart and evidence suggesting that most galaxies have massive *black holes* in their centers. A black hole is a region of space whose pull of gravity is extremely strong. Perhaps the most important scientific breakthrough connected with Hubble was the discovery that the universe is expanding at an ever-faster rate. Scientists have also combined Hubble's images with those of other observatories to create incredibly detailed images of cosmic objects.

Continued on the next page

Glowing arms of dust in the Whirlpool Galaxy are revealed in an *infrared* (heat) photo, taken by Hubble, from which most of the visible light has been removed.

Hubble orbits about 380 miles (610 kilometers) above Earth. It is a *reflecting telescope* with a large mirror that collects light. The mirror is 94 inches (240 centimeters) wide. The light is reflected to a small lens that focuses it for a camera. Hubble collects *infrared* (heat), visible, and ultraviolet light. Although Hubble is about the size of a tractor-trailer truck, it is actually much smaller than the biggest telescopes on Earth. But because it does not look through the *atmosphere,* Hubble can see about as far as any telescope on Earth. The atmosphere is the blanket of gases surrounding Earth. It *distorts* (bends) and dims light.

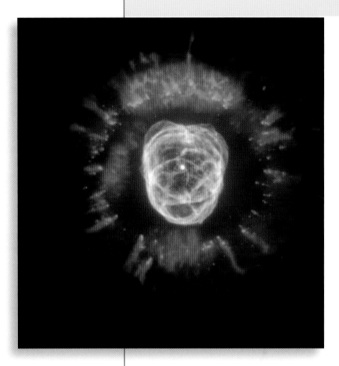

Gases and pieces of matter stream from a dying star in the Eskimo Nebula, in a false-color image from Hubble.

The space shuttle Discovery released Hubble into orbit in 1990. Unfortunately, astronomers soon discovered that the telescope's main mirror was incorrectly shaped. In 1993, astronauts on a servicing mission successfully installed corrective lenses that functioned like spectacle lenses for human eyes.

From 1993 to 2003, astronauts conducted a number of missions to repair or upgrade equipment on Hubble. But in 2002, NASA officials canceled a final servicing mission scheduled for 2006. After many protests from scientists and the public, NASA rescheduled the mission. In 2009, astronauts successfully repaired a camera and upgraded several other instruments. As a

Continued on the next page

Hot gas ejected from a dying, sunlike star in the Ant Nebula is captured in a false-color image by Hubble.

Hubble Space Telescope *Continued from the previous page*

result of all these missions, Hubble has greater abilities than its designers planned.

Other articles to read include: **Black hole; Hubble, Edwin Powell; James Webb Space Telescope; Satellite, Artificial; Telescope; Universe.**

A large storm with particles of water ice (shown in white) swirls near the north pole of Mars in a photograph taken by Hubble.

Christiaan Huygens

Huygens, Christiaan

Christiaan Huygens *(KRIHS tee ahn HOY gehns)* (1629-1695) was a Dutch astronomer, mathematician, and *physicist.* An astronomer studies objects beyond Earth. A physicist studies matter and energy.

In 1678, Huygens proposed that light is made up of a series of waves. Another scientist, Sir Isaac Newton, believed that light was made up of particles. Today, we know that light acts as both a particle and a wave.

Huygens made important advances in other fields. In 1651, he described a new way to measure the area of a circle. He worked with his brother Constantijn to develop more powerful telescopes. He also discovered Saturn's moon Titan. He figured out that what astronomers called "Saturn's arms" was a ring.

The European Space Agency honored Huygens's discovery of Titan by naming a space probe after him. The Huygens probe landed on Titan in 2005. It was carried and released by the Cassini spacecraft of the United States.

Other articles to read include: **Cassini; Electromagnetic waves; Light; Saturn; Telescope; Titan.**

Iapetus

Iapetus *(eye AP uh tuhs)* is the third-largest moon of Saturn. It has a surface marked by noticeable light and dark halves. Its dark half appears nearly as black as tar. Its bright half resembles dirty snow. No other body in the solar system is colored in this way.

Scientists think that the surface of Iapetus is mostly water ice. On the dark half, however, dark material covers the normally bright ice. The dust that darkens one side of Iapetus comes from another nearby moon, Phoebe. Large craters lie within the dark half. The appearance and age of the craters there suggest that the dark material settled after the incoming meteors or asteroids created the craters.

A vast ridge runs along the equator of Iapetus within the dark half. This ridge measures about 12 miles (20 kilometers) wide and stretches for at least 800 miles (1,300 kilometers). Some mountainous parts of the ridge rise at least 13 miles (21 kilometers) high. Scientists think the ridge may have folded upward, like some mountain ranges on Earth. It may have been built up by eruptions from the moon's interior.

Images taken by the Cassini space probe show Iapetus's lighter and much darker sides. Scientists believe the darker side is coated with dust from Phoebe, another of Saturn's moons.

The Italian-born French astronomer Giovanni Domenico Cassini discovered Iapetus using a telescope in 1671. In the early 1980's, the United States spacecraft Voyager 1 and Voyager 2 took photographs of Iapetus. In the 2000's, the U.S. Cassini spacecraft flew by Iapetus several times. Cassini's images revealed the ridge and other details on the dark half of the moon and in the small area between the dark and bright regions.

Iapetus's diameter measures roughly 900 miles (1,450 kilometers). The moon orbits Saturn every 79.3 Earth days at an average distance of about 2,213,000 miles (3,561,000 kilometers). Iapetus is named for one of the Titans, the first gods in Greek mythology.

Other articles to read include: **Cassini; Cassini, Giovanni Domenico; Enceladus; Mimas; Rhea; Satellite; Saturn; Titan; Voyager.**

Meteor Crater in Arizona is a popular tourist attraction. The crater is about 4,180 feet (1,275 meters) across.

Impact crater

An impact crater is a hole made when a *meteorite* strikes the surface of a planet, moon, or other solid body in space. A meteorite is a chunk of stone or metal from outer space, usually from an asteroid or comet. When the object is flying through space, it is called a *meteoroid (MEE tee uh royd)*. Once the object lands, it is called a *meteorite*. Particularly large impact craters are often called *impact basins*.

The impact of an meteorite releases a tremendous amount of energy in the form of *shock waves*. Shock waves are waves of energy that travel away from the impact. The shock waves travel through the surface until their energy is used up. As they travel, they push material away from the impact site, forming the crater. The shock waves force some of this material upward and outward to form the wall of the crater. The impact also tosses some of the material into the air. This material, called *ejecta,* settles around the crater in a layer.

Small impact craters are often bowl-shaped. Larger impact craters and basins tend to have flatter bottoms and more complex features. After a large impact, the center of the crater can bounce back up, producing a central peak. The steep walls can collapse under the force of gravity, forming *terraces* (layered areas).

Impact craters of many sizes mark the surfaces of the planets, moons, and other bodies in the solar system. Callisto, a large moon of Jupiter, is one of the most heavily cratered bodies in the solar system. In fact, its surface is almost completely covered by impact craters. Craters also cover much of the surface of Earth's moon.

Some impact craters on Mars have unusual-looking deposits of ejecta. These deposits resemble mudflows that have become solid. This appearance suggests that the impacting bodies may have encountered water or ice beneath the ground. Mercury has many deep impact craters. The planet does not have enough *atmosphere* (protective layer of air) to burn up meteoroids by friction.

Venus has fewer craters than do the moon, Mars, and

Continued on the next page

Mercury. This fact suggests that Venus's present surface is less than 1 billion years old. It also suggests, along with other evidence, that Venus remains volcanically active.

Earth has few impact craters even though millions of meteoroids approach Earth every day. Most of these meteoroids are the size of pebbles. They burn up in the atmosphere. Also, over the ages, many of Earth's impact craters have been heavily worn away by water or wind. Many craters have been buried by rocks and dirt as Earth's surface has changed.

More than 120 impact craters and basins have been found on Earth. One of the most famous is Meteor Crater in Arizona. It is about 4,180 feet (1,275 meters) across and 570 feet (175 meters) deep. It formed about 50,000 years ago when an iron meteorite weighing 330,000 tons (300,000 metric tons) struck Earth.

One of the largest buried craters is the Chicxulub *(CHEEK shoo loob)* Crater centered in Mexico's Yucatán Peninsula. The crater is about 112 miles (180 kilometers) in diameter. Rock samples obtained by drilling into the crater indicate that an asteroid or comet struck Earth there 65 million years ago. Many scientists believe that climate changes caused by the impact led to the extinction of many forms of life, including the dinosaurs.

Astronomers study impact craters to learn more about the surfaces of heavenly bodies. The number of craters on a surface gives astronomers some idea of the surface's age. The depth and shape of craters provide scientists with clues about the materials that make up the surface of a planet or other body.

Other articles to read include: **Callisto; Iapetus; Mars; Mercury; Meteor and meteorite; Moon; Venus.**

A massive impact crater about 315 miles (500 kilometers) wide covers a large section of Saturn's moon Iapetus. The impact that created this bowl-shaped depression destroyed about half of an even older crater.

Indian Space Research Organization

The Indian Space Research Organization (ISRO) manages much of India's space program. The organization designs and operates satellites and the rockets that carry them into space. The agency also processes information collected by the satellites.

India's first satellite, the scientific satellite Aryabhatta, was put into orbit by the Soviet Union in 1975. The ISRO's first successful launch was of the satellite Rohini in 1980.

India now has satellites for communications, *meteorology* (the study of weather conditions), and *remote sensing*. Remote-sensing satellites gather information about the surface of Earth. Such information helps India's researchers estimate the size of crops and determine damage from floods, among other uses.

In 2008, India launched the Chandrayaan-1 lunar orbiter. The satellite entered lunar orbit in November with the objective of mapping the moon's surface. Later that month, the satellite released a probe that landed on the surface. With that mission, India became the fifth space agency to reach the surface of the moon.

The ISRO was established in 1969. It was brought under the Department of Space in 1972. Its headquarters are in Bengaluru. India launches its rockets from the island of Sriharikota in the Bay of Bengal.

Other articles to read include: **Satellite, Artificial; Space exploration.**

A rocket carrying an Indian remote-sensing satellite blasts off from the Indian Space Research Organization's space center in Sriharikota, India.

Inflation theory

Inflation theory describes events in the universe in the first few seconds of its history. Inflation theory is an important addition to the *big bang theory,* the most widely accepted theory about the origin of the universe. Inflation theory helps explain the development and structure of the universe. The universe's structure features clumps of galaxies separated by vast regions of relatively

Continued on the next page

empty space. Inflation theory predicts that matter should clump in this way. It also predicts the average number of clumpy and empty regions inflation would produce.

According to this theory, the universe began about 13.8 billion years ago in a cosmic explosion called the big bang. Inflation theory suggests that after the big bang, the universe expanded very rapidly in only a few seconds. In this time, the universe grew from less than the size of a pinpoint to the size of a galaxy.

The American physicist Alan H. Guth developed inflation theory in the late 1970's. In 2002, scientists announced that a satellite called the Wilkinson Microwave Anisotropy Probe (WMAP) had produced detailed images of the radiation left over from the early universe. Studies of the images revealed that matter in the early universe clumped much as inflation theory had predicted.

Other articles to read include: **Big bang; Cosmic microwave background radiation; Galaxy; Universe.**

International Space Station

The International Space Station is a large *artificial satellite* in space. An artificial satellite is an object made by human beings that is put into space by a rocket. More than 15 countries worked together to build the International Space Station. The first part of the station was launched in 1998. The space station was completed in 2011. Astronauts continue to add improvements to the station.

Continued on the next page

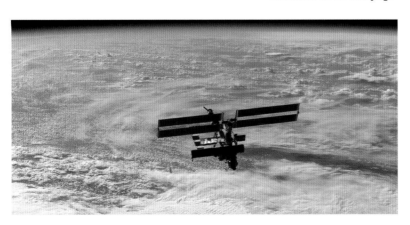

The International Space Station seems to hover above the clouds in an image taken from the space shuttle Atlantis in 2002. The ISS orbits about 250 miles (400 kilometers) above Earth.

American astronaut C. Michael Foale refills a water bag at the *galley* (kitchen) in a section of the ISS called the Zvezda Service Module. The module holds living quarters for the crew and some life-support systems.

An astronaut works in space to complete a section of the International Space Station.

International Space Station   *Continued from the previous page*

Three astronauts live in the International Space Station at one time. For a short period in 2009, 13 people were aboard the station at the same time. People first lived on the station in 2000. The International Space Station is about 250 miles (400 kilometers) above Earth.

The International Space Station is used to conduct scientific experiments. Some of these experiments measure how conditions in space can affect living things, including the astronauts.

A major advantage of a space station is that much of the equipment needs to be carried into space only one time. Spacecraft from several countries regularly visit the station. They bring new supplies and astronauts. In May 2012, SpaceX became the first private company to send a spacecraft to the station.

Other articles to read include: **Astronaut; Mir; Satellite, Artificial.**

Interstellar medium

Interstellar medium is all the ordinary matter between the stars in a *galaxy*. A galaxy is a vast system of stars, gas, dust, and other matter held together in space by their mutual gravitational pull. The interstellar medium includes gases and tiny solid particles known as *interstellar dust*. Most of the gas in our Milky Way

Continued on the next page

Galaxy consists of *molecules* (tiny bits) and single atoms of the *chemical element* hydrogen. A chemical element is a substance with only one kind of atom. The next most common element is helium. The dust particles come in a range of sizes. But the vast majority of them are millions of times smaller than the dust on your desk.

Like ordinary smoke, interstellar dust blocks visible light. Thus, the Milky Way's interstellar medium first appeared to astronomers as oddly shaped dark patches in photographs taken in visible light. The patches appeared against the background "sea" of stars.

The interstellar medium is distributed unevenly within a galaxy. In the Milky Way and other spiral galaxies, the gas is *denser* (more tightly packed) in the star-studded arms than in the regions between the arms.

Extremely hot stars heat the interstellar gas near them. As a result, this gas often glows in beautiful colors. New stars form when cold, especially dense regions of the interstellar medium collapse due to their own gravity.

Other articles to read include: **Dark matter; Galaxy; Star.**

Clouds of interstellar dust and gas surround newly formed stars, in an image take by the Hubble Space Telescope.

Io

Io is a moon of the planet Jupiter. It has more volcanic activity than any other planet or moon in the solar system. Lava flows and more than 200 large volcanic depressions cover the surface. Io's temperature reaches about –260 °F (–160 °C) during the day. But lava from the volcanoes can be hotter than 3,100 °F (1,700 °C).

Io has an iron-rich *core* (center) that is probably liquid. It has a thick *mantle* (middle layer) of *dense* (tightly packed) rocks and a *crust* (outer surface) of lighter rocks and sulfur compounds. Its thin, patchy atmosphere is mainly sulfur dioxide above the volcanoes.

Io's heat comes from the gravitational forces of Jupiter and its other large satellites. These forces pull Io's interior in different directions. As a result, the interior twists, producing heat and partially melting the rock in the mantle.

Continued on the next page

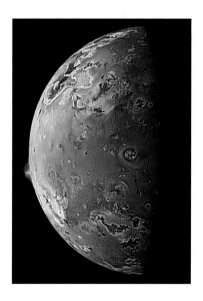

A *plume* (rising column of gas) erupts far into space from a volcano on Io.

Io *Continued from the previous page*

Many of Io's volcanic eruptions resemble those of *geysers*. In these eruptions, sulfur and sulfur dioxide gases may shoot hundreds of miles (kilometers) into space. There, the gases form umbrella-shaped plumes and produce a sulfurous "snow." Sulfur that has settled or flowed onto the surface makes Io one of the most colorful bodies in the solar system. The sulfur creates a rich array of yellows, greenish-yellows, and oranges.

Io is 2,264 miles (3,643 kilometers) in diameter, slightly bigger than Earth's moon. Io *orbits* (travels around) Jupiter every 1.77 Earth days at a distance of about 262,000 miles (421,600 kilometers). Io was discovered in 1610 by Galileo, a famous Italian astronomer and *physicist* (scientist who studies matter and energy).

Other articles to read include: **Callisto; Europa; Ganymede; Jupiter; Satellite.**

Ionosphere

The ionosphere *(eye ON uh sfeer)* is a layer of Earth's *atmosphere*. The atmosphere is the blanket of air around Earth. The ionosphere contains many electrically charged particles called *ions*.

The ionosphere begins about 34 miles to 55 miles (55 to 89 kilometers) above Earth. It ends about 190 miles (306 kilometers) up. It runs through the two highest layers of the atmosphere, called the *mesosphere* and the *thermosphere*.

Electrically charged particles in the ionosphere can produce ribbons of colors in the sky called *auroras.*

The height of the ionosphere depends on the amount of *radiation* (energy) reaching Earth from the sun. During the night, the ions in the ionsphere lose some of their electrical charge. As a result, the lowest layer of the ionosphere almost disappears and the other layers rise.

The ionosphere plays an important role in radio communication. It *reflects* (returns) certain kinds of radio waves back to Earth. Radio signals can be sent thousands of miles (kilometers) by bouncing them off the ionosphere. Otherwise, they would simply escape into space.

Other articles to read include: **Aurora; Magnetic storm.**

James Webb Space Telescope

James Webb Space Telescope, abbreviated JWST, is to be an orbiting space telescope. It will replace some of the abilities of the Hubble Space Telescope. The JWST is expected to be launched in 2018. It will have a main mirror that is 6.5 meters (21 feet) across. This mirror will be about seven times as large as Hubble's mirror. The JWST is designed to study *infrared* light. This type of light wave is invisible to humans but can be felt as heat. Thus, the JWST will not replace Hubble's ability to see in visible light.

The JWST will enable scientists to study the history of the universe, nearly all the way back to the cosmic explosion called the *big bang.* The telescope will collect information on the first stars and galaxies that formed after the big bang. The JWST will also help astronomers to study the forma-tion of stars and their planets and the evolution of the planets in the solar system.

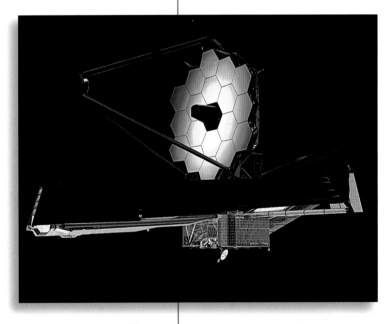

The JWST will orbit 930,000 miles (1.5 million kilometers) from Earth, observing the skies for up to 10 years. During that time, it will be the world's most important space obser-vatory and will be used by thousands of astronomers worldwide.

The JWST is being built by NASA, the United States space agency, the European Space Agency, and the Canadian Space Agency. The Space Telescope Science Institute, which currently operates Hubble, will operate the JWST after its launch.

The telescope is named after James Webb, the former NASA administrator who helped to develop and direct the Apollo program. Apollo was the U.S. space program that carried people to the moon.

Other articles to read include: **Hubble Space Telescope; Satellite, Artificial; Telescope.**

The James Webb Space Telescope is expected to launch in 2018. It will be the most powerful telescope ever launched into space.

Karl Jansky stands before his radio antenna. He became the first person to detect radio waves from space.

Jansky, Karl Guthe

Karl Guthe Jansky *(JAN skee)* (1905-1950) was an American engineer. He was the first person to detect radio waves from outside the *solar system* (the sun, the planets, and everything else that orbits the sun). Jansky's discovery led to the development of *radio astronomy,* a branch of astronomy that studies radio waves given off by objects in space.

In 1931, Jansky began to study the *static* in radio messages beamed across the Atlantic Ocean. Static is a disturbance in radio signals, usually caused by electricity in the atmosphere. In 1932, Janksy heard static he could not identify. He soon determined that the static came from outside the solar system. The source was located in the constellation Sagittarius. Jansky reported his findings in 1932 and 1933. His discovery marked a great advance in astronomy. Today, scientists use radio waves to observe objects in space that cannot be seen with other telescopes.

Jansky was born in Norman, Oklahoma. He graduated from the University of Wisconsin.

Other articles to read include: **Sagittarius; Telescope.**

Mae Jemison

Jemison, Mae Carol

Mae Carol Jemison (1956-) is an American doctor who became an astronaut. She was the first African American woman to travel in space.

Jemison was born in Decatur, Alabama. She grew up in Chicago and studied medicine at Cornell University in Ithaca, New York. For two years, she worked for the Peace Corps in Africa.

In September 1992, Jemison flew on the space shuttle Endeavour. She spent eight days in space. While on the Endeavour, she performed many scientific experiments.

Jemison left the space program in March 1993. She went to work on other projects, including the improvement of health care in western Africa.

Other articles to read include: **Astronaut; Space exploration.**

Jet Propulsion Laboratory

The Jet Propulsion Laboratory (JPL), in Pasadena, California, is a center for the design and control of *robotic* (unpiloted) spacecraft. The California Institute of Technology manages JPL for NASA, the United States space agency. Many JPL probes explore the other planets and moons of the solar system. The laboratory also participates in satellite missions to study Earth's atmosphere and surface. It operates NASA's Deep Space Network, a group of ground stations that track space probes and communicate with them.

A few students at the California Institute of Technology established the laboratory in 1936 as a place for rocket research. The laboratory performed research and development work on rockets for the U.S. Army from 1939 until 1958. In that year, JPL was taken over by NASA.

On January 31, 1958, JPL engineers launched Explorer 1, the first U.S. *artificial satellite* (human-made satellite). From 1962 to 1968, the laboratory guided the Ranger lunar probes and the Surveyor lunar landers. These craft helped prepare the way for astronauts to land on the moon. Mariner probes controlled by the laboratory visited Venus, Mars, and Mercury in the 1960's and early 1970's. The laboratory also participated in the Viking mission. This mission studied the *atmosphere* (blanket of gases) and soil of Mars during the mid-1970's. JPL designed the Voyager probes, which flew past Jupiter, Saturn, Uranus, and Neptune in the late 1970's and the 1980's. The Voyager probes are expected to be the first artificial object to leave the solar system.

In the late 1980's, JPL began launching a series of probes that studied the planets in greater detail. The Magellan spacecraft mapped the surface of Venus from 1990 to 1994. Galileo studied Jupiter and its moons from 1995 to 2003. Cassini began studying Saturn and its moons and rings in 2004. The laboratory also designed and controlled several orbiters and rovers sent to Mars. These include the Mars Science Lab, also called Curiosity. That rover landed in 2012.

Other articles to read include: **National Aeronautics and Space Administration; Rocket; Space exploration.**

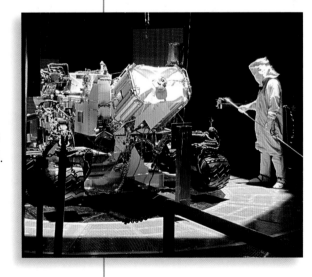

A heavily suited technician at JPL works on the Mars Science Laboratory, nicknamed Curiosity. The probe was built under *sterile* (germ-free conditions) to keep the probe from carrying life from Earth to Mars.

Jodrell Bank Observatory

The Jodrell *(JOH druhl)* Bank Observatory is one of the world's leading *radio astronomy* observatories. Radio astronomy observes radio waves instead of visible light waves. Jodrell Bank is located near Manchester, England. The Lovell telescope, the first giant radio telescope, began operating there in 1957. It has a dish-shaped reflector 250 feet (76.2 meters) across. The dish focuses radio waves on an antenna in the center of the dish. The observatory serves as a research and teaching department of the University of Manchester.

Astronomers at Jodrell Bank study objects called *pulsars*. Pulsars are the remains of exploded stars. Most give off pulses of radio waves, much like a ticking clock gives off pulses of sound. Jodrell scientists also study the gas and dust in galaxies. With the help of a radio telescope network called MERLIN, astronomers at Jodrell have mapped the location of many different sources of radio waves in the sky. These objects include distant galaxies and glowing objects called *quasars*. Quasars are galaxies that give off huge amounts of energy.

Other articles to read include: **Observatory; Pulsar; Telescope.**

The antenna at the center of the Lovell telescope translates radio waves collected by the dish-shaped reflector into electrical signals. Astronomers study the signals to learn about the objects that gave off the radio waves.

Johnson Space Center

The Johnson Space Center is the headquarters for all United States spacecraft projects involving astronauts. It is run by NASA, the United States space agency. The center's full name is the Lyndon B. Johnson Space Center. It was formerly called the Manned Spacecraft Center. The center covers about 1,600 acres (647 hectares) in Houston.

The space center serves as training headquarters for U.S. astronauts. After astronauts lift off from Cape Canaveral, Florida, the Mission Control Center at the space center takes control of

Continued on the next page

the flight. Mission Control monitors the systems that keep the astronauts alive and the spacecraft functioning.

Engineers at the space center design, develop, and help construct spacecraft. The vehicles are built in factories and then checked thoroughly at the space center. Special chambers at the space center reproduce flight vibrations, the vacuum of space, and the great temperature changes in space.

The construction of the Manned Spacecraft Center began in 1962. The center became the headquarters of the U.S. piloted space program in 1964. Scientists and engineers at the center directed the first landing of astronauts on the moon in July 1969. The space center was renamed in February 1973, after the death of former U.S. President Lyndon B. Johnson.

Other articles to read include: **National Aeronautics and Space Administration; Space exploration.**

Visitors to the Johnson Space Center in Houston view a Saturn V rocket, the type of rocket used to launch U.S. astronauts to the moon.

Jupiter

Jupiter is the fifth planet from the sun. It is the largest planet in the solar system. More than 1,000 Earths could fit inside Jupiter. When viewed from Earth, Jupiter appears brighter than most stars. Among the planets, only Venus is brighter. Jupiter is named after the king of the Roman gods.

Jupiter lies at the center of a system of cosmic objects so vast and varied that it resembles a miniature solar system. Jupiter has at least 63 *satellites* (moons) that *rotate* (spin) around it the way our moon rotates around Earth. Some 16 of these moons measure at least 6 miles (10 kilometers) in diameter. Scientists have discovered volcanoes on the moon called Io. They believe the moons Europa and Ganymede may have deep oceans of liquid water or slushy water ice beneath their solid surfaces. Four faint rings of dust particles encircle Jupiter.

Jupiter also has a strong *magnetic field*. A magnetic field is the area around a magnet in which its influence can be detected.

Continued on the next page

Jupiter's colorful bands of clouds are on display in an image taken by the Cassini space probe on its way to Saturn.

The crash of pieces of Comet Shoemaker-Levy 9 into Jupiter in 1994 is recorded in images taken by the Hubble Space Telescope. About five minutes after impact (1), a plume rises from the site (far left in photo). Darker gases brought to the surface by the impact clearly mark the site about 1 ½ hours after the collision (2). At 1 ½ days (3) and 5 days (4) after impact, Jupiter's high-speed winds have scattered the gases across the surface.

Jupiter   *Continued from the previous page*

Jupiter's magnetic field extends beyond the planet throughout a huge region of space called the *magnetosphere.* Astronomers sometimes refer to the planet together with its rings, satellites, and magnetosphere as the *Jovian system.*

Jupiter is a *gas giant,* a ball of gas and liquid. It has little or no solid surface. The planet's colorfully swirled appearance comes from thick red, brown, yellow, and white clouds in the lower *atmosphere* (blanket of gases). The clouds have dark areas called *belts* and light-colored areas called *zones.* These areas circle the planet and give it a striped appearance. In the zones, winds blow at speeds that reach up to 400 miles (650 kilometers) per hour near the *equator* (imaginary line around the middle of the planet).

Jupiter's most outstanding surface feature is the Great Red Spot, a swirling mass of gas. The color of the Great Red Spot varies from brick-red to brownish. The spot is so large that Earth could fit inside. The Great Red Spot is only one of the many oval or circular features in the atmosphere.

In addition to ovals, belts, and zones, Jupiter has storms and lightning. The lightning flashes on Jupiter are much more powerful than those on Earth.

Jupiter gives off about twice as much energy as it *absorbs* (takes in) from the sun. This indicates that some of Jupiter's energy comes from a source other than the sun. The energy may be heat left over from Jupiter's formation. It might also come from heat created as the planet slowly shrinks under the influence of gravity.

Jupiter *rotates* (spins) faster than any other planet. Jupiter's day—that is, the time it takes to rotate once—equals only about 9 hours and 55 minutes on Earth. By comparison, Earth's day is 24 hours long. Jupiter takes about 12 Earth years to travel once around the sun.

Astronomers have made detailed observations of Jupiter for centuries. It was one of the first planets studied by the famous Italian astronomer Galileo in the early 1600's. In 1610, Galileo discovered the four moons that later became known as the Galilean satellites. At the time, many people believed that every

Continued on the next page

Kk

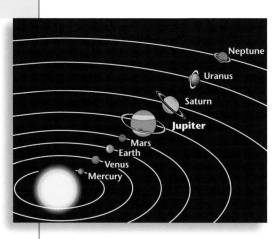

cosmic body revolved around Earth. The discovery of moons orbiting another planet helped convince Galileo and others that Earth was not at the center of the universe.

In 1995, the Galileo spacecraft became the first craft to orbit Jupiter. On the day the spacecraft arrived, a probe Galileo had released months earlier entered Jupiter's atmosphere. The probe made the first precise measurements of the atmosphere's helium, ammonia, and many other substances. It also recorded the speed of the winds below the cloud tops. The main Galileo spacecraft continued to orbit Jupiter for eight years. The Cassini spacecraft, designed to study Saturn, flew by Jupiter in December 2000. Galileo and Cassini helped astronomers study Jupiter's moons, atmosphere, and weather from two locations.

Other articles to read include: **Callisto; Cassini; Europa; Galileo** (scientist); **Galileo** (space probe); **Ganymede; Gas giant; Io; Planet; Satellite.**

Jupiter is the largest planet in the solar system and the fifth planet from the sun.

The twin domes of the Keck Observatory share the top of Mauna Kea with a number of other telescopes, including the Subaru telescope (left in photo).

Keck Observatory

The Keck Observatory includes two giant telescopes. It is on Mauna Kea *(MOW nuh KAY uh),* an inactive volcano on the island of Hawaii. At the observatory, scientists called *astronomers* study planets, stars, and other objects in the sky. The Keck telescopes are among the largest *optical telescopes* in the world. An optical telescope collects visible light.

The telescopes at the observatory are called Keck I and Keck II. Along with visible light, the Keck telescopes gather

Continued on the next page

Keck Observatory   *Continued from the previous page*

infrared (heat) waves from space. Keck I and II are *reflecting tele-scopes*. Each uses a large mirror to collect and focus light.

Each of the two mirrors actually consists of 36 smaller mirrors mounted together. Together, the 36 mirrors form a reflecting surface 33 feet (10 meters) in diameter. The two telescopes are sometimes used together. Used in this way, they act like a single larger telescope.

Keck I was completed in 1992. Keck II was built in 1996. The full name of the station is the W. M. Keck Observatory. It is named for a charitable foundation established by the American businessman William Myron Keck. The W. M. Keck Foundation funded the observatory's construction.

Other articles to read include: **Observatory; Telescope.**

Kennedy Space Center

The space shuttle Discovery exits the Kennedy Space Center's Vehicle Assembly Building in preparation for a launch to the International Space Station.

The Kennedy Space Center is a launching site for spacecraft. It is on the east coast of Florida.

The full name of the center is the John F. Kennedy Space Center of the National Aeronautics and Space Administration (NASA). It is on Merritt Island, across from a point of land called Cape Canaveral. The center used to be at Cape Canaveral. For this reason, people sometimes call the center *Cape Canaveral*.

NASA tests, fixes, and launches spacecraft at the Kennedy Space Center. Parts of the center are available for tour by the public.

Other articles to read include: **National Aeronautics and Space Administration; Space exploration.**

Kepler (spacecraft)

Kepler is a telescope that orbits Earth in space. It is designed to search for planets orbiting stars other than the sun. Scientists refer to planets outside the solar system as *extrasolar planets* or *exoplanets.*

Kepler collects light from stars with a *primary* (main) mirror measuring about 4.6 feet (1.4 meters) across. The craft measures the light using 42 sensors called *charge-coupled devices* or CCD's, the same devices found in digital cameras.

Kepler looks for small changes in brightness that occur when a planet passes in front of its star. These events are called *transits.* The tiny dimming lasts from a few hours to as long as 16 hours. Kepler hunts for transits that repeat. A transit that repeats after the same amount of time might be caused by a planet. Kepler watches about 100,000 stars at the same time.

Kepler's main goal is to find small, rocky planets, like Earth, that orbit within their star's *habitable zone.* In this zone, temperatures allow for liquid water on the planets. Scientists think liquid water is needed for life as we know it. The mission will also help scientists understand the variety of *planetary systems* (stars and their planets) in the universe.

NASA, the United States space agency, launched Kepler in March 2009. The telescope began making observations several months later. Kepler trails behind Earth in its *orbit* (path) around the sun. The mission was originally planned to last for 3½ years. But in April 2012, the mission was extended through 2016.

The Kepler telescope is named for Johannes Kepler, a German astronomer and mathematician. Kepler discovered the three laws of *planetary motion.* These laws describe the movements of the planets around the sun.

Other articles to read include: **Extrasolar planet; Habitable zone; Kepler, Johannes; Space exploration; Transit.**

The Kepler spacecraft is prepared for fueling at a hazardous operations facility in Florida. Technicians wear protective clothing to prevent dust and other particles from contaminating the satellite.

Johannes Kepler

Kepler, Johannes

Johannes *(yoh HAHN uhs)* Kepler (1571–1630) was a German *astronomer (uh STRON uh muhr)* and mathematician. An astronomer is a scientist who studies the planets, stars, and other objects in the sky. Kepler helped to change many long-held beliefs about the solar system.

Kepler discovered three laws that explained how the planets move around the sun. The English scientist Sir Isaac Newton later used Kepler's laws to create his laws about *gravitation*. Gravitation, also known as the force of gravity, keeps the planets in orbit around the sun and your feet firmly on the ground.

Kepler was one of the first astronomers to support the ideas of the Polish astronomer Nicolaus Copernicus *(koh PUR nuh kuhs)*. Copernicus had proposed that the planets *revolve* (travel around) around the sun. At the time, people believed that the sun revolved around Earth.

Kepler's most important discovery was that planets follows an *elliptical* (oval-shaped) orbit around the sun. This discovery disproved the belief that planets follow circular orbits, which was more than 2,000 years old. The results were published in Kepler's book *New Astronomy* (1609).

Kepler made important contributions to other areas of science, including *optics* (the study of light). For example, he helped explain how lenses work. Kepler was born in Weil, near Stuttgart, Germany.

Other articles to read include: **Copernicus, Nicolaus; Gravitation; Kepler; Orbit; Planet; Solar system.**

Kuiper, Gerard Peter

Gerard Peter Kuiper *(KY pur)* (1905-1973) was Dutch-born American astronomer. He made important studies of the planets. He became known for his work in the United States space program during the mid-1960's. Kuiper was a leading scientist in the Ranger space project. This project provided the first close-up photographs of the moon. These photographs helped scientists choose landing sites on the moon for U.S. astronauts. Kuiper's other achievements included the discovery of the second moon of

Continued on the next page

Neptune and the fifth moon of Uranus. The Kuiper belt, an area of rocky objects lying beyond the orbit of Neptune, is named in his honor. This area has several known *dwarf planets,* including Pluto and Eris.

Kuiper was born in Harenkarspel, the Netherlands, near Alkmaar. He received a Ph.D. degree from the State University of Leiden in 1933. Later that year, he moved to the United States. He served on the faculty of the University of Chicago from 1936 to 1960. Kuiper then became director of the Lunar and Planetary Laboratory at the University of Arizona.

Other articles to read include: **Astronomy; Kuiper belt; Moon.**

Kuiper belt

The Kuiper *(KY pur)* belt is a band of objects in the outer regions of the solar system. These objects are called Kuiper belt objects or KBO's. They are probably made of ice and rock. Scientists believe that KBO's are "building blocks" left over from the formation of the planets. Astronomers think that there may be as many as 100 billion KBO's larger than 0.6 mile (1 kilometer) across. About 100,000 may measure more than 60 miles (100 kilometers) across. Some KBO's are large enough to be considered *dwarf* planets.

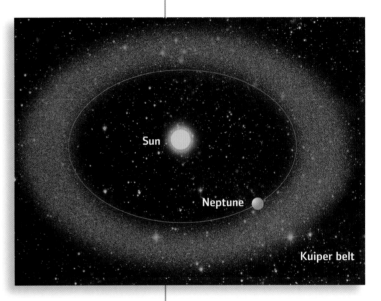

The Kuiper belt lies far beyond the orbit of Neptune. (Neither the size of objects nor the distance between objects in this illustration is drawn to scale.)

Most KBO's orbit the sun beyond the planet Neptune. Pluto is one of the larger Kuiper belt objects. Another large KBO is named Eris. Some KBO's become comets. These objects stray so close to Neptune that Neptune's gravity hurls them toward the sun. The objects may turn into comets by taking in enough heat to turn some of its ice into a gas.

An Irish scientist named Kenneth E. Edgeworth first suggested that KBO's existed. They were described in more detail in 1951 by the Dutch-born American astronomer Gerard P. Kuiper. The belt is named for him. The United States New Horizons probe, launched in 2006, was designed to explore the Kuiper belt after visiting Pluto in 2015.

Other articles to read include: **Dwarf planet; Eris; Kuiper, Gerard Peter; Neptune; New Horizons; Pluto; Solar system.**

Laplace, Marquis de

The Marquis de Laplace *(mar KEE duh la PLAS)* (1749-1827) was a French astronomer and mathematician. In his *Exposition of the System of the Universe* (1796), Laplace set out his ideas about the beginning of the solar system. He believed that a huge, lens-shaped cloud of gas spinned, cooled, shrank, and threw off planets and satellites. The remaining matter formed the sun. Laplace's theory was accepted by scientists for a long time. But it has since been replaced by other theories.

Laplace also made contributions to mathematical astronomy. He helped people understand the complicated movements of the heavenly bodies. In *Celestial Mechanics* (1799–1825), he wrote of

many of the achievements in astronomy from the time of Sir Isaac Newton.

Pierre Simon Laplace was born at Beaumont-en-Auge, France. He became a professor of mathematics in Paris at the age of 20. He was probably made a *marquis* (nobleman) in 1817.

Other articles to read include:
Astronomy; Planet; Solar system.

Marquis de Laplace

Large Binocular Telescope

The Large Binocular Telescope (LBT) is an observatory on Mount Graham, about 75 miles (120 kilometers) northeast of Tucson, Arizona. The LBT is built like a giant pair of binoculars. It consists of two identical telescopes connected side by side. Together, they make up one of the largest telescopes in the world. Scientists in Italy, Germany, and the United States worked together to build the observatory.

Continued on the next page

Each of the LBT's twin telescopes gathers light through its own *primary* (main) mirror. Each large mirror measures 27.6 feet (8.4 meters) in diameter. The light from the two telescopes are combined to make one image. By combining the light, the telescopes can see with greater *resolution* than either single telescope can see by itself. Resolution is the ability to produce images of faraway or very faint objects in great detail. The combined light is then directed into cameras and other instruments.

Astronomers took their first images using both mirrors of the LBT in 2008. In 2012, scientists began using new instruments to combine the light from the twin telescopes. The new instruments greatly increase the LBT's resolution. Such high resolution enables astronomers to study such faint objects as planets orbiting nearby stars and distant galaxies.

Other articles to read include: **Observatory; Telescope.**

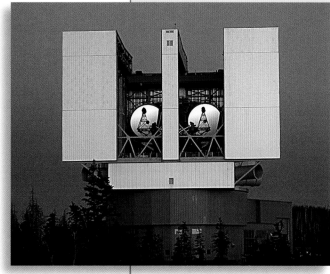

The Large Binocular Telescope on Mount Graham in Arizona is one of the largest optical telescopes on Earth. The two mirrors can be used together or separately.

Leavitt, Henrietta Swan

Henrietta Swan Leavitt (1868-1921) was an American astronomer. Her work helped later astronomers establish the size of the universe.

Leavitt became famous for her study of *Cepheid variables* in the galaxies called the Magellanic Clouds. A Cepheid variable is a type of star whose brightness changes regularly with time. The *period* of such a star is the time its light takes to change from bright to dark and back to bright. Leavitt discovered that stars with longer periods were, on average, brighter than those with shorter periods. Often, this difference can be used to measure the distances to different stars and galaxies.

Leavitt was born in Lancaster, Massachusetts. In 1892, she graduated from the Society for the Collegiate Instruction of Women (now Radcliffe College). She joined the Harvard College Observatory in 1902 and spent her entire career there.

Other articles to read include: **Astronomy; Magellanic Clouds; Star; Universe.**

The constellation Leo, the Lion, can be drawn in a number of ways.

Leo

Leo is a *constellation* known as the Lion. A constellation is a grouping of stars in the night sky. Leo sits between the constellations Cancer and Virgo. It is best viewed around March through May. A well-known meteor shower called the *Leonids* appears to originate in Leo. *Leo* means *lion* in the Latin language.

Leo can be drawn in several ways using different numbers of stars. One of these ways includes 13 main stars. Four stars define the lion's head. A *pentagon* (five-sided figure) of stars forms its neck and mane. The remaining stars mark out a rectangular-shaped body with two legs and a tail. Drawings that use a smaller number of stars typically leave out the legs and use fewer stars for the head, neck, and mane.

Leo was among the 48 constellations defined by the ancient Greek mathematician Ptolemy. Today, it is one of 88 constellations recognized by the International Astronomical Union, the leading authority in the naming of heavenly objects.

Other articles to read include: **Astrology; Constellation; Leonids; Ptolemy; Star; Zodiac.**

Meteors from the Leonid meteor shower streak the sky above an observation tower in Spain, in a time-lapse photograph taken over 20 minutes.

Leonids

The Leonids *(LEE uh nihds)* are meteors that seem to come from the *constellation* Leo. A constellation is a grouping of stars in the night sky. The *meteoroids* (particles or chunks of matter in space) that cause the Leonids travel around the sun in a path that Earth crosses about November 17 each year. The meteoroids become visible when they enter Earth's *atmosphere* (blanket of air).

In most years, few Leonids are seen. However, heavy Leonid meteor showers occur every 33 years when Earth passes through the thickest part of the meteoroid swarm. A heavy Leonid shower occurred in 1999. The next such shower is expected to take place in 2032.

Other articles to read include: **Leo; Meteor and meteorite.**

Libra

Libra is a *constellation* that is also called the Scales. A constellation is a grouping of stars in the night sky. Libra is easiest to see from the Southern Hemisphere. The best time to view Libra is from April though June.

Libra can be drawn in several different ways. One way of connecting the stars creates the image of a *balance scale.* A balance scale is a beam with a cup hanging from each end. In Greek mythology, the blindfolded goddess of justice holds the Scales. Statues of the goddess and the Scales are in many modern courthouses. The name *Libra* means *scales* or *balance* in the Latin language.

Libra was among the 48 constellations defined by the ancient Greek mathematician Ptolemy. Today, it is one of 88 constellations recognized by the International Astronomical Union, the leading authority in the naming of heavenly objects.

Other articles to read include: **Astrology; Constellation; Ptolemy; Star; Zodiac.**

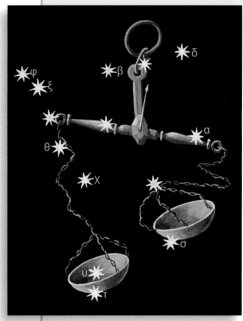

The constellation Libra, also called the Scales, is often shown as a type of scale called a balance scale.

Light

Light is a kind of energy that comes in a range of forms. All these forms are called *electromagnetic energy.* Electromagnetic energy is made of tiny individual packets of energy called *photons.* This energy travels freely through space in patterns of electric and magnetic influence called *electromagnetic waves.*

Human beings can see only a small part of this range. This part is called *visible light.* We see objects because visible light bounces off them and enters our eyes. This bouncing is called *reflection.* In the eye, light causes chemical and electrical changes that make it possible for us to see.

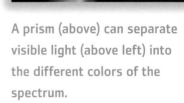

A prism (above) can separate visible light (above left) into the different colors of the spectrum.

Continued on the next page

Light *Continued from the previous page*

There are several sources of visible light in the universe. Stars produce much of this light. Many scientists believe that the centers of most galaxies produce at least some visible light. Some galaxies, called *quasars,* produce tremendous amounts of energy. Some of it can be seen as visible light. When larger stars reach the end of their lives, they can explode. An exploding star is called *supernova.* A supernova can produce millions of times as much light as a single star.

Most visible light comes from tiny particles within atoms called *electrons.* Electrons have a tiny negative electric charge. Light is produced by electrons that have gained energy from an outside source. They may have absorbed light from another source. They may also have been struck by other particles.

Heat can also provide energy to electrons. An atom with such an "energized" electron is said to be "excited." Ordinarily, an atom stays excited briefly. It de-excites by giving up the extra energy. It can transfer the energy to another atom in a collision. It can also *emit* (give off) a photon of visible light or another kind of electro-magnetic energy. The light carries away the extra energy. The energy given off by most artificial lights is provided by electricity.

Light waves have *crests* (peaks) and *troughs* (lows), like waves in the sea. The distance between two crests or troughs in a row is called the wave's *wavelength.* In addition to visible light, electro-magnetic energy includes radio waves, infrared rays (also called *heat rays*), ultraviolet rays, X rays, and gamma rays. Most scientists consider microwaves to be a form of radio waves.

Ultraviolet rays have wave-lengths too short to be detected by the human eye. Ultraviolet rays cause sunburn and suntan. Infrared rays have wavelengths too long to be detected by the human eye. Infrared rays cause the warming sensation we feel

Continued on the next page

A band of colors called the *visible spectrum* forms when white light passes through a prism. The prism bends the shortest light waves the most. They appear violet. It bends the longest waves the least. They appear red. All other colors lie in-between. The length of light waves is measured in nanometers. One nanometer is one-billionth of a meter, or about ¹⁄₂₅,₀₀₀,₀₀₀ inch.

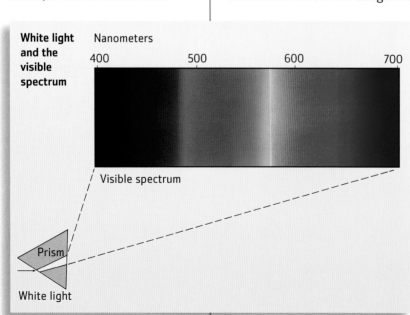

White light and the visible spectrum

Nanometers

400   500   600   700

Visible spectrum

Prism

White light

from sunlight. The entire range of wavelengths, from radio waves at the longest to short gamma rays at the shortest, is called the *electromagnetic spectrum*.

The shorter the wavelength, the more energy a wave has. Radio waves have long wavelengths. They have the least energy. Radio waves are fairly harmless to people. Gamma rays have the shortest wavelengths. They have the most energy. Gamma rays can be harmful to people, even in small amounts.

In addition to ultraviolet and infrared rays, sunlight is also part white light. When white light passes through a *prism (PRIHZ uhm)*, it separates into the colors of the rainbow. Violet light has the shortest wavelength we can see, and red light has the longest. When light passes through something, it may bend and change its direction. This bending is called *refraction (rih FRAK shuhn)*.

Scientists measure the wavelength, brightness, and speed of light. The speed of light in empty space is always the same. In space, light travels at 186,282 miles (299,792 kilometers) per second. The wavelengths of electromagnetic radiation can be lengthened by two means. Such a lengthening is called *redshift*. The longest wavelengths of visible light are red, while the shortest are blue. Lengthening the wavelength of visible light "shifts" the wavelength towards the red end of the spectrum. Shortening the wavelength shifts it towards the blue end.

The first way to lengthen wavelengths is called *Doppler redshift*. The motion of the wave source compared to the viewer causes this redshift. Light waves given off by an object moving away from an observer will spread out to longer wavelengths. The Doppler effect can work in reverse. Light waves given off by an object moving toward an observer will push together into shorter wavelengths. This is often called blueshift.

The second redshift is called *cosmological redshift*. It is produced by the *expansion* (stretching out) of the universe. Most scientists believe that the universe began expanding about 13.8 billion years ago in a cosmic explosion called the *big bang*. As the universe expands, the distance between most galaxies increases. The wavelength of light also steadily grows as it travels through the expanding space. The farther the radiation travels—that is, the more space it travels through—the more its wavelength stretches.

Other articles to read include: **Aurora; Big bang; Electromagnetic waves; Gamma rays; Light pollution; Light-year; Magnitude; Redshift.**

The bright lights of such urban areas as New York City can wash out the incoming light from stars and planets.

Light pollution

Light pollution is unwanted light in the night sky caused by *artificial* (human-made) lighting. Such lighting includes street lights and the lights in and on buildings. Many street and building lights in towns and cities are not aimed at only the ground. Instead, their light goes in many directions, including up into the sky. Such lights, combined over the area of a city, create a type of light pollution called *sky glow*. This glow is often brighter than starlight.

Light pollution hides stars' light in much the same way that the sunlit sky does during the day. Light pollution interferes with people's view of the stars. Astronomers at nearby observatories may not be able to observe the sky. Light pollution can also harm wildlife. The light can change animals' natural behavior and movements. Light affects the behavior of many animals, including migrating birds, frogs, and sea turtles. Such animals may be attracted to artificial light sources. In addition, many outdoor light fixtures waste energy by shining light where it is not needed.

Some communities and organizations work to fight light pollution. Communities may limit the kind and position of lighting fixtures. For example, street lights and other artificial lights can be shielded so they shine only on the ground. Some national parks in the United States, Canada, New Zealand, and the United Kingdom have been recognized as *dark-sky parks* or *reserves*.

Other articles to read include: **Astronomy; Light; Star.**

Light-year

A light-year is the distance that light travels in a *vacuum* in one year. A vacuum is a space that contains little matter. The light-year is used by scientists called *astronomers (uh STRON uh muhrz)* to describe the vast distances between stars, galaxies, and other objects in space.

Continued on the next page

Light travels at a speed of 186,282 miles (299,792 kilometers) per second. Therefore, one light-year equals about 5.88 trillion miles (9.46 trillion kilometers). A jet moving at a speed of 500 miles (800 kilometers) per hour would need to fly for 1.34 million years to travel one light-year.

Objects in space are usually very far from one another. Even the star nearest to Earth—other than the sun—is 4.3 light-years away. The Andromeda Galaxy, the large galaxy nearest to our own Milky Way, is about 2.5 million light-years away.

Other articles to read include: **Astronomical unit; Andromeda Galaxy; Light.**

Local Group

The Local Group is the small group of *galaxies* that includes our own galaxy, the Milky Way. A galaxy is a huge collection of stars, gas, and dust held together by gravity. The sun, Earth, and all the other planets in the solar system are located in the Milky Way. Astronomers have found about 40 galaxies in the Local Group. These galaxies occupy a roughly ball-shaped region of space around 10 million *light-years* in diameter. One light-year is the distance light travels in a vacuum in a year—about 5.88 trillion miles (9.46 trillion kilometers).

The Andromeda Galaxy and the Milky Way are the largest galaxies in the Local Group. They have more matter than all the other galaxies in the group combined. The Local Group also includes many much smaller galaxies, called *dwarf galaxies*. Many of these galaxies orbit the Milky Way or the Andromeda Galaxy, much like the moon orbits Earth.

Today, the Milky Way and the Andromeda Galaxy are pulling closer together. In a few billion years, they will collide to form a larger galaxy.

With the unaided eye or binoculars, we can see the Milky Way and four other galaxies in the Local Group. The Andromeda Galaxy and Triangulum Galaxy appear in the northern sky. The Magellanic Clouds, two dwarf galaxies, appear in the southern sky.

Other articles to read include: **Andromeda Galaxy; Galaxy; Milky Way.**

Galaxies in the Local Group include NGC 224 (center) and its small companion NGC 221 (lower center). Another galaxy in the group, known as NGC 205, appears upper right in the image.

Lowell, Percival

Percival Lowell (1855–1916) was an American astronomer. He became best known for his belief in the possibility of life on Mars. Lowell based this belief on what he thought were canals there. But later astronomers proved that canals do not exist on Mars.

Lowell began his career as a businessman. Soon, however, his interests turned to astronomy. In 1894, he completed the Lowell Observatory in Flagstaff, Arizona. He wrote several books, which had wider popular appeal than scientific value.

In 1905, his studies led him to predict the discovery of a planet beyond Neptune. He proposed that the force of gravity of some unknown object was affecting the orbits of Neptune and Uranus. He began an intensive search for it from his observatory. But he died in 1916 without finding it. In 1930, Clyde W. Tombaugh, an assistant at the Lowell Observatory, discovered Pluto. The planet was named after the Roman god of the dead. The name also honors Percival Lowell, whose initials are the first two letters of Pluto. Lowell was born in Boston.

Other articles to read include: **Astronomy; Extraterrestrial intelligence; Mars; Pluto.**

Percival Lowell

Lyra

Lyra *(LY ruh)* is a small *constellation* that is also called the Harp. A constellation is a grouping of stars in the night sky. Lyra is named for an ancient stringed musical instrument that resembles a small harp. The lyre was especially popular amomg the ancient Greeks.

Lyra can be seen from the Northern Hemisphere. Its brightest star, Vega, is about 26 *light-years* from Earth. One light-year equals 5.88 trillion miles (9.46 trillion kilometers). Vega is the fifth-brightest star visible from Earth, excluding the sun.

Lyra can be drawn in several ways using a different number of stars. It is often shown with 10 stars.

Continued on the next page

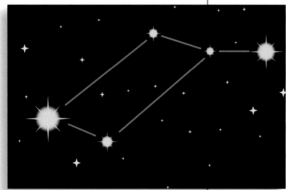

The constellation Lyra is also known as the Harp.

Lyra has two notable features that can be seen through a small telescope. One of them is Epsilon Lyrae, a *binary star* (pair of stars that orbit each other). Another is the *Ring Nebula,* a ring-shaped cloud of dust and gas surrounding a very faint star. The nebula formed when the star blew off an outer layer of its atmosphere.

Other articles to read include: **Binary star; Constellation; Nebula; Star.**

Magellanic Clouds

The Magellanic Clouds are two nearby galaxies. They can be seen from Earth's Southern Hemisphere. They look like small, hazy patches of light. They are the galaxies closest to our galaxy, the Milky Way.

The Large Magellanic Cloud is about 160,000 *light-years* from Earth. A light-year is the distance that light travels in a vacuum in one year. It is about 5.88 trillion miles (9.46 trillion kilometers). The Small Magellanic Cloud is about 180,000 light-years away. They are both a type of galaxy called a *dwarf galaxy.* They are called dwarf galaxies because they are quite small compared with the largest galaxies.

The Magellanic Clouds have billions of stars. But single stars can only be seen with the most powerful telescopes. The Magellanic Clouds also have a huge amount of gas. New stars form from the gas. Much of the light from the Magellanic Clouds comes from young, extremely *luminous* (bright) hot blue stars.

The Magellanic Clouds were first reported in the early 1500's by the Portuguese explorer Ferdinand Magellan.
It was not until the early 1900's that people realized the "clouds" were actually galaxies outside the Milky Way.

Other articles to read include: **Galaxy; Milky Way; Star.**

New stars pierce through clouds of dust and gas in a star-forming region of the Large Magellanic Cloud, in a photograph taken by the Hubble Space Telescope.

Magnetic storm

A magnetic storm is a large change in Earth's *magnetic field*. The area around a magnet where its magnetism can be felt is called a magnetic field. Because Earth is a giant magnet, it has a magnetic field. The field goes out many miles into space. The change in Earth's magnetic field is caused by the sun.

The sun is constantly producing a stream of particles and energy called the *solar wind*. The wind flows out into the solar system. These particles are responsible for auroras. Every so often, the solar wind becomes more powerful. The two events that most often produce this extra power are *solar flares* and *coronal mass ejections* (CMEs). A flare is a sudden brightening of a part of the sun. Flares are strong sources of X rays and gamma rays as well as particles. CME's are large eruptions of matter into space. Both of these events send out a huge amount of energy. The energy can affect the magnetic field around Earth. The energy may even pass throught the field and strike Earth directly.

The particles and energy produced by the sun are often called *space weather.* Most space weather does little to change activity on Earth. But every once in a while, a CME or flare can knock out a satellite in space or, if powerful enough, can disrupt electric transmission on Earth. For example, a magnetic storm in 1987 knocked out power across the Canadian province of Quebec. Scientists believe that an extremely powerful CME or a flare directed straight at Earth could knock out the electrical power over an entire continent.

Other articles to read include: **Corona; Coronal mass ejection; Solar wind; Sun.**

Much of the material that comes from the sun is directed around Earth by the planet's magnetic field. Coronal mass ejections and solar flares are two types of solar eruptions that can alter Earth's magnetic field and cause a magnetic storm.

Magnitude

Magnitude is the scale used by astronomers to measure the brightness of objects in space. The brighter a star or planet, the lower its magnitude number. The magnitude system is based on the work of the ancient Greek astronomer Hipparchus. About 125 B.C., Hipparchus classified the stars according to brightness. He called the brightest stars first magnitude; the next brightest, second magnitude; and so on down to the faintest stars. He called the faintest stars sixth magnitude.

Later astronomers found that first magnitude stars were about 100 times as bright as sixth magnitude stars. A star of any magnitude is about 2 ½ times as bright as a star of the next brightest magnitude. This scale has been extended to zero and negative magnitudes because some stars and planets are brighter than first magnitude ones. For example, the sun has a magnitude of minus 27.

The word *magnitude* usually refers to *apparent magnitude,* or the brightness of a star as seen from Earth. To compare actual brightness, astronomers use *absolute magnitude,* which shows how bright stars would appear if they all were the same distance from Earth. The sun is a fifth magnitude star on the absolute magnitude scale.

Other articles to read include: **Hipparchus; Light; Planet; Star.**

Main Belt

The Main Belt is a region of the *solar system* between the orbits of Mars and Jupiter. The vast majority of asteroids lie in the Main Belt. The solar system is the sun and all the objects that orbit the sun. The Main Belt is sometimes called the *Main Asteroid Belt.*

The Main Belt stretches more than 100 million miles (160 million kilometers) across. Most Main Belt asteroids orbit the sun at distances between roughly 2 and 3 *astronomical units.* An astronomical unit (AU) equals about 93 million miles (150 million kilometers). It is the same as the average distance between Earth and the sun.

Main Belt asteroids occur in *families.* These families are groups of tens to hundreds of asteroids that are about the same distance

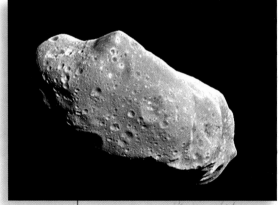

The oddly shaped asteroid Ida orbits among what may be millions of objects in the Main Belt.

Continued on the next page

Main Belt *Continued from previous page*

from the sun. Some groups, such as the Eos family, are made of similar material. This suggests that the Eos members are broken pieces of a larger body or group of bodies. Other families have members made with many different materials. This suggests that their members were not made in the same way.

Other articles to read include: **Asteroid; Ceres; Dawn; Solar system; Vesta.**

Makemake

Makemake *(MAH kee MAH kee)* is a *dwarf planet.* A dwarf planet is a round object in space that is smaller than a planet and larger than a comet or meteor. Makemake was the fourth dwarf planet discovered. It is found in a part of the solar system beyond the farthest planet, Neptune. This area, called the *Kuiper Belt,* is home to several dwarf planets, including Pluto and Eris, as well as millions of other smaller objects. Makemake is the second-brightest object in the Kuiper Belt after Pluto, as seen from Earth.

Makemake has a slightly reddish color. Scientists have found traces of frozen nitrogen on its surface. Scientists think Makemake takes about 310 Earth years to circle the sun. It does this at an average distance of about 50 *astronomical units.* An astronomical unit is the average distance from Earth to the sun. It equals about 93 million miles (150 million kilometers).

Scientists have not found any moons orbiting Makemake. If so, Makemake is the only known dwarf planet without moons.

Makemake was discovered in March 2005. It was named for the god of *fertility* (ability to produce offspring) in the mythology of the Rapanui people of Easter Island.

Other articles to read include: **Ceres; Dwarf planet; Eris; Kuiper belt; Pluto.**

The dwarf planet Makemake is the second-brightest object in the Kuiper belt, behind Pluto, when viewed from Earth.

Maria

Maria *(MAHR ee uh)* are dark areas on Earth's moon. The word *maria* is Latin for *seas;* its singular is *mare (MAHR ee).* The name comes from the smoothness of the dark areas and their resemblance to bodies of water. The maria were created when the parts of the moon were partly flooded by lava from erupting volcanoes. The lava then froze, forming rock. Since that time, meteoroid impacts have created craters in the maria.

The different maria are named "Seas." For example, the first mission to land on the moon set down on the Sea of Tranquility. There are over 20 named maria.

Other articles to read include: **Impact crater; Moon.**

Maria, Latin for *seas,* are the smooth dark areas on the moon's surface.

Mars

Mars is the fourth planet from the sun. It is a reddish planet covered with rocks and *craters (KRAY tuhrz),* or bowl-shaped holes. Mars was named for the ancient Roman god of war because of its bloodlike color. It owes its color to iron-rich minerals in its soil. Mars is sometimes known as the *red planet.*

Scientists have found strong evidence that water once flowed on the surface of Mars. The evidence includes channels, valleys, and gullies on the planet's surface. Some scientists also think that water may still lie in cracks and pores in rocks below the surface. Space probes have also discovered vast amounts of ice in the polar regions.

Some scientists believe life may have existed on Mars billions of years ago and that living things might exist there today. Water is one of three ingredients that scientists believe are necessary for life as we know it. Mars also has the two other ingredients. They are chemical elements that form the building blocks of living things and a source of energy that living organisms can use.

Mars travels around the sun in an *elliptical* (oval-shaped) orbit. It takes about 687 Earth days for Mars to go all the way around

The planet Mars, like Earth, has clouds in its atmosphere and a deposit of ice at its north pole. But unlike Earth, Mars has no liquid water on its surface.

Continued on the next page

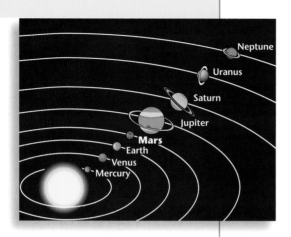

Mars is the fourth planet from the sun.

Olympus Mons is the tallest volcano in the solar system. It rises about 16 miles (25 kilometers) above the surface and spreads over an area as large as the state of Arizona (outlined in white).

Mars *Continued from the previous page*

the sun. The length of a day on Mars is just a bit longer than Earth's. The Martian *solar day* is 24 hours 39 minutes 35 seconds long. Mars has two small moons called Phobos and Deimos.

The *atmosphere* of Mars is about 100 times less *dense* (tightly packed) than the atmosphere of Earth. The atmosphere is the blanket of gases around a planet or moon. But the Martian atmosphere is dense enough to support a weather system that includes clouds and winds. Tremendous dust storms sometimes rage over the entire planet.

The surface of Mars looks more like the surface of Earth than that of any other planet. Like Earth, Mars has plains, canyons, volcanoes, valleys, gullies, and polar ice. Unlike Earth, Mars has many *impact craters* (holes formed when asteroids or comets crashed into the surface).

Mars has the largest volcanoes in the solar system. The tallest volcano is Olympus Mons (Latin for *Mount Olympus*). It rises about 16 miles (25 kilometers) and is more than 370 miles (600 kilometers) across. Martian volcanoes have slopes that rise gradually, much like the slopes of volcanoes in Hawaii. Both the Martian and Hawaiian volcanoes are *shield volcanoes*. They formed from eruptions of lavas that can flow for long distances before becoming solid.

Along the Martian *equator* (imaginary line around the middle) lies one of the most striking features on the planet—a system of canyons known as the Valles Marineris. The canyons run for

about 2,500 miles (4,000 kilometers)— nearly the width of Australia. Individual canyons of the Valles Marineris are as much as 60 miles (100 kilometers) wide and 5 to 6 miles (8 to 10 kilometers) deep. Large channels emerge from

Continued on the next page

the eastern end of the canyons. The channels suggest that the canyons may once have been partly filled with water. Scientists believe that the Valles Marineris formed mostly by *rifting,* a splitting of the *crust* (outer layer) due to being stretched.

Although Mars and Earth are alike in some ways, the plants and animals that live on Earth could not live on Mars. The average temperature on Mars is about –80 °F (–60 °C). Temperatures at the Martian poles drop to as low as about –195 °F (–125 °C) during the winter. But temperatures at midday at the *equator* rise to as high as 70 °F (20 °C). Also, the air of Mars has almost no oxygen. People and animals need oxygen to breathe.

Scientists have studied Mars through telescopes for many years. As yet, no people have set foot on the red planet. In 1965, the United States spacecraft Mariner 4 flew near Mars and took pictures of its surface. It was one of several Mariner missions. In 1976, the U.S. Viking 1 and Viking 2 became the first space-craft to land on Mars. They took pictures and collected soil samples. The U.S. Pathfinder probe landed on Mars in 1997. All these spacecraft were controlled by radio signals from Earth.

In early 2004, the United States sent the rovers Spirit and Opportunity to Mars. The rovers transmitted photographs of ground features and checked rocks and soil for evidence that liquid water once existed on the surface. In 2006, the U.S. Mars Reconnaissance Orbiter went into orbit around Mars. The craft was designed to study the planet's structure and atmosphere and to look for landing sites for future lander and rover missions.

The U.S. Phoenix Mars lander operated on the planet's surface from May to November 2008. Its chief discovery was water ice just below the surface of the Martian soil.

In 2012, a rover called the Mars Science Laboratory descended to the surface on a scheduled 98-week mission. The rover, nick-named Curiosity, is the largest rover to reach the Martian surface. Curiosity has provided scientists with clear evidence that Mars could have been hospitable to microbial life.

Other articles to read include: **Deimos; Mars Exploration Rover Mission; Mars Pathfinder; Mars Science Laboratory; Olympus Mons; Phobos; Planet; Space exploration.**

Seas spill across Mars in an artist's illustration showing how the planet might have appeared billions of years ago.

Mars Exploration Rover Mission

The Mars Exploration Rover Mission consists of two robotic *rovers* sent to Mars. A rover is a remotely controlled vehicle that can move around. The rovers are nicknamed Spirit and Opportunity. They were sent to study the history of water on the planet. Engineers and scientists at the Jet Propulsion Laboratory designed and built the rovers for NASA, the United States space agency. Since landing on Mars in 2004, the rovers have found convincing evidence that the planet's surface and underground once held water. The two rovers are equipped with scientific instruments created by American and European scientists and engineers.

NASA launched Spirit on June 10, 2003, and Opportunity on July 7. Spirit landed on January 4, 2004, in Gusev Crater. The crater is an *impact basin,* a vast hollow created by a large asteroid or comet strike. Scientists suspect the crater once held an ancient lake. Opportunity landed three weeks later in Meridiani Planum, a broad plain on the opposite side of the planet. That site contains a mineral that forms on Earth in the presence of water.

Spirit and Opportunity each have rolled over 4 miles (6 kilometers) on their investigations. The rovers were sent for a 90-day mission. But both Spirit and Opportunity continued to gather information for more than five years. In 2009, Spirit became trapped in a bed of loose soil. Spirit continued to gather information for about two more years. Then NASA ended its mission. Opportunity continues to study Mars.

Other articles to read include: **Mars; Mars Pathfinder; Mars Science Laboratory; Space exploration.**

The Spirit rover examines a rock on Mars, in an artist's illustration.

Mars Pathfinder

The Mars Pathfinder was a United States spacecraft that landed on Mars on July 4, 1977. The space probe sent images and other data from the surface of Mars for nearly three months.

Pathfinder actually "bounced-down" on the Ares Vallis flood plain of Mars. Part of its mission was to test a new landing system that used parachutes and air bags. Just before landing, the air bags filled to completely enclose the spacecraft. This cushioning enabled Pathfinder to land in a rocky valley filled with boulders.

After landing, Pathfinder released the Mars Sojourner Rover. The rover was a small, six-wheeled robot that analyzed the rocks and soil on Mars. The rover circled Pathfinder, roaming as far as 35 feet (12 meters) from the craft. The Pathfinder mission returned more than 16,500 images to scientists on Earth. The photos included spectacular color pictures of the planet's surface and views of the planet's moons and the sun.

Pathfinder identified volcanic rocks that scientists had not expected to find on Mars. It also found that a cloud layer covered the Martian sky in the morning.

Other articles to read include: **Mars; Mars Exploration Rover Mission; Mars Science Laboratory; Space exploration.**

The Sojourner rover studies rock and soil around the Mars Pathfinder's landing site, in a photograph taken by Pathfinder.

Mars Science Laboratory

Mars Science Laboratory is a robotic space mission to the planet Mars. It consists of a six-wheeled *rover* (robotic vehicle) called Curiosity. Curiosity is the largest rover ever sent to Mars. It is the size of a small automobile and weighs nearly 1 ton (900 kilograms). It is controlled from a command center in California. The goal of the Mars Science Laboratory is to look for certain conditions supportive to living things. Such conditions include the presence of liquid water; a source of energy, such as sunlight; and nutrients, including nitrogen, phosphorous, and oxygen. Curiosity was built by the United States National Aeronautics and

Continued on the next page

The Mars Science Laboratory appears in a "self portrait," a combination of several images taken by a camera on its robotic arm.

Mars Science Laboratory *Continued from previous page*

Space Administration (NASA) in partnership with agencies in several other countries. The other countries include Canada, Russia, and several European countries.

Curiosity carries many scientific instruments. They include color cameras and a laser mounted atop a tall mast. The laser can vaporize small pieces of rock from a distance of up to 23 feet (7 meters). Curiosity can then check the vaporized material to determine what the rock was made of. The body of the rover holds instruments that can analyze samples and check for many different chemicals. Curiosity also has a 7-foot (2.1-meter) robotic arm that can make up-close measurements of the surface, drill into rocks, and scoop up soil.

Curiosity launched on Nov. 26, 2011. The rover landed on Aug. 6, 2012, in a depression called Gale Crater. The craft landed using a novel system called a *sky crane.* A parachute slowed the craft after it entered the Martian atmosphere. A set of rockets then lowered the rover to the ground on a long line. Curiosity is designed to drive about 12 miles (20 kilometers) during a mission lasting one Martian year, about 98 weeks.

Other articles to read include: **Mars; Mars Exploration Rover Mission; Mars Pathfinder; Space exploration.**

Christa McAuliffe

McAuliffe, Christa

Christa McAuliffe *(muh KAW lihf)* (1948–1986) was chosen to become the first schoolteacher to travel in space. She blasted off aboard the space shuttle Challenger on Jan. 28, 1986. But the shuttle blew up shortly after take-off. The accident killed McAuliffe and the six other crew members. McAuliffe was selected by NASA, the United States space agency, from more than 11,000 teachers who had asked for the job. She planned to record her thoughts and experiences before, during, and after her space flight.

Sharon Christa Corrigan was born in Boston. She married Steven McAuliffe in 1970. She earned a bachelor's degree in 1970 and a master's degree in 1978. From 1982 until her death, McAuliffe taught social studies at Concord High School in Concord, New Hampshire.

Other articles to read include: **Astronaut; Challenger disaster; Onizuka, Ellison Shoji; Space exploration.**

Mercury

Mercury is the planet closest to the sun. Its average distance from the sun is 35,980,000 miles (57,910,000 kilometers). The ancient Romans named Mercury after the speedy messenger of the gods in ancient stories. They chose that name because Mercury goes around the sun faster than any other planet.

Mercury is only about 3,032 miles (4,879 kilometers) across, about two-fifths of Earth's diameter. It is smaller than Jupiter's moon Ganymede and Saturn's moon Titan. Because Mercury is so small and near the sun, it is hard to see from Earth without a telescope. Sometimes Mercury can be seen in the sky just after sunset or just before sunrise.

Mercury takes about 88 Earth days to complete one orbit around the sun. A day on Mercury—from sunrise to sunrise—is about 59 Earth days. Sometimes Mercury is directly between the Earth and the sun. When this occurs, every 3 to 13 years, the planet can be seen as a black spot against the sun.

Mercury is dry and very hot and has almost no *atmosphere* (blanket of gases). The sun's rays are approximately seven times as strong on Mercury as they are on Earth. The temperature on the planet may reach 840 °F (450 °C) during the day. At night, the temperature may drop as low as –275 °F (–170 °C). Scientists doubt that the planet has any form of life. Because of its lack of atmosphere, Mercury's sky is black. Stars probably would be visible from the surface during the day.

The surface of Mercury has wide, flat areas, steep cliffs, and *impact craters*. The craters formed when meteors or small comets crashed into the planet. Mercury does not have enough atmosphere to slow down these objects and burn them up by friction. Studies of Mercury indicate that the craters at Mercury's poles contain water ice. The floors of the craters are permanently shielded from sunlight, so the temperature never gets high enough to melt the ice.

Scientists think the inside of Mercury is much like the inside of Earth. Both planets have an outer layer called the *crust* and a rocky layer called a *mantle* beneath the crust. Scientists think Mercury has an iron core like Earth's.

Continued on the next page

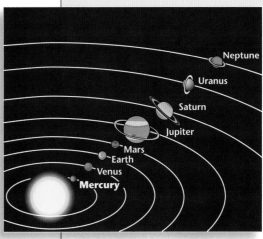

Mercury is the closest planet to the sun.

Never-before-seen details of Mercury's surface are captured in one of the first close-up photographs of the planet, taken by the U.S. probe Mariner 10 in 1974.

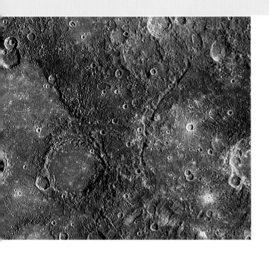

The surface of Mercury is covered with craters and with plains created by lava flows.

Mercury   *Continued from the previous page*

The United States Mariner 10 became the first spacecraft to reach Mercury. The remotely controlled spacecraft flew to within 460 miles (740 kilometers) of Mercury on March 29, 1974. It swept past the planet again on September 24, 1974, and on March 16, 1975. During those flights, the spacecraft photographed portions of the surface of Mercury. It also detected Mercury's *magnetic field*. A magnetic field is the influence that a magnet or an electric current creates in the region around it.

In 2004, the United States launched the Messenger probe to map the planet's surface and study its structure. Messenger went into orbit around Mercury in 2011. It has revealed surprising findings about the geology of the planet.

Other articles to read include: **Evening star; Impact crater; Messenger probe; Planet; Space exploration; Transit.**

A bulging plateau (whitish area at left) surrounded by narrow ridges (pink) rises above volcanic plains in Mercury's northern hemisphere, in a false-color image based on measurements from Messenger.

Messenger probe

The Messenger probe is a spacecraft sent to the planet Mercury. The craft was launched on August 3, 2004, and reached orbit around the planet in March 2011. The craft was launched by NASA, the United States space agency. Messenger was designed to study Mercury's surface, interior, and *magnetic field*. A magnetic field is the influence that a magnet or an electric current creates in the region around it.

Information from the probe has revealed that geological activities on Mercury did not end billions of years ago, as scientists had believed. The probe found more recent evidence for active volcanoes and a shifting crust. Some of these activities may be occuring because Mercury is slowly shrinking. The shrinking would explain why the outer layer of the planet is buckling and cracking. A closer look at the surface also showed that lava flows occurred more recently than previously thought.

The Messenger mission was originally scheduled for one year. The mission has since been extended.

Other articles to read include: **Mercury; Space exploration.**

Meteor and meteorite

Meteors are bright streaks of light that appear for a short time in the sky. They are often called shooting stars or falling stars, because they look like stars falling from the sky. The brightest meteors are sometimes called *fireballs*.

A meteor appears when a *meteoroid* (a piece of hard material) enters Earth's *atmosphere (AT muh sfihr)* from outer space. Earth's atmosphere is all of the air that surrounds our planet. Air rubs against the meteoroid, causing friction, and heats it. This makes the meteor glow. Most meteors glow for only about a second, but they leave a shining trail.

Meteoroids usually break up into tiny pieces before reaching Earth. Meteoroids that reach Earth's surface are called *meteorites*. Meteorites reach Earth because they are the right size to travel through the atmosphere. If they are too small, they break up. If they are too big, they may explode. Most meteorites are quite small, about the size of a pebble.

Millions of meteors occur in Earth's atmosphere every day. At certain times every year, Earth meets a number of clusters of tiny meteoroids. At such times, the sky seems to be filled with a shower of sparks. This is called a *meteor shower*.

Some meteorites are pieces of the same material that formed the planets. Scientists study meteorites for clues to how planets form and to the early history of the solar system.

Other articles to read include: **Impact crater; Leonids; Perseid meteor shower.**

A meteoroid travels through outer space, which has no atmosphere.

The thin air of the upper atmosphere begins to heat the object, causing it to glow and create a trail of melted particles and hot gases.

The friction caused by a denser atmosphere makes the trails so hot that the meteoroid becomes visible as a meteor.

The object usually breaks apart completely before reaching the ground.

A meteor appears in the sky when an object called a meteoroid enters the atmosphere from space.

Meteor Crater in Arizona was created by a meteor strike about 50,000 years ago. It measures about 4,180 feet (1,275 meters) wide and 570 feet (175 meters) deep.

Milky Way

The Milky Way is the home galaxy for the sun, Earth, and all the other objects in the solar system.

The Milky Way is the *galaxy* (system of stars) that contains the sun, Earth, and other objects in the solar system. The name *Milky Way* also refers to the part of the galaxy that people can clearly see without a telescope or other light-gathering instrument. On clear, dark nights, this part of the galaxy appears as a wide, milky-looking band stretching across the sky. If you look at this band for a whole year, the band seems to completely circle Earth in the sky. Dark gaps in the band consist of clouds of gas and dust that block out light from the stars behind them. The Milky Way, in turn, is part of a collection of about 40 galaxies called the *Local Group.*

The Milky Way is shaped like a thin disk with a *bulge* (swelling) in the center. This bulge is a thick bar of stars. The bar stretches for about 15,000 *light-years* across the center of the galaxy. A light-year is the distance light travels in a vacuum in one year, about 5.88 trillion miles (9.46 trillion kilometers). All of the stars and star groups in the Milky Way orbit the center of the galaxy.

Stars, dust, and gas spread out from the central bulge in a *spiral* (coiled) pattern. To someone far above the Milky Way, the galaxy would resemble a huge pinwheel. But our view of the Milky Way is dominated by the hazy light from a strip of nearby stars. There are two reasons why we have this view. First, we are inside the galaxy. Second, *interstellar dust* (dust between the stars) partially blocks the starlight.

The Milky Way measures about 100,000 light-years from one side to the other. The galaxy is about 10,000 light-years thick at the central bulge. The Milky Way is so huge that about 10 smaller galaxies *orbit* (travel around) it like moons around a planet.

The solar system lies in one of the galaxy's spiral arms, about 25,000 light-years from the center. The distance between the stars in our section of the Milky Way averages about 5 light-years. Stars in the center of the galaxy are about 100 times as close together.

Continued on the next page

Clouds of gas and dust prevent astronomers from using visible light to see into the center of the Milky Way. However, other forms of light can penetrate the clouds. By studying these kinds of light, astronomers have found unusual objects in the central region,

Studies have also shown that a powerful gravitational force comes from the exact center of the galaxy. This force is so strong that the *mass* (amount of matter) responsible for it must be about 4 million times as great as the mass of the sun. Furthermore, this tremendous mass must be packed into a volume of space smaller than the solar system. The only known kind of object that could be both that massive and that small is a *black hole*. A black hole is an invisible object whose gravitational pull is so great that not even light can escape from it.

Other articles to read include: **Black hole; Galaxy; Gravitation; Light-year; Interstellar medium; Local Group; Shapley, Harlow; Star.**

Mimas

Mimas *(MY muhs)* is the seventh-largest moon of Saturn. It is only 247 miles (397 kilometers) wide. Mimas has a bright, icy suface marked with many *impact craters.* An impact crater is a hole created when an object is struck by a smaller fast-moving object, such as a asteroid or comet.

A vast impact crater named Herschel is the most obvious feature on the surface of Mimas. The crater measures measures about 80 miles (130 kilometers) across, about one-third the width of the satellite. Its outer walls are about 3 miles (5 kilometers) tall. It also features a central peak that rises 4 miles (6 kilometers) above the crater floor. Scientists do not know for sure what kind of collision created the crater. But such a large impact probably nearly destroyed Mimas.

Mimas *orbits* (travels around) Saturn at a relatively close distance—about 115,300 miles (185,500 kilometers). It follows a path within the planet's outermost ring. Scientists think that Mimas may be so bright because small, icy particles from the ring

The huge Herschel impact crater on Mimas is a scar left from a collision with another object that almost tore the moon apart.

Continued on the next page

Mimas   *Continued from the previous page*

coat the moon. The amount of light reflected by Saturn's rings often outshines the light reflected by Mimas. As a result, astronomers have difficulty observing Mimas from Earth.

The British astronomer Sir William Herschel discovered Mimas using a telescope in 1789. The United States Voyager 1 spacecraft flew by Mimas in 1980. It discovered the crater that was later named in Herschel's honor. Voyager 1 also found a series of long grooves on Mimas's surface. These grooves might be linked to the impact that created the Herschel crater.

The U.S. Cassini spacecraft has visited Mimas several time since arriving at Saturn in 2004. Cassini's images have revealed details of the Herschel crater and of the grooves.

Other articles to read include: **Cassini; Dione; Enceladus; Iapetus; Rhea; Satellite; Saturn; Titan; Voyager.**

Russian astronauts aboard a Soyuz space capsule captured this photo of the space shuttle Atlantis docked with the Mir space station in 2005.

Mir

Mir *(meer)* was a long-running space station built by the Soviet Union (now Russia). Mir was made up of several units, called *modules.* The modules were launched separately. The first module went up in 1986. The space station was destroyed in 2001. *Mir* is the Russian word for *peace.*

The Soviet Union began to put Mir together during its "space race" with the United States. The Soviets wanted to operate Mir for five years. But the country collapsed in 1991. The Russians decided to leave Mir in space longer. During one period, the station was occupied by at least one person for almost 10 straight years.

Russia ended the Mir program in March 2001. It sent Mir into Earth's *atmosphere* (blanket of gases), causing it to burn up.

Other articles to read include: **International Space Station; Space exploration.**

Miranda

Miranda is one of the largest moons of the planet Uranus. It is about 290 miles (470 kilometers) wide.

The surface of Miranda has certain surface features not seen anywhere else in the solar system. These are three oddly shaped regions called *ovoids (OH voyds)*. Each ovoid is 120 to 190 miles (200 to 300 kilometers) across. The outer area of each ovoid resembles a racetrack. It has parallel ridges and canyons wrapped about the center. In the center, however, ridges and canyons crisscross one another randomly. Miranda has some of the highest cliffs of any planet or moon in the solar system. Scientists think that geological activity within Miranda created the ovoids, probably in the past 2 billion years.

Miranda was discovered by the Dutch-born American astronomer Gerard Kuiper on February 16, 1948. The space probe Voyager 2 flew close to Miranda in 1986. The probe took photographs of the moon.

Other articles to read include: **Kuiper, Gerard Peter; Satellite; Uranus; Voyager.**

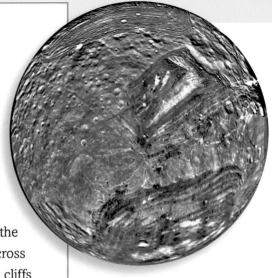

The weird ovoids on Miranda were captured by Voyager 2 on its journey to Uranus.

Mitchell, Maria

Maria Mitchell (1818–1889) was an American *astronomer* (scientist who studies outer space). She became known for her studies of the sun, the spots that form on the sun's surface, and of the moons surrounding other planets. She discovered a new comet in 1847.

Mitchell was born in Nantucket, Massachusetts. For the most part, Mitchell taught herself. She also learned astronomy from her father. In 1848, she became the first woman to join the American Academy of the Arts and Sciences. She became a professor of astrononomy at Vassar College in 1865. In 1905, she was elected to the Hall of Fame for Great Americans.

Other articles to read include: **Astronomy; Sun.**

Maria Mitchell

Moon

The moon is a huge, rocky object that travels around Earth. It is Earth's only natural *satellite* (object that orbits a planet). The moon is the brightest object in Earth's night sky. On some nights, it looks like a giant shining circle of light. On other nights, it looks like a thin, silver fingernail. Although the moon is bright, it does not give off its own light, the way the sun does. Moonlight is *reflected* (bounced off) sunlight.

The moon is the only place in the solar system other than Earth that has been visited by people. Scientists believe that the moon is about 4.6 billion years old. That is about the same age as Earth.

The moon is much smaller than Earth. If the moon and Earth were side by side, it would be like looking at a tennis ball next to a basketball. The moon looks bigger than any star because it is so much closer to Earth than anything else. The moon is about 238,897 miles (384,467 kilometers) from Earth. A rocket journey from Earth to the moon and back takes about six days.

The moon also has much less *mass* (amount of matter) than Earth. As a result, its *gravitational force* is much less. An object that weighs 6 pounds (3 kilograms) on Earth would weigh only 1 pound (0.5 kilogram) on the moon. Despite its relatively weak gravitational force, the moon is close enough to Earth to produce tides in Earth's waters. The moon is moving away from Earth at the rate of about 1 ½ inches (3.8 centimeters) per year.

A person on Earth looking at the moon with the unaided eye can see light and dark areas on the lunar surface. The light areas are rugged highlands known as *terrae (TEHR ee)*. The word *terrae* is Latin for *lands*. The terrae have many craters. They are the original crust of the moon. But they have been broken by the impact of *meteoroids* (rocky objects in space) and *comets* (icy balls).

The dark areas on the moon are known as *maria (MAHR ee uh)*. The word *maria* is Latin for *seas;* its singular is *mare (MAHR ee)*. The term comes from the smoothness of the dark areas and their resemblance to bodies of water. The maria are cratered landscapes that were partly flooded by lava when volcanoes erupted. The lava then froze,

Continued on the next page

Striking contrasts of light and dark reflect differences in the geology of the moon. The light areas are rugged highlands. The dark zones were partly flooded by volcanic lava that froze to form smooth rock.

Most of the water on the moon (blue areas) can be found near the poles, as shown in a false-color image taken by India's Chandrayaan-1 moon probe.

forming rock. Since that time, meteoroid impacts have created craters in the maria.

Nothing lives on the moon. It has no air and no wind. The sky is always dark, the way it is on Earth at night. A person can always see the stars from the moon.

At night, the moon gets very cold. The temperature can be as cold as −280 °F (−173 °C). That is colder than any place on Earth. It can be as hot as 260 °F (127 °C) in the daytime. That is hotter than boiling water.

The moon travels around Earth in an *elliptical* (oval-shaped) path about once every 27 days. Earth's gravity keeps the moon on this path. The moon spins around once during each trip around Earth. One full day on the moon lasts about 30 days on Earth.

As the moon orbits Earth, an observer on Earth can see the moon appear to change shape. It changes from a crescent to a circle and back again. This change occurs because of the way the moon orbits Earth. Sometimes, the moon is on the side of Earth opposite the sun. Then, the whole sunlit side of the moon can be seen from Earth. Other times, we can see only part of its sunlit side. This is why the moon sometimes looks like a tiny sliver. The different appearances are known as the *phases of the moon*.

Scientists believe that the moon formed as a result of a collision commonly known as the "Big Whack." According to this idea, Earth collided with a planet-sized object 4.6 billion years ago. After the impact, a cloud of *vaporized rock* (rock turned to gas) shot off Earth's surface and went into orbit around Earth. The cloud cooled and *condensed* (collected) into a ring of small, solid bodies. These bodies gathered together, forming the moon.

Some ancient peoples believed that the moon was a spinning bowl of fire. Others thought it was a mirror that reflected Earth's lands and seas. But philosophers in ancient Greece understood that the moon is a *sphere* (ball-like object) in orbit around Earth. They also knew that moonlight is reflected sunlight.

The Italian scientist Galileo in 1609 made the first scientific study of the moon. He used a simple telescope. Beginning in 1959, the Soviet Union (now Russia) and the United States sent a series of robot spacecraft to examine the moon in detail. Their ultimate

Continued on the next page

A combined image of the moon and Earth show the size difference between the two bodies.

A map of the moon showing the stronger gravitational pull of mountains and other high areas (red) and the lower gravitation pull of craters and other low areas (blue) was created using data collected by the twin Gail space probes.

Moon *Continued from the previous page*

goal was to land people safely on the moon. On July 20, 1969, the United States Apollo 11 lunar spacecraft landed on the moon. Astronaut Neil A. Armstrong became the first person to set foot on the lunar surface. Since then, the United States, China, Japan, India, and the European Space Agency have sent probes to the moon to map its surface.

Other articles to read include: **Armstrong, Neil Alden; Blue moon; Eclipse; Gravitation; Impact crater; Maria; Orbit; Satellite.**

Mount Wilson Observatory

Mount Wilson Observatory is a telescope observatory in southwestern California. It stands on Mount Wilson, 5,710 feet (1,740 meters) above sea level, about 10 miles (16 kilometers) northeast of Pasadena. George Ellery Hale, an American astronomer, founded the observatory in 1904. It originally focused on the study of the sun. It is still a leading center for research in this area. The observatory has two solar telescopes, which are mounted in towers 150 and 60 feet (46 and 18 meters) high.

The observatory also operates two *reflecting telescopes* (telescopes that use mirrors to collect light). One has a diameter of 60 inches (1.5 meters), and the other has a diameter of 100 inches (2.5 meters). These instruments are used to study stars. American astronomer Edwin P. Hubble used the 100-inch reflecting telescope to discover that the universe is *expanding* (growing larger).

An observation dome houses one of several telescopes on Mount Wilson.

Until 1980, the Mount Wilson Observatory was operated jointly by the Carnegie Institution of Washington, D.C., and the California Institute of Technology at Pasadena. In 1980, the Carnegie Institution assumed control of the Mount Wilson Observatory. The Carnegie Institution continued to operate the observatory until 1989. That year control of the observatory was transferred to the Mount Wilson Institute, a private organization.

Other articles to read include: **Hale, George Ellery; Observatory; Palomar Observatory; Telescope.**

National Aeronautics and Space Administration (NASA)

The National Aeronautics and Space Administration (NASA) is a United States government agency. It researches flight within and beyond Earth's *atmosphere* (blanket of gases). NASA employs thousands of scientists, engineers, and technicians. One of NASA's major facilities is the John F. Kennedy Space Center on Merritt Island, in Florida. Another is the Lyndon B. Johnson Space Center in Houston.

In 1957, President Dwight D. Eisenhower gave responsibility for a United States space program to the National Advisory Committee for Aeronautics (NACA). NACA had been founded in 1915. NACA became NASA in 1958. Its headquarters are in Washington, D.C. NASA has launched many space flights. Some have carried astronauts and some have not. The flights without astronauts have included those of *artificial* (human-made) satellites and space probes. These craft are used for scientific research and for such purposes as communication systems and weather forecasting.

In 1969, NASA's Apollo 11 spacecraft became the first craft to land human beings on the moon. In 1981, NASA launched Columbia, the first space shuttle. In 1986, however, NASA suffered one of the worst accidents in its history. The shuttle Challenger broke apart shortly after launch. All seven crew members were killed.

In 1993, the United States and Russia agreed to work toward the construction of a space station. It became known as the *International Space Station (ISS)*.

In 2003, the shuttle Columbia broke apart as it reentered Earth's atmosphere. All seven crew members were killed. NASA introduced new safety measures after the accident.

NASA's space exploration goals include more missions to the

Continued on the next page

A NASA astronaut works in space on the International Space Station.

The NASA logo was designed in 1959.

National Aeronautics and Space Administration (NASA) *Continued from the previous page*

moon, possibly to an asteroid, and eventually, getting humans to Mars. NASA is working on several new space vehicles. It is working with private companies to achieve many of its goals.

Over the years, NASA has started and supported many science programs. These programs do not only involve space flight. They also involve astronomy, aviation, *meteorology* (the study of weather), oceanography, and many other fields.

Other articles to read include: **Astronaut; Challenger disaster; Columbia disaster; International Space Station; Satellite, Artificial; Space exploration.**

Historic planes hang from the ceiling of the National Air and Space Museum in Washington, D.C.

National Air and Space Museum

The National Air and Space Museum, in Washington, D.C., features exhibits on *aviation* (flying) and space flight. It is part of the Smithsonian Institution. The museum holds the largest collection of historic aircraft and spacecraft in the world. It has more than 20 galleries, a theater, and a planetarium. Its displays include the Wright brothers' 1903 *Flyer;* Charles A. Lindbergh's *Spirit of St. Louis;* X-1 and X-15 aircraft; and Mercury, Gemini, and Apollo spacecraft. Museum visitors can touch a rock from the moon and walk through a space station.

The museum sponsors and conducts research into the history, science, and technology of aviation and space flight. Further museum research includes planetary science, geology, and geophysics.

Congress created the National Air Museum in 1946. The museum was given its present name in 1966. The museum's main building opened in 1976. In 2003, the museum opened the Steven F. Udvar-Hazy Center at Washington Dulles International Airport

Continued on the next page

in Virginia. The center displays many more objects. These objects include the Lockheed SR-71 Blackbird, the Boeing B-29 Superfortress *Enola Gay,* and the space shuttle *Discovery.* The museum pieces are maintained and restored at the Paul E. Garber Preservation, Restoration, and Storage Facility in Suitland, Maryland.

Other articles to read include: **Planetarium; Space exploration.**

National Optical Astronomy Observatories (NOAO)

The National Optical Astronomy Observatories (NOAO) are a group of astronomy research centers. They are funded by the United States government. The NOAO includes Kitt Peak National Observatory near Tucson, Arizona; Cerro-Tololo Inter-American Observatory in northern Chile; and the National Solar Observatory in Arizona and New Mexico.

The NOAO was established in 1982 to combine the nation's major centers for *optical astronomy* into one organization. Optical astronomy uses telescopes that capture visible light and *infrared* (heat) radiation to form images.

The NOAO provides facilities to astronomers. Any astronomer can ask for time on NOAO telescopes. The NOAO also maintains a staff of astronomers. They improve and develop the observatories' instruments, as well as do research.

Other articles to read include: **Observatory; National Radio Astronomy Observatory; Telescope.**

A faint *nebula* (cloud of gas and dust) that looks like a bird about take flight is captured in an image from a telescope at the Kitt Peak Observatory.

National Radio Astronomy Observatory (NRAO)

National Radio Astronomy Observatory (NRAO) is an organization that operates radio telescopes. The telescopes are in Socorro, New Mexico, and Green Bank, West Virginia. The NRAO is financed by the United States National Science Foundation and has scientific offices in Charlottesville, Virginia.

The telescope in Socorro, the Expanded Very Large Array (VLA), is one of the world's most powerful radio telescopes. This instrument consists of 27 large, dish-shaped metal mirrors called *reflectors* that operate as a single telescope. Each reflector measures 82 feet (25 meters) across.

Another NRAO instrument, the Very Long Baseline Array (VLBA) telescope, consists of 10 reflectors. They are at sites across U.S. territory, from Hawaii to the Virgin Islands. Like the VLA, the VLBA acts as a single telescope. At Green Bank, the NRAO operates the Robert C. Byrd Green Bank Telescope and a smaller radio telescope.

Scientists using NRAO telescopes have detected radio waves given off by nearly all types of objects in space. These objects range from nearby planets to distant quasars.

Other articles to read include: **Observatory; Telescope.**

The Very Large Array (VLA) consists of 27 dishes. Each reflector is 82 feet (27 meters) across.

Naval Observatory, United States

The U.S. Naval Observatory is the country's oldest national observatory. It was founded in 1830 and is operated by the U.S. Navy. It is headquartered in Washington, D.C.

The United States Naval Observatory is responsible for measuring the positions and motions of the sun, moon, planets, and stars. It monitors the position of Earth. It also maintains the precise time for the United States.

Scientists using the Washington, D.C., telescope discovered the two moons of Mars in 1877. In 1978, scientists at the Flagstaff, Arizona, branch discovered Pluto's satellite Charon.

Other articles to read include: **Observatory; Telescope.**

Near-Earth Object Program

The Near-Earth Object Program tracks objects in space that pass close to Earth. The program identifies and tracks comets and asteroids that move around the sun near Earth's orbit. These comets and asteroids are called near-Earth objects or NEO's. The program consists of several smaller programs spread around the world.

The history of the solar system includes many impacts between different bodies. Earth has been hit by countless asteroids and comets during its existence. Several of these impacts have been large enough to change the climate all around the globe. Many scientists believe one such impact is responsible for the extinction of the dinosaurs.

The major role of the program is to determine if any NEO's could strike Earth. In 1998, the National Aeronautics and Space Administration (NASA) began its part of the "Spaceguard" effort. Spaceguard is a group of several countries and institutions around the world tracking NEO's. The countries include Australia, Italy, Japan, and the United Kingdom. The first goal of the program was to discover and track over 90 percent of the NEO's larger than 0.62 mile (1 kilometer) by the end of 2008. After succeeding in that mission, Spaceguard began focusing on finding 90 percent of NEO's larger than 450 feet (140 meters). As of mid-2013, the program had found 9,858 NEO's. At least 860 of them have a diameter of approximately 0.62 mile.

Other articles to read include: **Asteroid; Comet; Impact crater.**

Comet C/2001 Q4 was discovered on August 24, 2001, by the Near-Earth Asteroid Tracking (NEAT) system, a division of the Near-Earth Object Program. The program identifies and tracks comets and asteroids moving around the sun near Earth's orbit.

Nebula

A nebula *(NEHB yuh luh)* is a cloud of dust particles and gas in space. The term *nebula* comes from the Latin word for *cloud.* Scientists use the term *nebulae (NEHB yuh lee)* for more than one of these clouds. Nebulae can be found in the Milky Way and

Continued on the next page

The Cat's Paw is a diffuse nebula in a region of star formation.

Nebula *Continued from the previous page*

other systems of stars called *galaxies*. Nebulae are called either *diffuse (dih FYOOZ)* or *planetary*.

Diffuse nebulae are the larger of the two types. Scientists believe that new stars are forming in many diffuse nebulae. Some contain enough dust and gases to make 100,000 stars the size of the sun.

Planetary nebulae are balls of clouds made up of dust and gases. These nebulae surround some old stars. They form when a star starts to collapse and throw off the outer layers of its *atmosphere* (surrounding blanket of gases).

Other articles to read include: **Galaxy; Interstellar medium; Milky Way; Star.**

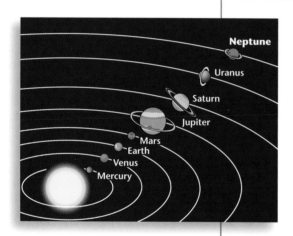

Neptune is the farthest planet from the sun.

Neptune

Neptune is the farthest planet from the sun. It is the only planet that cannot be seen from Earth without a telescope. Bright blue clouds cover Neptune's surface. Because these clouds look like water, the planet was named after the ancient Roman god of the sea.

Scientists believe that Neptune is a *gas giant*, made up mostly of gases, water, and minerals. They also believe that Neptune has three layers. The *core* (innermost layer) probably consists of mostly iron, nickel, and *silicates*. Silicates are minerals that also make up much of Earth's rocky *crust* (outer layer). Unlike Earth, Neptune has no solid surface. The layer above the core is a slushy *mantle* (middle layer) made of mostly ammonia, methane, and water ices. The large amount of ice within Neptune, as well as Uranus—leads astronomers to label both planets *ice giants*. Neptune's slushy mantle blends smoothly into its uppermost layer, a gaseous atmosphere of mostly hydrogen and helium. A small amount of methane gives the atmosphere a blue color.

High in Neptune's atmosphere, thick layers of clouds are in rapid motion. Winds blow these clouds at speeds up to about 900 miles (1,450 kilometers) per hour. The highest clouds in Neptune's

Continued on the next page

atmosphere consist mainly of frozen methane. In 1989, the Voyager 2 spacecraft found that Neptune had a dark area of violently swirling gas that resembled a hurricane. This area, called the Great Dark Spot, was similar to the Great Red Spot on Jupiter. In 1994, the Hubble Space Telescope found that the Great Dark Spot had vanished.

Like the other giant planets in the solar system, Neptune has rings. Neptune's six rings are much fainter and darker than those of Saturn. The rings consist of orbiting particles of dust. Neptune's outer ring is unlike any other planetary ring in the solar system. It has five curved sections, called *arcs*. The arcs are brighter and thicker than the rest of the ring. Scientists believe small moons cause the dust to spread unevenly in the ring.

Neptune travels around the sun in an *elliptical* (oval-shaped) orbit. It takes about 165 Earth years for Neptune to go around the sun. Neptune's day—the time it takes to rotate once on its *axis*—lasts about 16 hours and 3 minutes. An axis is an imaginary line through the middle of a planet around which a planet *rotates* (spins). Like Earth and the other planets, Neptune's axis is tilted. Neptune's tilt causes the planet to have seasons. Each season on Neptune lasts about 40 years.

Neptune is about four times as big as Earth. Scientists know of at least 13 moons, but the planet probably has many more. Triton, Neptune's largest satellite, orbits in the opposite direction to that of Neptune's rotation. It is the only major satellite in the solar system to do so.

Neptune was discovered by mathematics by scientists studying another planet, Uranus. Astronomers observing Uranus noticed a difference between the planet's actual orbit and the orbit they thought it should be following. They concluded that the gravitational force of some unknown planet was pulling on Uranus.

Scientists first saw Neptune through a telescope in 1846. The United States spacecraft Voyager 2 took the first close-up pictures of Neptune in 1989. Voyager also allowed scientists to locate six moons and the rings.

Other articles to read include: **Gas giant; Planet; Planetary ring; Satellite; Triton; Uranus; Voyager.**

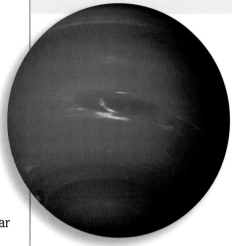

Neptune is thought to be blue due to a small amount of methane, the main ingredient in natural gas, in the planet's outermost layer of gas.

Instruments aboard Voyager 2 photographed rings around the planet Neptune. The rings are extremely thin compared with the rings around Saturn.

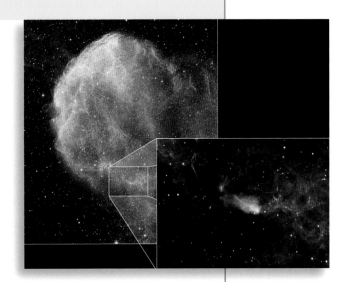

Several telescopes were used to create one image of a neutron star (cutout). The star is part of the remains of a *supernova* (exploded star) (above left).

A magnetar is a rare type of pulsar that has a much stronger magnetic field than other pulsars.

Neutron star

A neutron *(NOO tron)* star is the smallest and *densest* type of star known. A dense object has its particles packed together very tightly. Neutron stars measure only about 12 miles (20 kilometers) across. But they have a *mass* almost three times that of the sun, which is much larger than a neutron star. Mass depends on an object's weight and *gravity,* the amount of pull it has. Neutron stars do not burn brightly like the stars that can be seen from Earth.

A neutron star forms when a large star runs out of fuel. The star's strong gravity causes it to collapse. Gravity squeezes together particles in the center of the star. The star later explodes as a *supernova* (an exploding star that can be seen from Earth), leaving behind its spinning center. That center is a neutron star. Some neutron stars spin so fast that they go around many times a second.

Scientists have identified several different neutron stars. One, called a *pulsar,* has two jets of energy that shoot out at opposite ends of the star. As the star spins, the jets sometimes point toward Earth, much like a lighthouse spins a light. Another type of neutron star is called a *magnetar.* Magnetars have some of the strongest magnetic fields in the universe.

Other articles to read include: **Gravitation; Pulsar; Star; Supernova.**

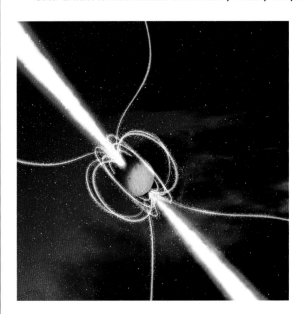

New Horizons

New Horizons is the first space probe sent to study Pluto and its large moon Charon. Instruments on New Horizons will photograph the surfaces of Pluto and Charon and measure their surface temperatures. They will study Pluto's thin *atmosphere* (blanket of gases).

New Horizons is a mission of NASA, the United States space agency. NASA launched New Horizons on Jan. 19, 2006. The probe was scheduled to reach its closest point to Pluto and Charon on July 14, 2015.

After leaving Pluto, the probe is scheduled to pass through the *Kuiper belt,* a band of icy bodies largely beyond the orbit of Neptune. The measurements made by New Horizons will help scientists learn about the nature of these *Kuiper belt objects* (KBO's). They are thought to be the remains of the material that came together to form the planets. Scientists hope that the probe will glimpse other objects as it continues away from the sun.

Other articles to read include: **Kuiper belt; Pluto; Satellite; Space exploration.**

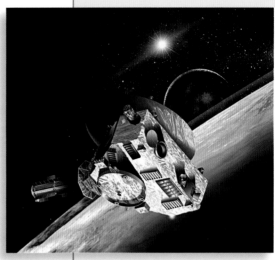

The New Horizons probe will be the first space probe to visit Pluto.

Newton, Sir Isaac

Sir Isaac Newton (1642-1727) was an English scientist. He is sometimes described as "one of the greatest names in the history of human thought" because of his great contributions to astronomy, mathematics, and *physics*. Physics is the study of energy and matter.

Newton showed that all the objects in the universe are attracted to one another by an invisible force. He realized that the force that makes a pebble fall to the ground is the same force that keeps planets traveling around the sun. This force is called *gravitation*.

Newton later discovered that sunlight is a mixture of all the colors of light. He passed a beam of sunlight through a glass *prism,* which separated it into colors. Then he studied the colors. He was able to show that objects have color

Sir Isaac Newton

Continued on the next page

Newton, Sir Isaac   *Continued from the previous page*

because they reflect light. For example, grass looks green because it reflects green light.

Newton's study of light led him to make a new kind of telescope with a reflecting mirror instead of lenses. Through it he observed the moons of Jupiter. Newton's telescope proved to be much better than any previous telescope. Many modern telescopes use a similar design.

Newton invented a new kind of mathematics, called *calculus (KAL kyuh luhs).* (Calculus was also invented independently by the German mathematician Gottfried Leibniz.) Calculus can answer questions about things that are changing.

Newton also made important discoveries about motion. His book explaining his discoveries, *Philosophiae naturalis principia mathematica* (Mathematical Principles of Natural Philosophy), was published in 1687. This book is thought to be one of the greatest single works in the history of science. Later scientists, such as the German-born physicist Albert Einstein, challenged and changed Newton's work. But Einstein admitted that his own work would have been impossible without Newton's discoveries.

Other articles to read include: **Gravitation; Light; Telescope.**

The current North Star is named Polaris.

North Star

North Star

The North Star is a bright star above the North Pole. It is sometimes called the *polestar.* It can only be seen from the Northern Hemisphere. Its position in the sky does not change as do those of other stars. When the North Star is in sight, all the other stars in the sky seem to revolve around it.

For many years, people have used the North Star as a guide. It has also been used to measure *latitude* (position in relation to Earth's equator). In addition, many cultures have told stories based on the North Star.

Right now, Polaris *(poh LAIR ihs)* is the North Star.

Continued on the next page

Polaris is the brightest star of a group called the Little Dipper. But Polaris will not always be the North Star. Earth's *axis* (the imaginary line through Earth that connects the poles) slowly moves in a circle. As it does, it will eventually point to a different star. In about 12,000 years, Earth's axis will point north to a spot near Vega in the *constellation* Lyra. A constellation is a grouping of stars in the night sky. In about 22,000 years, Thuban in the constellation Draco will become the North Star. About 26,000 years from now, Polaris will again become the North Star.

Other articles to read include: **Big and Little Dippers; Constellation; Lyra; Star.**

Nova

A nova is an explosion on a star. The star may become from 10,000 to 100,000 times as bright as the sun. A nova may shine from a few days to several years. The explosion hurls a huge shell of gas and dust away from the star. The word *nova* comes from the Latin word for *new*. People once thought *novae* (the plural of nova) were new stars.

Scientists believe novae happen in *binary stars*. A binary star is actually two stars that closely *orbit* (travel around) each other. In the case of a nova, one of the stars is about the size of the sun. The other is a kind of small, compact star called a *white dwarf*. The white dwarf's strong gravitational pull draws material off the larger star and onto the white dwarf. Once the white dwarf collects enough material, a sudden and violent reaction occurs. The white dwarf undergoes a nova.

Most white dwarfs survive a nova. Many scientists think that some binary stars may produce many novae over their lifetime.

Some stars produce a different kind of explosion called a *supernova*. A supernova is thousands of times as bright as a nova.

Other articles to read include: **Binary star; Star; Supernova; White dwarf.**

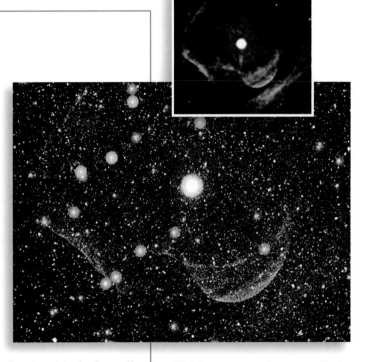

Within a group of stars called Z Camelopardalis flashes a nova (above). Many of the stars around the nova have been filtered out in the smaller image (inset).

Observatory

The Hubble Space Telescope (top), one of the most important telescopes of all time, has allowed scientists to see far into the universe. The Gran Telescopio Canarius in the Canary Islands (above) is one of the largest and most powerful telescopes on Earth.

An observatory *(uhb ZUR vuh TAWR ee)* is a place where scientists can study planets, stars, galaxies, and other objects in space. An observatory has at least one telescope or similar device. Most observatories are built on the ground. But observatory equipment is also used underground, in the atmosphere, and in space. The word *observatory* can also mean an old structure that people once used to note important days of the year.

Earth's atmosphere helps determine where telescopes are placed. The atmosphere distorts light passing through it. Observatories on Earth are usually placed high on a mountain, above most clouds, where the atmosphere is thin. During the 2000's, many telescopes on Earth were fitted with a machine called *adaptive optics*. These machines are able to detect how the atmosphere is distorting the incoming light and can remove the distortion. This has greatly increased the power of telescopes that observe from Earth.

Many telescopes work with visible light. Other types of light arriving from space are invisible to the human eye. Telescopes have been made to detect these invisible forms of light. These include telescopes that detect gamma rays, infrared light, microwaves, radio waves, ultraviolet light, and X rays. The light detected by these telescopes is often changed into images people can see. The images from telescopes that detect different forms of light are often combined into one image. These images can give scientists clues as to what is happening in different areas of the area being studied.

The staff of an observatory includes engineers, astronomers, telescope operators, and others. Astronomers who are not on the staff do most of the research. There are many scientists and only a few large telescopes. Therefore, scientists often must schedule a time to use them. Often, the scientists that are using the telescopes are not at the observatory. Many modern telescopes can be programmed to complete a task or can be controlled remotely by scientists from any location.

Other articles to read include: **Light pollution; Mount Wilson Observatory; Palomar Observatory; Pierre Auger Observatory; Telescope; Yerkes Observatory.**

Ochoa, Ellen

Ellen Ochoa *(oh CHOH ah)* (1958-) is a United States astronaut. She was the first Hispanic American woman to travel in space. Her first space flight took place in April 1993. Ochoa and other astronauts were on the space shuttle Discovery. They spent nine days in space doing research on the sun and its effects on Earth's climate and environment. Ochoa has made several other space flights since then. In 2013, she became the director of the Johnson Space Center in Houston.

Ochoa was born in Los Angeles. She earned a bachelor's degree in physics from San Diego State University in 1980. In 1981, Ochoa received a master's degree in electrical engineering from Stanford University. She also earned a doctor's degree in electrical engineering from Stanford in 1985. Ochoa joined the astronaut program in 1990.

Other articles to read include: **Astronaut; Space exploration.**

Ellen Ochoa

Olympus Mons

Olympus Mons is a volcano on Mars that is the largest volcano in the solar system. Olympus Mons (Latin for *Mount Olympus*) rises about 16 miles (25 kilometers) above the surrounding plains. It is nearly three times the height of Mount Everest, the tallest mountain on Earth.

Three other large volcanoes, called Arsia Mons, Ascraeus Mons, and Pavonis Mons, sit atop a broad raised region called Tharsis. All these volcanoes have slopes that rise gradually, much like the slopes of Hawaiian volcanoes. Both the Martian and Hawaiian volcanoes are *shield* volcanoes. They formed from eruptions of lava that can flow for long distances before cooling into rock.

Olympus Mons is more than 370 miles (600 kilometers) in diameter. It is so large that the entire chain of Hawaiian islands from Kauai to Hawaii would fit inside it.

Other articles to read include: **Mars; Volcano.**

The gigantic volcano Olympus Mons on Mars is the largest volcano in the solar system. It is about as large as the state of Arizona.

Ellison Onizuka

Onizuka, Ellison Shoji

Ellison Shoji Onizuka *(ahn uh zoo kah, EHL uh suhn SHOH jee)* (1946-1986), was the first Asian American in space. He was also one of the seven United States astronauts killed in the 1986 Challenger disaster.

On his first space flight in January 1985, Onizuka and his fellow astronauts on the space shuttle Discovery completed a secret three-day mission. As part of his second mission, Onizuka and the other astronauts aboard the space shuttle Challenger planned to release two satellites. One was a retrievable satellite to study Halley's Comet. The other was a communications satellite. On Jan. 28, 1986, an accident destroyed the shuttle shortly after liftoff.

Onizuka was born June 24, 1946, in Kealakekua, Hawaii. His grandparents immigrated to Hawaii from Japan to work on sugar plantations. In 1964, he enrolled at the University of Colorado, where he joined the Air Force Reserve Officer Training Corps. In 1970, he went on active duty with the Air Force. NASA selected him as an astronaut in 1978 for the first team of space shuttle crew members.

Other articles to read include: **Astronaut; Challenger disaster; Space exploration.**

Oort cloud

The Oort *(oort* or *ohrt)* cloud is a cluster of comets, smaller objects, and perhaps even planets in the outermost region of the solar system. The Oort cloud is shaped like a slightly flattened, hollow ball. The nearest part of the cloud may be roughly 500 billion miles (800 billion kilometers) from the sun. The farthest part may be up to 18 trillion miles (30 trillion kilometers) from the sun.

The Oort cloud is the source of *long-period comets*—comets that take 200 years or longer to *revolve* (travel around) the sun. The cloud may hold up to 1 trillion comets. Comets may leave the Oort cloud and enter the inner solar system when they are disturbed by a large gravitational force, such as the gravity of a

Continued on the next page

passing star. Many objects in the cloud may have formed around other stars but were pulled away by the sun's gravity.

In 2004, a team of United States scientists announced the discovery of a body later found to be about two-fifths the diameter of Pluto. It is nearly three times as far from the sun as Pluto.

The object, named Sedna, lies about 8 billion miles (13 billion kilometers) from the sun. This distance is much closer than the point where scientists thought the Oort cloud began. Some scientists concluded that Sedna belonged to the Oort cloud and that the cloud's inner boundary lies closer to the sun than previously thought.

The Oort cloud is named for the Dutch astronomer Jan H. Oort. In 1950, he predicted that the cloud might exist.

Other articles to read include: **Comet; Planet; Solar system.**

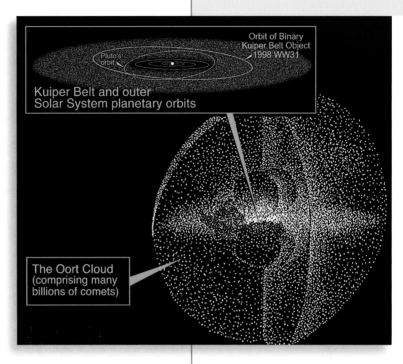

Kuiper Belt and outer Solar System planetary orbits

Orbit of Binary Kuiper Belt Object 1998 WW31

Pluto's orbit

The Oort Cloud (comprising many billions of comets)

Many scientists believe that the solar system of planets and the Kuiper Belt beyond Neptune (top) are surrounded by a huge gathering of small icy objects called the Oort cloud (above).

Orbit

An orbit is the path an object takes as it *revolves* (goes around) another object. The word *orbit* is most often used in *astronomy,* the study of stars, planets, and other objects in space. All objects pull on other objects around it. This pull is called *gravitation* or *the force of gravity.* The larger an object, the more pull it has on the objects around it. In astronomy, an object in orbit is revolving around a larger object. Earth and the other planets travel in orbit around the sun. The moon moves in orbit around Earth. A planet's orbit makes an oval-shaped curve called an *ellipse.*

Scientists call the bigger object or planet being orbited the primary and the smaller object or planet in orbit the secondary.

Continued on the next page

Satellites are placed into different orbits depending on their functions.

Orbit   *Continued from the previous page*

Spacecraft can become secondaries of Earth or another planet. Not all objects that orbit each other differ greatly in sizes. Some are very close to the same size. In cases such as this, the two objects orbit a spot in between the two objects. The two objects can be thought of as two people twirling around each other as they hold hands.

Other articles to read include: **Ellipse; Gravitation; Planet; Satellite; Satellite, Artificial.**

Orion is easily found in the northern sky by looking for his "belt," three bright stars roughly lined up in a row.

Orion

Orion *(aw RY uhn* or *oh RY uhn),* the Hunter, is a brilliant *constellation* that includes two of the brightest stars in the sky. A constellation is a grouping of stars in the night sky. Orion is most easily seen from the Northern Hemisphere.

Orion is often portrayed holding a raised weapon in one hand and an animal skin or shield in the other. He is often pictured with his back turned toward us. In this view, the bright red star Betelgeuse *(BEE tuhl jooz, BEHT uhl juhz)* marks his left shoulder. A blue-white star called Rigel *(RY juhl* or *RY guhl)* marks his right foot. Orion is easily identified by a row of three stars forming his belt. A sword, made of faint stars, dangles from the belt.

The ancient Greeks named this constellation Orion because its shape reminded them of a handsome and energetic hunter in Greek mythology. He was a giant who could walk through the sea and on its surface. But he had a troubled love life.

Two well-known *nebulae* (clouds of gas and dust) are located in Orion. The Orion Nebula makes up part of Orion's sword. The Horsehead Nebula in Orion's belt is very difficult to see.

Other articles to read include: **Betelgeuse; Constellation; Nebula; Star.**

Pp

Palomar Observatory

Palomar *(PAL uh mahr)* Observatory is a telescope
observatory in southwestern California. It is about 45
miles (72 kilometers) northeast of San Diego, atop
Palomar Mountain, 5,597 feet (1,706 meters) above
sea level. The observatory is best known for the Hale
Telescope, one of the world's largest *optical telescopes.*
An optical telescope collects and focuses visible light
reflected (given off) by objects. In 1963, astronomers
using the Hale Telescope first identified *quasars,*
extremely bright objects in the center of some distant
galaxies. Energy from quasars takes billions of years
to reach Earth. For this reason, the study of quasars
can provide information about early stages of the universe.

The Hale Telescope is a *reflecting telescope.* Such telescopes
collect and focus light with a mirror. The telescope can also be
equipped with detectors that observe and photograph *infrared
rays* (heat rays). Studying infrared light can help scientists study
the formation of stars.

Palomar also has the Oschin Telescope. Astronomers using
the Oschin Telescope discovered several large objects beyond
the orbit of Neptune, including Orcus, Quaoar, and Sedna and
the dwarf planets Eris, Haumea, and Makemake. The Hale
Telescope was named for American astronomer George Ellery
Hale, who planned its construction. It began operations in 1948.

Other articles to read include: **Hale, George Ellery; Mount Wilson Observatory;
Quasar; Telescope.**

The Palomar observatory in
southern California houses the
Hale Telescope, which was the
most powerful telescope in the
world for 45 years.

Pegasus

Pegasus *(PEHG uh suhs)* is a *constellation* named for a winged
horse in Greek mythology. A constellation is a grouping of stars
in the night sky. Pegasus lies in the northern sky. It is best viewed
from around September through November.

As commonly drawn, the constellation Pegasus includes about
13 to 15 main stars. A square of four stars marks the horse's

Continued on the next page

The constellation Pegasus represents a winged horse sent by the Greek gods to aid the hero Perseus.

Pegasus *Continued from the previous page*

body or wing. A line and an arc of stars extend from one corner. They can be taken to represent the horse's two front legs. A curved line of four stars from another corner marks the head and neck.

In 1995, scientists discovered in Pegasus the first planet known to orbit a star similar to the sun. The planet orbits the star 51 Pegasi.

Pegasus was among the 48 constellations described by the ancient Greek mathematician Ptolemy. Today, it is one of 88 constellations recognized by the International Astronomical Union, the leading authority in the naming of heavenly objects. The constellation is named for a winged horse in ancient Greek stories. He was the offspring of Medusa, a monstrous, snake-haired woman, and Poseidon, god of horses and of the sea. The hero Perseus slew Medusa by cutting off her head. Pegasus sprang full-grown either from her head or neck, or from the blood from her neck.

Other articles to read include: **Constellation; Extrasolar planet; Ptolemy; Star.**

Saul Perlmutter

Perlmutter, Saul

Saul Perlmutter (1959-) is an American scientist. He won the 2011 Nobel Prize in *physics* (the study of matter and energy). Perlmutter shared the prize with American scientists Adam Riess and Brian Schmidt for their discovery that the *expansion* (spreading apart) of the universe is *accelerating* (speeding up). The discovery led scientists to think that the universe is filled with a mysterious energy, called *dark energy*. Scientists think dark energy is pushing the universe apart faster and faster.

Perlmutter was born in Champagne-Urbana, Illinois. He became a physics professor at the University of California at Berkeley in 2004. He has also worked at the United States Lawrence Berkeley National Laboratory.

Other articles to read include: **Big bang; Reiss, Adam Guy; Schmidt, Brian Paul; Universe.**

Perseid meteor shower

The Perseid meteor shower is a group of shooting stars seen on Earth in July and August. The meteors seem to come from the *constellation* Perseus. A constellation is a grouping of stars in the night sky. A shooting star, also called a meteor, appears when a piece of matter enters Earth's atmosphere from space at high speed. Such a piece of matter is called a *meteoroid.*

The meteoroids that cause the Perseid shower travel around the sun in an orbit that Earth crosses in mid-summer each year. They become visible when they enter Earth's atmosphere. The Perseids are caused by a *comet* called Swift-Tuttle. A comet is a ball of ice and rock that orbits the sun. The shower is caused when Earth passes through the debris left behind when the comet passed close to the sun. Small pieces of the comet that have broken off strike Earth.

The Perseid meteor shower consist of small pieces of the comet Tuttle-Swift. They occur each year in July and August.

The Swift-Tuttle comet last passed close to Earth in 1992. It will not return for about another 133 years. Even though the comet passed in 1992, scientists think that most of the debris in the shower was broken off thousands of years ago.

Other articles to read include: **Comet; Leonids; Meteorite.**

Phobos

Phobos *(FOH buhs* or *FOB uhs)* is a moon of the planet Mars. It is the larger of the planet's two tiny moons. The other moon is named Deimos *(DY mos).* The American astronomer Asaph Hall discovered both of them in 1877. He named them for the sons of Ares, the Greek god of war. Neither of the two moons is perfectly round. They are both shaped more like a common rock. At its widest, Phobos has a diameter of about 17 miles (27 kilometers).

The two satellites have many craters that formed when *meteoroids* (rocky objects in space) struck them. The surface of Phobos also has a complicated pattern of grooves. These may be cracks that developed when an impact created the satellite's largest crater.

Phobos, one of two moons that orbit Mars, has a distinctive large impact crater.

Continued on the next page

Phobos   *Continued from the previous page*

Scientists do not know where Deimos and Phobos formed. They may have come into existence in orbit around Mars at the same time the planet formed. Another possibility is that the satellites formed as asteroids near Mars. The gravitational force of Mars then pulled them into orbit around the planet. Both satellites are a dark gray color that is similar to the color of some kinds of asteroids.

Other articles to read include: **Deimos; Impact crater; Mars; Satellite.**

Pierre Auger Observatory

Pierre Auger *(pyair oh zhay)* Observatory is the world's largest facility for detecting *cosmic rays.* Cosmic rays are electrically charged particles smaller than most atoms. Such particles continuously rain down on Earth from space. The Pierre Auger was designed to find the source of cosmic rays with the greatest energies. These particles are called *ultra-high-energy cosmic rays.*

The observatory consists of 1,600 detectors spread over about 1,200 square miles (3,000 square kilometers) of a plain in Argentina. Each detector includes a tank that holds about 3,000 gallons (11,400 liters) of pure water. When a particle enters the water, it produces a flash of light that can be measured by the detector. Using information from many detectors, scientists can calculate the direction the cosmic ray came from.

The Pierre Auger began collecting information in 2004. In 2007, a study of this information produced the first evidence that ultra-high-energy cosmic rays come from the centers of certain galaxies. Scientists think that such centers are powered by massive *black holes.* A black hole is a region of space whose gravity is so strong that nothing can escape it, not even light.

The observatory takes its name from the French scientist Pierre V. Auger. He studied cosmic rays during the 1930's.

Other articles to read include: **Black hole; Cosmic rays; Observatory.**

The Pierre Auger Observatory uses 1,600 tanks of water (above, right) to detect particles created by cosmic rays. Fluorescence detectors (above, left) look for flashes of light in the sky created by the shower of cosmic ray particles.

Pisces

Pisces *(PIHS eez, PY seez)* is a *constellation* (a grouping of stars in the night sky). Pisces can be seen from much of the Northern and Southern hemispheres. It is best viewed from September to November. It has few bright stars and so can be difficult to see. It is best viewed far from bright city lights.

Pisces is said to represent two fish. The word *pisces* means *fish* in the Latin language. The constellation can be drawn in several ways. Its stars are commonly connected in a "V" shape. Each arm of the "V" represents a fish.

Pisces was among the 48 constellations defined by the ancient Greek mathematician Ptolemy. Today, it is one of 88 constellations recognized by the International Astronomical Union (IAU), the leading authority in the naming of heavenly objects.

Other articles to read include: **Astrology; Constellation; Ptolemy; Star; Zodiac.**

The constellation Pisces is represented by two fish.

Planck

Planck is an Earth-orbiting spacecraft launched on May 14, 2009. It was designed to measure the *cosmic microwave background* (CMB) radiation. Scientists believe that the CMB radiation is energy left over from the early universe, immediately after the *big bang* (the event that began the expansion of the universe). The CMB was produced about 380,000 years after the big bang.

Planck has produced detailed maps of the CMB radiation. It improved on measurements made by earlier spacecraft. By studying these maps, scientists can see how matter spread in the early universe. Areas of the CMB with more energy contain more matter.

Planck is named in honor of the German scientist Max Planck. It was launched by the European Space Agency (ESA), but Canada and the United States contributed to its development.

Other articles to read include: **Big bang; Cosmic microwave backgound radiation; Planck, Max; Satellite, Artificial**

The mission of the space telescope Planck was to map the cosmic microwave background (CMB) radiation. The CMB radiation is the remains of the big bang, the event that created the universe.

Max Planck

Planck, Max

Max Karl Ernst Ludwig Planck *(plahngk)* (1858-1947) was an important German scientist. He studied how objects absorb and release heat and other kinds of energy. In 1900, Planck developed an idea called *quantum (KWON tuhm) theory.*

Quantum theory totally changed the field of physics. Scientists had thought that energy flows continuously. Planck showed that energy actually flows in tiny units that he called *quanta* (plural of quantum). One example of such a unit is called a *photon.* A photon is the smallest unit, or quantum, of light energy. All forms of light, including visible light and X rays, are composed of photons.

Planck was born in Kiel, Germany, on April 23, 1858. He studied at the universities of Munich and Berlin. He taught physics at the universities of Munich, Kiel, and Berlin. In 1918, Planck was awarded the Nobel Prize in physics.

Other articles to read include: **Electromagnetic waves; Light; Planck.**

Planet

Earth is the only known planet with liquid water on its surface.

A planet is a large, round object that *orbits* (travels around) the sun or another star. Earth is one of the eight planets in the solar system. Planets are much smaller than the sun and almost all other stars. There are many planets outside the solar system.

To the unaided eye, the planets look much like the background stars in the night sky. However, the planets move slightly from night to night in relation to the stars. The name *planet* comes from a Greek word meaning *to wander.* Planets also shine with a steady light, but stars seem to twinkle. Planets do not produce their own light the way the sun and other stars do. Planets can be seen only because light from the sun shines on them.

Planets move in two main ways. They travel around their parent star in paths called *orbits.* As each planet

Continued on the next page

orbits its star, it also rotates on its *axis,* an imaginary line through its center.

For many years, the word *planet* has had no formal definition in *astronomy* (the study of objects and forces in space). Scholars struggled to create a simple system for explaining the differences between the smallest worlds and the largest comets, asteroids, and other bodies. In 2006, the International Astronomical Union (IAU), a widely recognized authority in naming heavenly bodies, voted to establish a standard definition of the term *planet.* Some astronomers welcomed the decision. Other astronomers thought the definition was not clear enough and refused to accept it.

The IAU divides objects that orbit the sun into three major classes: (1) planets, (2) dwarf planets, and (3) small solar system bodies. A planet orbits the sun and no other body. It has so much *mass* (amount of matter) that its own gravitation pulls it into a *sphere* (round shape). In addition, a planet has a strong enough gravitational pull to sweep the region of its orbit relatively free of other objects.

A dwarf planet also orbits the sun and is large enough to be round. However, its gravitational pull is not strong enough to clear the region of its orbit. Small solar system bodies, including most asteroids and comets, have too little mass for gravity to force their irregular shapes into spheres.

Continued on the next page

Mercury is the smallest planet and is also the closest planet to the sun.

The Mars Curiosity rover discovered rock formations that may have been formed in the presence of liquid water.

An artist's depiction of a planet orbiting the star Gliese 436. A number of planets orbiting stars other than the sun have been discovered by astronomers using powerful telescopes and other instruments.

Four objects in the Kuiper belt have been identified as dwarf planets—Eris, Pluto, Makemake, and Haumea. Sedna and Quaoar, which orbit beyond the Kuiper belt, may also be dwarf planets.

Planet *Continued from the previous page*

Going outward from the sun, the eight planets are Mercury, Venus, Earth, Mars, Jupiter, Saturn, Uranus, and Neptune. From its discovery in 1930, Pluto was generally considered a planet. However, its small size and irregular orbit led many astronomers to question whether Pluto should be grouped with such worlds as Earth and Jupiter. Pluto more closely resembles other icy objects found in a region of the outer solar system called the *Kuiper (KY pur)* belt. In the early 2000's, astronomers found several such Kuiper belt objects (KBO's) about the same size as Pluto. The IAU created the "dwarf planet" classification to describe Pluto and other nearly planet-sized objects.

Since 1992, astronomers have discovered more than 200 stars other than the sun with planets. Astronomers cannot see these planets. However, they can detect the planets from tiny changes in the stars' movement and tiny decreases in the amount of light coming from the stars.

Other articles to read include: **Dwarf planet; Extrasolar planet; Gas giant; Jupiter; Kuiper belt; Mars; Mercury; Neptune; Orbit; Planetary ring; Pluto; Satellite; Saturn; Solar system; Sun; Uranus; Venus.**

Largest known Kuiper Belt objects
Dysnomia
Charon
Eris
Pluto
Makemake
Haumea
Sedna
Quaoar
Earth

Planetarium

A planetarium *(plan uh TAIR ee uhm)* is a device that shows where planets, stars, and other objects are in the sky. Many planetariums are rooms inside a building. Others take up an entire building.

Some early planetariums showed movable pictures of the starry sky painted on the inside of a dome. Modern planetariums use projectors to show pictures of the sun, moon, planets, stars, and other objects on the inside of a dome-shaped screen. Many use computers to control the projectors. Planetariums also use computers to show visitors what the universe might look like from other planets or points in space. Many projectors can also show standard video formats to show movies or to enhance the projections.

One of the first planetariums was a *sphere* (round object) made in Germany during the mid-1600's. The stars were copper nail-heads coated with gold. Light from an oil lamp made these "stars" shine. Possibly the greatest breakthrough in planetariums came in 1923 with the introduction of a projector casting images in a dark room. The projector, produced by the Carl Zeiss Company in Germany, would become the basic projector design well into the 20th century.

Other articles to read include: **Planet; Star; Tyson, Neil deGrasse.**

Most planetariums use complex projectors to cast images and maps of the universe and the objects in it.

The Frederick Phineas and Sandra Priest Rose Center for Earth and Space in New York City was built on the site of the original Hayden Planetarium. The new planetarium, part of the larger center, is also called the Hayden.

Make your own planetarium

Like other people through the ages, you may have imagined pictures in the stars. You may have found different groups of stars named after ancient Greek gods and fantastic beasts.

If you enjoy looking at the stars and the patterns they make in the sky, make your own version of the sky, called a planetarium. In a planetarium, light is used to form patterns on the walls or ceiling of a room. It's like bringing the night sky inside. With your planetarium, you can stargaze during the day and on rainy nights. But on clear nights, go out and look at the real thing. The constellations will seem like old friends whom you recognize at a glance.

What you need:

- a round oatmeal container with lid
- scissors
- a pen
- tracing paper
- black construction paper
- different size paper punches
- a pencil
- a flashlight

1. Cut out the bottom of the oatmeal box or similar large tube container.

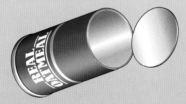

2. Cut the center out of the lid, leaving at least a half-inch space at the edge.

3. Using the tracing paper, trace the dots in the constellation Leo, the Lion, on this page.

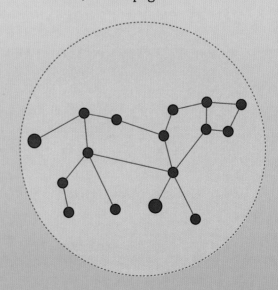

Continued on the next page

4. Trace the outside of the box lid on the construction paper. Cut out the circle. Trim it just inside the line, so that it fits inside the lid.

5. Place the tracing of the constellation over the construction paper circle. Use the large, medium, and small punches to make different holes for stars of different sizes. Or punch the holes with a pencil, making the ones for big stars larger.

6. Fit the construction paper circle inside the lid. Place the lid on the box.

7. Go into a totally dark room. Put the flashlight into the box from the bottom and turn it on. Look up. You should see the constellation on the ceiling.

8. Find constellations in books and trace them. Then make more construction paper circles and punch the constellations into them.

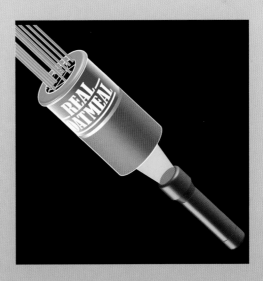

http://bit.ly/15q4yFw

A dark, previously unknown ring much larger than any other known planetary ring in the solar system surrounds Saturn. The ring (reddish oval in an artist's illustration) extends about 7.4 million miles (12 million kilometers) from Saturn (shown as a dot in the center of the image and magnified in the inset).

Planetary ring

A planetary ring is a disk-shaped region of rocky or icy particles around a planet. From a distance, such regions can appear as solid rings. In the solar system, the planets Jupiter, Saturn, Uranus, and Neptune have rings. We can see these rings because their particles reflect sunlight. Saturn's *densest* (most tightly packed) rings reflect so much sunlight that they can be seen through even small telescopes. The rings around Jupiter, Uranus, and Neptune are much less dense. Rings with fewer particles spread over a wider area can appear so faint that only powerful telescopes or nearby spacecraft can detect them. Such rings are called *diffuse rings.*

The particles in planetary rings can range in size from tiny grains to boulders. The particles all circle the planet on individual orbits. Astronomers often refer to all of a planet's rings and the small moons inside them as the planet's *ring system.*

Astronomers are not certain when and how planetary rings originated. Evidence shows that most rings formed fairly recently, perhaps within the last 100 million years. Diffuse rings appear to be made up of small particles continually cast off from *satellites* (moons) within them. Dense rings may be made of fragments of a large body that was destroyed in a collision.

Other articles to read include: **Jupiter; Neptune; Planet; Satellite; Saturn; Uranus.**

Pluto

Pluto is an icy body in the outer reaches of the solar system. Pluto was once considered a planet. But many astronomers now consider Pluto a *dwarf planet.* Pluto cannot be seen from Earth without a telescope.

From its discovery in 1930, Pluto was widely considered the ninth planet of the solar system. But its small size and irregular orbit led many astronomers to question whether Pluto should be

Continued on the next page

grouped with such worlds as Earth and Jupiter. Pluto more closely resembles other icy objects found in a region of the outer solar system beyond the orbit of Neptune called the *Kuiper (KY pur) belt.* In the early 2000's, astronomers found several other Kuiper belt objects (KBO's) about the same size as Pluto. In 2006, the International Astronomical Union (IAU), a widely recognized authority in naming heavenly bodies, created the "dwarf planet" classification to describe Pluto and these other objects. Some astronomers welcomed the decision. Other astronomers thought the definition was not clear enough and refused to accept it. In 2008, the IAU named the dwarf planets beyond Neptune *plutoids* in honor of Pluto.

Astronomers know little about Pluto's size or surface conditions because the dwarf planet is so far from Earth and is relatively small. Pluto is about 39 times as far from the sun as Earth is. It takes about 248 Earth years for Pluto to orbit the sun. For about 20 years of each orbit, Pluto comes closer to the sun than Neptune does. Pluto has an estimated diameter of 1,460 miles (2,350 kilometers), less than one-fifth that of Earth.

Pluto's surface is one of the coldest places in the solar system. The temperature on parts of Pluto may be about –385 °F (–232 °C). Pluto is mostly light brown. It appears to be partly covered with frozen methane and to have a thin atmosphere made mostly of nitrogen. Studies of Pluto suggest that the planet is made of rock and ice.

Pluto has at least five moons. One of the moons, Charon, is roughly half as wide as Pluto. This makes it the largest moon, compared to the body it orbits, in the solar system.

Pluto was discovered in 1930 by Clyde W. Tombaugh, an assistant at the Lowell Observatory in Arizona. He used predictions made by American astronomer Percival Lowell and other astronomers to find it.

The Hubble Space Telescope took the first good pictures of Pluto in 1996. In 2006, NASA, the United States space agency, launched the New Horizons probe. The probe was expected to fly by Pluto in 2015.

Other articles to read include: **Dwarf planet; Kuiper belt; New Horizons; Satellite; Tombaugh, Clyde.**

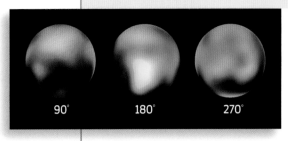

Bright and dark regions swirl across the surface of Pluto in images made by the Hubble Space Telescope. The bright areas are frozen nitrogen and methane. The methane ice may be growing and shrinking because of changes in the seasons on Pluto.

Pluto has five known moons. Two of the moons, P4 and P5, were discovered by the Hubble Space Telescope in 2011 and 2012, respectively. These two satellites have not yet received official names.

Porco, Carolyn

Carolyn C. Porco (1953-   ) is an astronomer. She has worked on several space probe missions, including Voyager 1 and Voyager 2. The probes photographed Jupiter, Saturn, Uranus, and Neptune. In the early 1990's, Porco became the leader of the *imaging* (photography) team for the Cassini probe to Saturn and its moons. Porco's team made many discoveries with Cassini's cameras. For example, they found *geysers* (jets spewing water) and ice on Saturn's moon Enceladus.

Porco was born in New York City. She completed her doctorate degree at the California Institute of Technology in 1983. Porco has taught at the University of Arizona and the University of Colorado. She has also done scientific research at the Space Science Institute in Boulder, Colorado.

Other articles to read include: **Astronomy; Cassini; Voyager.**

Proxima Centauri

Proxima Centauri is the closest star to Earth besides the sun. It is 4.2 *light-years* from Earth. One light-year equals the distance light travels in a vacuum in a year, about 5.88 trillion miles (9.46 trillion kilometers). Proxima can be found in the *constellation* Centaurus. A constellation is a grouping of stars in the night sky.

Proxima Centauri is a type of star called a *red dwarf.* Such stars are smaller than the sun. They are the most common star in our galaxy, the Milky Way.

Two stars near Proxima Centauri are Centauri A and Centauri B. These two stars *orbit* (travel around) each other. This type of double star is called a *binary star.* All together, the three stars are called Alpha Centauri. Many scientists believe Proxima Centauri orbits Centauri A and Centauri B. If this is true, Alpha Centauri is actually a triple star system.

Other articles to read include: **Alpha Centauri; Light-year; Red dwarf; Star.**

Proxima Centauri is a red dwarf, the most common type of star in the Milky Way.

Ptolemy

Ptolemy *(TOL uh mee)* (A.D. 100?-165?) was one of the greatest *astronomers (uh STRON uh muhrs)* and geographers of ancient times. He was also known as Claudius Ptolemaeus *(KLAW dee us TOL uh may us)*. The name *Claudius* meant that he was Roman. The name *Ptolemaeus* meant that he lived in Egypt. Almost nothing is known about his life. But scholars have determined that he made his astronomical observations in Alexandria, Egypt, about A.D. 150.

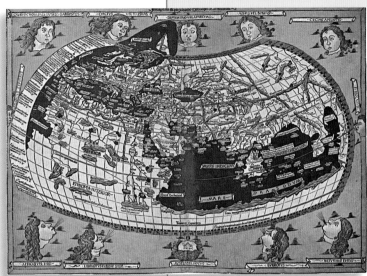

An early map of the world appeared in a 1482 edition of Ptolemy's eight-volume *Geography*. Scholars are not sure if this map was made by Ptolemy himself or by mapmakers who rediscovered his work after it had been lost for many centuries.

Ptolemy's observations and theories are preserved in a 13-part work entitled *Mathematike Syntaxis,* or *Mathematical Composition.* This work was so admired that it became known as the Almagest, meaning *the greatest.*

In his work, Ptolemy rejected the idea that Earth moves. He thought that everything in the universe moved either toward or around Earth's center. He said that the sun, stars, and planets moved around Earth at different speeds. Ptolemy's system of astronomy was widely accepted throughout Europe until 1543. That year, the Polish astronomer Nicolaus Copernicus *(koh PUR nuh kuhs)* formed his idea that Earth moves around the sun. This new idea took many years to be fully accepted.

Ptolemy devoted two parts of the *Syntaxis* to a catalog of the stars. This catalog included 1,022 stars grouped into 48 constellations. He gave a *magnitude* (brightness) for each star. Ptolemy also discovered that the moon travels in an irregular orbit.

Ptolemy's book *Geography* contains a map of the world, including Europe, northern Africa, and most of Asia, as well as 26 maps of specific areas. In his world map, Ptolemy showed the land mass from Spain to China as bigger than it really is. He showed the Atlantic Ocean as smaller than it really is. This mistake encouraged Christopher Columbus to make his famous voyage to what became known as the Americas in 1492.

Other articles to read include: **Astronomy; Copernicus, Nicolaus; Constellation; Orbit; Solar system.**

Qq

A pulsar (arrow) only about 12 miles (19 kilometers) wide is powerful enough to light up a *nebula* (cloud of gas and dust) more than 150 light-years across.

Monstrous jets of gas shoot from a quasar at the center of the galaxy Centaurus A, in an image taken by the Chandra X-ray Observatory.

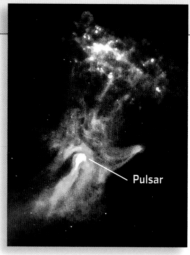

Pulsar

Pulsar

A pulsar *(PUHL sahr)* is an object in space that gives off light rays, usually radio waves, in *pulses* (regular patterns). Pulsars were named for these pulses. Although they are about 12 miles (20 kilometers) wide, pulsars may spin many times a second.

Pulsars seem to pulse because they give off light rays in only two directions, like a lighthouse. As the pulsar spins, the source of the light rays spins, too. If the light rays pass over Earth, they are detected as pulses.

Pulsars are an incredibly heavy kind of star called a *neutron star.* These stars form after stars of a certain size explode at the end of their lives. Scientists may find pulsars using several different kinds of telescopes.

Other articles to read include: **Light; Nebula; Neutron star; Star.**

Quasar

A quasar *(KWAY sahr* or *KWAY zahr)* is a very bright object at the center of some galaxies. Some quasars are 1 trillion times as bright as the sun. Some quasars are also some of the farthest known objects from Earth. A quasar is powered by a giant *black hole,* a region of space with a very strong gravitational pull. The central black hole in a quasar produces energy by swallowing clouds of gas from the surrounding galaxy.

Quasars give off huge amounts of energy. This energy is produced in different forms of light, including X rays, gamma rays, and radio waves. This energy may eventually reach Earth. Scientists can study this energy to learn about quasars and the early universe.

Astronomers at the Palomar Observatory, near San Diego, California, discovered quasars in 1963. Since then, they have found thousands of quasars.

Other articles to read include: **Black hole; Galaxy; Gamma rays; Light; Palomar Observatory.**

Red dwarf

A red dwarf is a small, relatively cool star. Red dwarfs glow with a dim, reddish light. Their reddish color results from their relatively low temperature. They are the most common type of star in the Milky Way, our galaxy.

Red dwarfs range in *mass* (amount of matter) from about $\frac{1}{12}$ to $\frac{1}{2}$ the mass of the sun. They generally give off from about $\frac{1}{10}$ to less than $\frac{1}{10,000}$ as much light as the sun. Red dwarfs shine so faintly that they are difficult to find at great distances. Red dwarfs include Proxima Centauri, the star closest to the sun.

Because red dwarfs have such low masses, they burn hydrogen—their fuel—very slowly. Their *cores* (centers) can continue to burn hydrogen for tens of billions or even several trillions of years. This amount of time is much longer than the current age of the universe. For this reason, scientists believe that no red dwarf has yet used up its hydrogen fuel.

Other articles to read include: **Brown dwarf; Proxima Centauri; Star; White dwarf.**

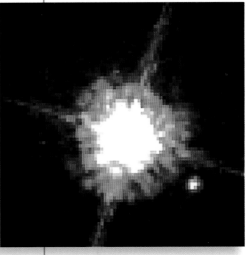

A red dwarf is circled by a much smaller companion in a false-color image taken by the Hubble Space Telescope.

Red giant

A red giant is a huge, extremely bright star that glows with a reddish light. Red giants range in size from about 10 times to 100 times as wide as the sun. They shine tens to hundreds of times as brightly as the sun. Their reddish appearance results from their relatively low temperatures, around 2000 to 4500 °C. Well-known red giants include Arcturus, the fourth-brightest star in the night sky, and Aldebaran, the brightest star in the *constellation* Taurus. A constellation is a grouping of stars in the night sky.

Each red giant was once a star like our sun. A red giant forms when a star with about $\frac{1}{2}$ to 8 times the *mass* (amount of matter) of the sun uses up most of the fuel in its *core* (center). The star then swells up to many times its original size.

Astronomers predict that, around 5 billion years from now, the

Continued on the next page

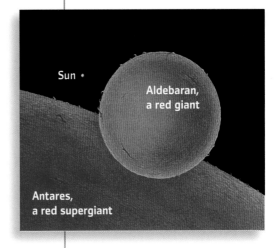

Red giants and supergiants range in size from about 10 to 1,000 times the diameter of the sun.

Red giant   *Continued from the previous page*

sun will become a red giant. Its outer layers will probably expand past the current orbit of Mercury. The sun will remain a red giant for about a billion years. Over the roughly 100 million years that follow, it will cast off its outer layers. These layers will cool as they expand, growing redder. Eventually, the red giant will become a small cool star called a *white dwarf.*

Other articles to read include: **Betelgeuse; Canopus; Star; Sun; White dwarf.**

Redshift

Redshift is a stretching of light. The stretching changes the *wavelength* of light. Wavelength is the distance between the crest of one light wave and the crest of the next.

Redshift results from two different causes—Doppler redshift and cosmological redshift. The motion of a wave source relative to an observer can cause a change in the wavelength. Objects moving away from the observer are stretched, increasing the wavelength. Scientists call this shifting in wavelength the *Doppler effect.* The wavelength of a light wave determines its color. Red has the longest wavelength of *visible light* (light we can see). The light being stretched will therefore appear redder, or *redshifted.*

Astronomers have found that nearly all cosmic objects far outside the Milky Way have only redshifts. They are all moving away from Earth. This *cosmological redshift* is produced by the expansion of the universe. Most scientists believe that the universe began expanding about 13.8 billion years ago. As the universe expands, the distance between most galaxies increases. The wavelength of light also steadily stretches as it travels through the expanding space.

Other articles to read include: **Big bang; Light; Universe.**

The light from extremely distant galaxies has been "stretched" toward the red end of the light spectrum because of the expansion of space, in an image taken by the Hubble Space Telescope.

Ride, Sally Kristen

Sally Kristen Ride (1951-2012) was the first woman United States astronaut to travel in space. In June 1983, she and four other astronauts made a six-day flight on the space shuttle Challenger. During the flight, Ride helped launch satellites and do experiments. Ride made her second shuttle flight in October 1984, also aboard Challenger. On that mission, she helped launch another satellite.

Ride was scheduled to fly a third flight in 1986. However, the Challenger was destroyed in an accident that year. Ride was assigned to a special group to investigate the accident.

Ride was born in Los Angeles. She earned a doctorate degree in physics in 1978. That same year, she was selected to become an astronaut. Beginning in 1987, she taught at Stanford University in California and then at the University of California at San Diego. She also served as director of the California Space Institute. In 2003, Ride helped to investigate the destruction of the shuttle Columbia, which broke apart as it returned to Earth.

Other articles to read include: **Astronaut; Challenger disaster; Space exploration.**

Sally Kristen Ride

Riess, Adam Guy

Adam Guy Riess (1969-   ) is an American scientist. He won the 2011 Nobel Prize in *physics* (the study of matter and energy). He shared the prize with American scientists Saul Perlmutter and Brian Schmidt. The three won for their discovery that the *expansion* (spreading apart) of the universe is *accelerating* (speeding up). The discovery led scientists to think that the universe is filled with a mysterious energy, called *dark energy.* Scientists think dark energy is pushing the universe apart faster and faster.

Adam Guy Riess was born in Washington, D.C. He became a professor at Johns Hopkins University in 2006.

Other articles to read include: **Big bang; Perlmutter, Saul; Schmidt, Brian Paul; Universe.**

Adam Guy Riess

Rocket

The Mars Science Laboratory rover, nicknamed Curiosity, blasts off atop a Saturn V rocket from Cape Canaveral, Florida, in November 2011.

A rocket is a device that pushes itself forward by shooting gases in the opposite direction. A rocket is a kind of *engine*. Like car engines and jet engines, rockets produce motion. Rockets are the most powerful kind of engine.

Most rockets produce motion by burning a fuel. These rockets are called *chemical* rockets. In addition to fuel, rockets carry a substance called an *oxidizer*. Burning fuel requires oxygen, which the oxidizer supplies. Jet engines work much like rockets, but they do not have an oxidizer. They get oxygen from the air. Because rockets do not need oxygen from the air, they can burn fuel in outer space. A rocket's mixture of fuel and oxidizer is called a *propellant.*

A chemical rocket burns fuel inside a *combustion (kuhm BUHS chuhn)* (burning) chamber. The burning creates hot gas. The gas rapidly *expands* (spreads out) in all directions. However, it can only escape the chamber through an opening in the back of the rocket called the *nozzle.* As the gas moves out from the nozzle, the rocket is pushed in the opposite direction. This movement can be explained by the laws of motion discovered by the English scientist Isaac Newton. Newton's laws say that for every action, there is an equal and opposite reaction.

Most space rockets have two or three sections, called *stages.* Such rockets are called *multistage (MUHL tih STAYJ)* rockets. Each stage has a rocket engine, propellant, and oxidizer. The first stage, the lowest, launches the rocket. After the first stage has burned its propellant, the rocket drops that section. The second stage then fires. The rocket uses one stage after another in this way.

Rockets are used to launch artificial satellites into a circular path, called an *orbit,* around Earth. Rockets that launch satellites and *space probes* (crewless spacecraft) are called *launch* vehicles.

Rockets carry space probes on long voyages to explore the solar system. Probes have explored the sun, the moon, and all the planets in the solar system. They carry scientific instruments that

Continued on the next page

gather information about the planets and transmit information back to Earth. Probes have landed on the surface of the moon, Venus, Mars, and Saturn's moon Titan.

A two-stage rocket is made of two parts called *stages*. Each stage has an engine, fuel, and a supply of oxygen. When the fuel in the first stage is used up, that stage falls away. Then, the second stage fires.

Rockets also launch vehicles carrying astronauts into space. The Saturn V rocket, which carried astronauts to the moon, was the most powerful launch vehicle ever built. It could send a spacecraft weighing more than 100,000 pounds (45,000 kilograms) to the moon. Space shuttles were reusable rocket-powered spacecraft that could fly into space and return to Earth repeatedly.

Engineers created the first launch vehicles by altering military or *meteorological* (atmospheric) rockets. For example, they added stages to some of these rockets to increase their speed. Today, engineers sometimes attach smaller rockets to a launch vehicle. These rockets, called *boosters,* provide additional power to launch heavier spacecraft.

Rockets are made by both governments and private companies. NASA, the American space agency, has produced its own rockets and has also helped private companies build their own.

Other articles to read include: **Jet Propulsion Laboratory; Orbit; Satellite, Artificial; Space exploration.**

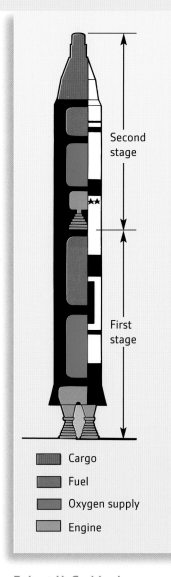

Second stage

First stage

Cargo
Fuel
Oxygen supply
Engine

Robert H. Goddard, an American rocket pioneer, stands next to the frame he used to launch the world's first successful liquid-propellant rocket, in March 1926. The rocket, which Goddard designed and built, reached an altitude of 41 feet (12 meters), flew for 2 seconds and averaged about 60 miles (96 kilometers) per hour. The rocket burned gasoline and liquid oxygen.

Rubin, Vera

Vera Rubin (1928-) is an American astronomer. She is best known for her work on *dark matter*. Dark matter is a mysterious form of matter that cannot be seen. But it may make up most of the matter in the universe.

Vera Rubin

Rubin worked with the American astronomer Kent Ford. The two studied how stars move in galaxies. These movements could not be explained based only on the matter that they saw. This provided evidence that dark matter really exists.

Rubin was born in Philadelphia. She graduated from Vassar College as the school's only astronomy major. She then studied astronomy and *physics* (the study of matter and energy) at Cornell University in Ithaca, New York, and Georgetown University in Washington, D.C. Rubin joined the Carnegie Institution of Science as a researcher. At Carnegie, she met and worked with Ford.

Other articles to read include: **Astronomy; Dark matter.**

Sagittarius was among the 48 constellations defined by the ancient Greek mathematician Ptolemy.

Sagittarius

Sagittarius is a *constellation* also known as the Archer. A constellation is a grouping of stars in the night sky. An *archer* is a person who shoots with a bow and arrow. Sagittarius is easiest to see from the Southern Hemisphere from June through August.

Sagittarius is most often shown as a mythical creature called a *centaur*. A centaur has the head and upper body of a human and the lower body of a horse. Sagittarius holds a bow and arrow. But the stars in the constellation can be connected in many ways.

Sagittarius is an ancient constellation. It remains one of 88 constellations recognized today by the International Astronomical Union (IAU), the main authority in the naming of heavenly objects.

Other articles to read include: **Astrology; Constellation; Sagittarius A*; Star; Zodiac.**

Sagittarius A*

Sagittarius *(SAJ uh TAIR ee uhs)* A* is a super-massive *black hole* at the center of our galaxy, the Milky Way. A black hole is an invisible region in space. Its gravitational force is so strong that nothing can escape from it, not even light. The name *Sagittarius A*<* is pronounced *Sagittarius A star.* The black hole got its name because the center of the galaxy lies in the direction of the constellation Sagittarius.

Astronomers have never seen Sagittarius A* *(SgrA*)*. The clearest sign that SgrA* is a supermassive black hole is the rapid movement of stars around it. The fastest of these stars appears to orbit SgrA* every 15.2 years at speeds that reach about 3,100 miles (5,000 kilometers) per second. Astronomers believe that an object about 4 million times as massive as the sun must lie inside the star's orbit. The only known object that could be that massive and fit inside the star's orbit is a black hole.

A black hole is smaller than an atom. But its *event horizon* can be very large. The event horizon is the area around a black hole from which nothing can escape. The event horizon around SgrA* is about 27 million miles (44 million kilometers) across. If SgrA* were placed where the sun is, its event horizon would reach out about half way to Mercury, the closest plane to the sun.

Other articles to read include: **Black hole; Gravitation; Sagittarius; Milky Way.**

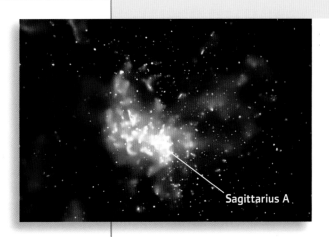

Sagittarius A

Superheated gas that gives off X rays surrounds the supermassive black hole, known as Sagittarius A*, at the center of the Milky Way Galaxy (shown in a false-color image taken by the Chandra X-ray Observatory).

Satellite

A satellite *(SAT uh lyt)* is an object that *orbits* (circles around) a planet or other larger body in space. A satellite can either be a natural object, like Earth's moon, or an artificial craft launched into orbit by rocket. This article is about natural satellites, which are also called *moons.*

All the planets in the solar system except Mercury and Venus have moons. Earth has one moon, and Mars has two moons. Jupiter, Saturn, Uranus, and Neptune have many moons.

Continued on the next page

None of the many cracks, valleys, ridges, pits, and icy flows on Jupiter's moon Europa extend more than a few hundred yards (meters) upward or downward, making the moon one of the smoothest bodies in the solar system.

Astronomers (scientists who study the universe) have also discovered satellites around dozens of *asteroids* and a number of *Kuiper belt objects* (KBO's). Asteroids are rocks that orbit the sun. KBO's are icy bodies found beyond the orbit of Neptune.

Satellites come in many different sizes. The largest is Jupiter's moon Ganymede. Ganymede is even larger than the planet Mercury. The smallest known satellite is the moon Dactyl, which orbits the asteroid Ida. Dactyl is only 4,600 feet (1.4 kilometers) across.

Moons are made up of different materials. The satellites closest to the sun are often made of a kind of rock called *silicate (SIHL uh kayt).* This is the same material that makes up most of Earth's outer surface. Some satellites are made up of both silicate and ice. Still other satellites are made up mostly of ice. In general, the farther a satellite is from the sun, the more ice it has. Most of the ice on satellites is water ice, like the ice we see on Earth.

Scientists generally believe that most of the satellites of the solar system formed at about the same time as planets did, and in the same way. According to this *theory* (idea based on scientific evidence), these bodies formed about 4.6 billion years ago from a huge, spinning cloud of gas and dust. Over time, *gravitation* pulled pieces of dust from the cloud together. Gravitation is a natural force that draws objects toward each other. The pieces of dust formed rocks. Gravitation pulled larger and larger pieces together. Eventually, some of the pieces became planets and moons.

Impact craters mark the surfaces of most satellites in the solar system. Many of these bowl-shaped holes were created billions of years ago in the early years of the solar system. At that time, planets, moons, and other bodies were frequently bombarded by leftover material from the formation of the solar system.

Some satellites have changed since they formed. These moons may have many kinds of surface features. For example, Jupiter's satellite Io has several active volcanoes. Space probes have detected erupting geysers on Saturn's moon Enceladus and Neptune's moon Triton. Jupiter's Europa is believed to have an ocean of liquid water beneath its icy surface. Some scientists think that life could exist there. Saturn's Titan has a dense atmosphere that may be similar in some important ways to the early atmosphere of Earth.

Scientists use telescopes and spacecraft to study satellites and

Continued on the next page

the planets they orbit. Many missions have visited Earth's moon. These missions include probes, landers, and the Apollo missions of the 1960's and 1970's, in which astronauts walked on the moon's surface. The moon is the only natural satellite on which human beings have set foot.

Spacecraft have flown near many other satellites in the solar system. Several spacecraft have imaged the moons of Mars. Two spacecraft have studied the moons of Jupiter and Saturn. Studying Saturn's system of satellites is a major focus of the Cassini spacecraft, which arrived at Saturn in 2004. Cassini also dropped a probe called Huygens that landed on Titan in 2005. Huygens was the first probe to land on a satellite besides Earth's moon. The New Horizons spacecraft will study Pluto and its moon Charon when it reaches Pluto in 2015.

Other articles to read include: **Cassini; Gravitation; Impact crater; Orbit; Moon; New Horizons; Phobos; Planet;** *and those on individual satellites.*

Jupiter's moon, or satellite, Io orbits the largest planet in the solar system. Io is more geologically active than any other satellite—or any planet—in the solar system.

Satellite, Artificial

An artificial satellite is an object made by people that *orbits* (travels around) a body in space. Most artificial satellites orbit Earth. Earth's moon is a natural satellite.

People use artificial satellites to study the universe and forecast the weather. Satellites relay Internet and telephone signals around the world. People use satellites to help steer ships and airplanes, to monitor crops and other natural resources, and to support military activities. Artificial satellites also have orbited and studied the moon, the sun, asteroids, and the planets Mercury, Venus, Mars, Jupiter, and Saturn. The space probe Voyager 2 flew past the planets Uranus and Neptune.

Spacecraft with people on board also are considered to be artificial satellites. These objects include space capsules and space stations. Pieces of *space debris,* also known as *space junk,* are also considered artificial satellites. Space debris includes

Continued on the next page

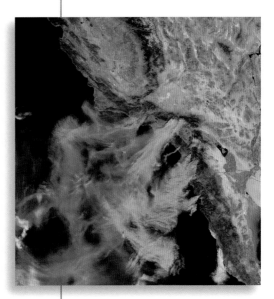

Clouds of smoke from wildfires raging across southern California blow toward the sea, in an image captured by the Terra Earth-observing satellite.

Satellite, Artificial *Continued from the previous page*

burned-out rocket boosters and empty fuel tanks that have not fallen to Earth.

The Soviet Union (now Russia) launched the first artificial satellite in 1957. It was called Sputnik 1. Since then, dozens of countries have developed, launched, and operated satellites. Today, thousands of working satellites orbit Earth.

Other articles to read include: **Communications satellite; Orbit; Rocket;** *and those on individual satellites.*

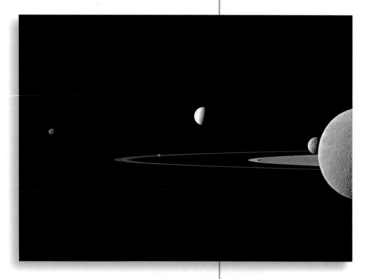

Five of Saturn's moons stand out against the blackness of space, in an image from the Cassini space probe. The moons are (from left to right) Janus, Pandora, Enceladus, Mimas, and Rhea.

Saturn

Saturn is a planet know for its spectacular rings. Saturn also ranks as the second-largest planet in the solar system. Only Jupiter is larger. Saturn is the sixth planet from the sun. It was the farthest planet from Earth known to ancient observers. The rings of Saturn can be seen from Earth with a small telescope. Saturn gets its name from the ancient Roman god of agriculture.

Saturn is about 74,900 miles (120,540 kilometers) wide, about 10 times as wide as Earth. It travels around the sun at an average distance of about 891 million miles (1.4 billion kilometers). Saturn takes about 29 Earth years to go around the sun.

Scientists think that Saturn is a giant ball of mostly gas, made of the chemical elements hydrogen and helium. It has no solid surface. However, many scientists believe the planet may have a hot, solid center of iron and rocky material.

Despite its huge size, Saturn has a lower *density* (matter packed together) than any other planet in the solar system. Saturn's density is even less than that of liquid water. As a result, Saturn would float—if there were a swimming pool big enough to hold it.

A thick layer of clouds covers Saturn. The clouds appear to us as *belts* (bands) of different colors that wrap around the planet.

Continued on the next page

Scientists believe the bands' appearance seems to be caused by differences in temperature and height among clouds of rising and falling gases.

Temperatures on Saturn are much lower than temperatures on Earth, mainly because Saturn is so far away from the sun. The average temperature at the top of Saturn's clouds is about –285 °F (–175 °C). The temperature rises below the clouds.

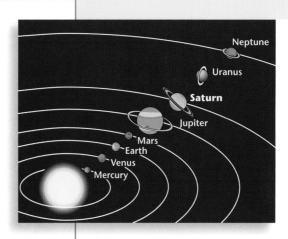

Saturn is the sixth planet from the sun.

Saturn has seven wide, flat rings. They surround the planet at its *equator* (imaginary line around the middle), but they do not touch it. The rings consist mainly of pieces of ice. They range from dust-sized grains to chunks more than 10 feet (3 meters) in diameter. The rings vary greatly in width. The outermost ring may measure more than 180,000 miles (300,000 kilometers) across. The rings also vary greatly in thickness. Most are probably under 100 feet (30 meters) thick.

Saturn has at least 60 *satellites* (moons) and probably many more. Titan, Saturn's largest moon, is larger than the planet Mercury. It is the second-largest moon in the solar system, behind Jupiter's moon Ganymede. Scientists are particularly interested in Saturn's moon Enceladus. Some scientists think that the presence of liquid water and *organic* (carbon-based) molecules on Enceladus suggest that life may exist there.

In 1610, the Italian astronomer Galileo Galilei discovered Saturn's rings using one of the first telescopes. Galileo could see faint bulges on each side of the planet. He concluded that the bulges were two large satellites. In 1656, the Dutch astronomer Christiaan Huygens *(HOY gehns)* used a more powerful telescope to describe a "thin, flat" ring around Saturn. In 1675, the Italian-born French astronomer Giovanni Domenico Cassini discovered that the single ring was actually two.

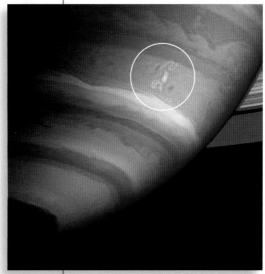

The United States has sent a number of space probes to Saturn. In 1979, the Pioneer-Saturn space probe took many pictures of Saturn. In 1980 and 1981, two Voyager space probes discovered several moons of Saturn. In 2004, the Cassini spacecraft became the first to orbit Saturn.

Other articles to read include: **Cassini; Galileo** (scientist)**; Dione; Enceladus; Huygens, Christiaan; Iapetus; Mimas; Planet; Planetary ring; Rhea; Satellite; Titan.**

The Dragon Storm on Saturn, shown in a false-color image taken by the Cassini spacecraft in 2004, generated lightning that was 10,000 times as strong as lightning on Earth.

Schmidt, Brian Paul

Brian Paul Schmidt (1967-) is an American scientist. He won the 2011 Nobel Prize in *physics*. Physics is the study of matter and energy. Schmidt shared the prize with the American scientists Saul Perlmutter and Adam Riess. The three won for their discovery that the *expansion* (spreading apart) of the universe is *accelerating* (speeding up). The discovery led scientists to think that the universe is filled with a mysterious energy, called *dark energy*. Scientists think dark energy is pushing the universe and the objects inside it apart faster and faster.

Schmidt was born in Missoula, Montana. He graduated from the University of Arizona in 1989 and then attended Harvard University for his master's and doctoral degrees. He joined the Mount Stromlo Observatory near Canberra, Australia, in 1995.

Other articles to read include: **Big bang; Perlmutter, Saul; Riess, Adam Guy; Universe.**

Brian Paul Schmidt

Scorpius

Scorpius is a *constellation* also known as the Scorpion. A constellation is a grouping of stars in the night sky. Scorpius sits in the southern sky between the constellations Libra and Sagittarius. It is best viewed around June through August.

As commonly drawn, Scorpius includes about 18 main stars. Most of these stars form a hook shape representing the scorpion's body and tail. A crossbar of stars near the head suggests the scorpion's arms and claws.

Scorpius was among the 48 constellations defined by the ancient Greek mathematician Ptolemy. Today, it is one of the 88 constellations recognized by the International Astronomical Union, the leading authority in the naming of heavenly objects.

Other articles to read include: **Astrology; Constellation; Ptolemy; Star; Zodiac.**

Many of the major stars in Scorpius form a hook, said to represent the scorpion's body and tail.

SETI Institute

The SETI Institute is a research group that is searching for life in space. The word SETI stands for the *Search for Extra-Terrestrial (ehks truh tuh REHS tree uhl) I*ntelligence. But researchers at the institute seek any form of life beyond Earth, however intelligent it may be. The institute is in Mountain View, California. SETI was started in 1984.

SETI research involves looking near other stars for signals sent by extraterrestrials in the form of light or radio waves. During the 1990's and early 2000's, scientists used telescopes that collect radio waves to hunt for signals coming from many hundreds of stars. Together with the University of California at Berkeley, the SETI Institute built the Allen Telescope Array. This group of 350 radio telescopes in California was designed to conduct SETI studies of about 1 million stars.

Other articles to read include: **Allen Telescope Array; Extraterrestrial intelligence.**

Shapley, Harlow

Harlow Shapley (1885–1972) was an American astronomer. He helped determine the size of the Milky Way Galaxy and the solar system's location within it.

Shapley studied *variable stars*. Variable stars change brightness in a regular cycle of dim and bright. These stars are often found in tightly bound groups of stars. Shapley observed a high number of these star groups, called *globular clusters,* near the center of the Milky Way. Shapley first measured the brightness of variable stars in these clusters. He then calculated their distance from Earth. He found that the solar system is closer to the edge of the galaxy than to its center. He also showed that the Milky Way is much larger than astronomers had believed.

Harlow Shapley was born in Nashville, Missouri. He earned a Ph.D. degree from Princeton University in 1913. Shapley served as director of the Harvard College Observatory from 1921 to 1952.

Other articles to read include: **Astronomy; Galaxy; Milky Way; Star cluster.**

Sharman, Helen

Helen Sharman

Sharman, Helen (1963-) was the first person from the United Kingdom to travel into space. On May 18, 1991, a Soviet Soyuz TM-12 spacecraft carrying Sharman and two Soviet cosmonauts lifted off from a launch site in Kazakhstan. After an eight-day stay aboard the Soviet Union's Mir space station, Sharman returned to Earth on May 26 in a TM-11 Soyuz craft.

Sharman's mission was a part of Project Juno, a British-Soviet space mission aboard Mir. Potential British astronauts were recruited for Project Juno through a national advertising campaign. Sharman was selected from among 13,000 applicants to participate in the project. She trained for her mission in Russia.

Helen Patricia Sharman was born in Sheffield, England. She studied chemistry at Sheffield University. Following her experiences as an astronaut, she began giving public lectures. She also became involved in a campaign to improve science education in the United Kingdom. Sharman wrote of her experiences in *Seize the Moment* (1993) and the children's book *The Space Place* (1997).

Other articles to read include: **Astronaut; Mir; Space exploration.**

Shepard, Alan Bartlett, Jr.

Alan B. Shepard, Jr.

Alan Bartlett Shepard, Jr. (1923-1998), was the first American to travel in space. He was also the fifth astronaut on the moon.

Shepard was born in East Derry, New Hampshire. He served in World War II (1939-1945) and became a Navy test pilot. In 1959, he was chosen as one of the first astronauts.

In April 1961, Yuri Gagarin *(YOOR ee gah GAHR ihn)* of the Soviet Union (now Russia) became the first person to travel in space. On May 5, 1961, less than a month later, Shepard rocketed 117 miles (188 kilometers) into space from Cape Canaveral, Florida. He landed 15 minutes later, 302 miles (486 kilometers) out in the Atlantic Ocean. In 1971, he commanded Apollo 14, the third landing on the moon.

Other articles to read include: **Astronaut; Gagarin, Yuri Alekseyevich; Space exploration.**

Shoemaker, Carolyn

Carolyn Jean Spellmann Shoemaker (1929-   ) is an American astronomer. She has discovered more than 800 *asteroids* (rocky objects in space) as well as more comets than any other person. She has won numerous scientific prizes.

Shoemaker may be best known for her codiscovery of the comet Shoemaker-Levy 9 with astronomer David Levy and her husband, planetary scientist Eugene Shoemaker. The comet drew worldwide attention when it collided with the planet Jupiter in 1994.

Carolyn Jean Spellmann was born in Gallup, New Mexico. She took up astronomy in 1980, at the age of 51.

Other articles to read include: **Asteroid; Astronomy; Comet; Shoemaker, Eugene Merle.**

Shoemaker, Eugene Merle

Eugene Merle Shoemaker (1928-1997) was an American planetary scientist and *geologist.* A geologist is a scientist who studies how the planet Earth formed and how it changes. Shoemaker founded *astrogeology,* the geological study of objects in outer space. He also warned people about the danger of a comet or *asteroid* hitting Earth. An asteroid is a rocky object in space.

Shoemaker studied what happens when asteroids and comets crash into planets and moons. He proved that Meteor Crater in Arizona was formed when an asteroid crashed into Earth.

Shoemaker discovered 32 comets and many asteroids. In 1993, he codiscovered the comet Shoemaker-Levy 9, along with his wife, Carolyn Shoemaker, and astronomer David H. Levy. In 1994, this comet was observed crashing into Jupiter.

Shoemaker was born in Los Angeles. He attended the California Institute of Technology and Princeton University.

Other articles to read include: **Asteroid; Astronomy; Comet; Shoemaker, Carolyn.**

Eugene and Carolyn Shoemaker

Sirius

Sirius is the brightest star in the night sky. It is also called the Dog Star. Sirius is twice as large as the sun and gives off 30 times as much light. Sirius is one of the stars nearest Earth. It is about 9 *light-years* away. A light-year is the distance that light travels in a vacuum in one year, about 5.88 trillion miles (9.46 trillion kilometers). Sirius forms part of the *constellation* Canis Major, or the Great Dog. A constellation is a grouping of stars in the night sky.

Sirius is part of a *binary system*. A binary system is actually two stars that *orbit* (travel around) each other. Sirius's companion star, Sirius B, is a *white dwarf*. A white dwarf is an extremely compact star. Sirius and Sirius B make a complete orbit around each other about every 50 years.

Other articles to read include: **Binary star; Light-year; Star; White dwarf.**

Brilliant Sirius and its faint, tiny companion star appear in an image taken by the Hubble Space Telescope. The crossed lines in the photograph were created by the telescope's imaging system.

Sloan Digital Sky Survey

The Sloan Digital Sky Survey (SDSS) is a project to map the night sky. It aims to create a census of the stars, galaxies, and other objects in a vast region of the universe. Professional astronomers and students use SDSS data in every field of astronomy. Astronomers conduct the survey using a telescope at the Apache Point Observatory near Sunspot, New Mexico.

The SDSS telescope features a primary mirror 2.5 meters (8.2 feet) in diameter. The telescope takes images of the night sky and records objects that appear in the images. The survey has cataloged hundreds of millions of objects since the project began operating in 1998. It is scheduled to continue through 2014.

The SDSS telescope is cataloging hundreds of millions of stars, galaxies, and other objects. Such information helps astronomers measure the objects' distance from Earth. The survey is producing the most detailed map of galaxies ever made. Astronomers can compare this map to various models to test *theories* (ideas based

Continued on the next page

on scientific findings) about the development of the universe and the objects in it. Information from the SDSS has confirmed, for example, that most of the universe consists of *dark energy,* a little-understood form of energy.

The survey has also cataloged stars in our own galaxy, the Milky Way. The results showed that the stars are spread in an uneven, "lumpy" fashion. This lumpiness appears to result from the Milky Way colliding with and absorbing small galaxies.

The SDSS has revealed many previously unknown objects. The survey discovered some of the most distant galaxies known. The light from these galaxies has taken about 13 billion light-years to reach Earth. In the Milky Way, the survey has found cool, dim objects called *brown dwarfs.* A brown dwarf has a greater *mass* (amount of matter) than a planet but less mass than a star. The SDSS has also provided evidence for the existence of *dark matter,* the invisible substance that makes up most of the matter in the universe.

A partnership of academic institutions called the Astrophysical Research Consortium manages the Sloan Digital Sky Survey.

Other articles to read include: **Brown dwarf; Dark matter; Galaxy; Star; Telescope.**

A 100-inch (2.5-meter) telescope that collects visible light is used to conduct the Sloan Digital Sky Survey, an ambitious survey of the night sky. The survey has cataloged more than 350 million objects.

Solar Dynamics Observatory (SDO)

The Solar Dynamics Observatory (SDO) is a space telescope *orbiting* (circling) Earth. Scientists use it to measure and image the sun's *magnetic field.* A magnetic field is the invisible region around a magnetic object where its influence can be felt. NASA, the United States space agency, launched the SDO in 2010.

The SDO observes the sun's magnetic field indirectly by recording changes in the sun's *plasma,* a hot gaslike material. Researchers study the changes in the plasma to understand how

Continued on the next page

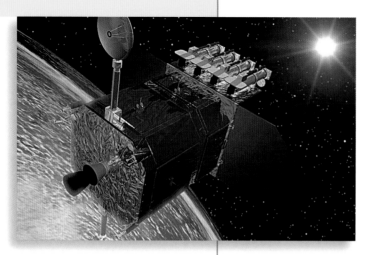

The SDO circles Earth once a day in an orbit that keeps it within sight of the sun and also of its communication station in New Mexico.

Solar Dynamics Observatory

Continued from the previous page

magnetic energy is created inside the sun and released as different types of energy at the surface. If a large release of this energy struck Earth directly, it could cut electric power, damage satellites, or disrupt radio transmissions.

The SDO is in a *geosynchronous orbit.* This means that it circles Earth at the same speed as Earth spins. This enables the SDO to stay directly above its communication station in New Mexico.

Other articles to read include: **Coronal mass ejection; Magnetic storm; Observatory; Satellite, Artificial; Sun; Telescope.**

The solar system is located on the outer edge of one of the *spiral* (curving) arms of the Milky Way Galaxy.

Solar system

The solar system is made up of the sun, the planets, and other smaller objects that *orbit* (travel around) the sun. These smaller objects include *dwarf planets,* moons, *asteroids, comets,* and *meteoroids.* Other systems that include a star and the objects that orbit it are called *planetary systems.* However, they are sometimes called "other" solar systems. Since the 1990's, *astronomers* (scientists who study outer space) have discovered a number of planetary systems.

The sun is the largest object in the solar system. It provides most of the light, heat, and other energy that makes life on Earth possible. The sun contains 99.8 percent of the solar system's *mass* (amount of matter).

The planets orbit the sun in *elliptical* (oval-shaped paths). The four inner planets—Mercury, Venus, Earth, and Mars—are made up mostly of iron and rocks. They are smaller than the outer planets. The outer planets are Jupiter, Saturn, Uranus, and

Continued on the next page

Neptune. All the outer planets are giant worlds surrounded by thick layers of gases.

Dwarf planets are round objects with less mass than the planets. Unlike a planet, a dwarf planet lacks the gravitational pull to sweep other objects from the region of its orbit. Nearly all the dwarf planets orbit beyond the orbit of Neptune in a band of rocky objects called the *Kuiper (KY puhr) belt*.

Moons orbit every planet except Mercury and Venus. Some dwarf planets and asteroids have moons, too. The inner planets have few moons. Earth has one moon, and Mars has two tiny moons. Each of the giant outer planets has many moons. The dwarf planet Pluto has at least five moons. The largest of Pluto's moons, Charon, is half as wide as Pluto. The asteroid Ida is also known to have a small moon. It is named Dactyl.

Asteroids are rocky objects much smaller than planets. Most asteroids orbit the sun between the orbits of Mars and Jupiter in a region called the *Main Belt*. One asteroid in the Main Belt, Ceres, is large enough to be called a dwarf planet. Some asteroids travel in *elliptical* (oval) orbits that pass inside the orbit of Earth or even that of Mercury. Astronomers believe there are hundreds of thousands of asteroids in the solar system.

Comets are made up mainly of ice and rock. When a comet gets close to the sun, some of the ice turns into gas. The gas and bits of dust shoot out of the comet, forming a long tail.

Continued on the next page

The solar system consists of the sun, eight planets, and everything else that orbits the sun. (The size of the sun and planets is shown to scale, though the distances between them are not.)

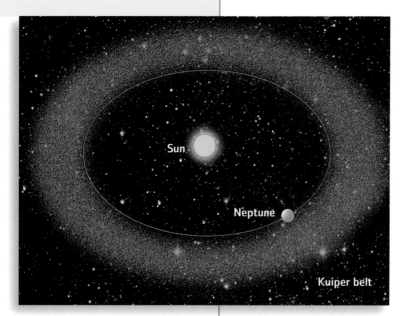

The Kuiper belt lies far beyond the orbit of Neptune. (Neither the size of objects nor the distance between objects in this illustration is drawn to scale.)

Solar system

Continued from the previous page

Scientists think that some comets come from the Kuiper belt. They think some come from the *Oort cloud,* a cluster of comets far beyond the Kuiper belt.

Meteoroids are chunks of metal or rock that are usually smaller than asteroids. When meteoroids fall into Earth's *atmosphere* (blanket of gases), they break up. As that happens, they form bright streaks of light called *meteors*. Meteoroids that reach the ground are known as *meteorites*. Most meteorites are broken chunks of asteroids. Some meteorites came from Mars or the moon.

Most scientists believe that the solar system formed from a giant, *rotating* (spinning) cloud of gas and dust known as the *solar nebula*. According to this theory, the solar nebula began to collapse because of its own gravity. Some astronomers think that a nearby *supernova* (exploding star) may have triggered the collapse. As the nebula shrank, it spun faster and flattened into a disk.

Most of the material in the solar nebula was pulled toward the center and formed the sun. As the flattened disk spun around this center, particles within it collided and stuck together. They eventually formed asteroid-sized bodies called *planetesimals*. Some of these planetesimals combined to become the planets. Other planetesimals formed moons, and at leadt one asteroid, Vesta. The planets and asteroids all *revolve* (travel) around the sun in the same direction. They also move more or less in the same *plane* (level), because they originally formed from this flattened disk.

At a certain point, the pressure at the center of the disk became great enough to trigger the nuclear reactions that power the sun. Eventually, eruptions on the surface of the sun produced a continuous flow of particles from the sun called the *solar wind*. In the inner solar system, many scientists believe the wind was so powerful that it swept away most of the lighter chemical

Continued on the next page

elements—hydrogen and helium. In the outer regions of the solar system, however, the solar wind was much weaker. As a result, much more hydrogen and helium remained in the outer planets. This process explains why the inner planets are small, rocky worlds and the outer planets are mostly hydrogen and helium.

The solar system is constantly changing. For example, many scientists believe that the four largest planets—Jupiter, Saturn, Uranus, and Neptune—formed much closer to the sun than they are today. The gravitational push and pull between the planets eventually threw them away from the sun into more distant orbits.

Other articles to read include: **Asteroid; Comet; Dwarf planet; Ellipse; Jupiter; Kuiper belt; Main Belt; Mars; Mercury; Meteorite; Nebula; Neptune; Orbit; Planet; Satellite; Saturn; Solar wind; Sun; Uranus; Venus.**

1. Many scientists think that the solar system began as a cloud of gas and bits of rock and metal.

2. The cloud began to spin and flattened into a disk.

3. Most of the cloud pulled together in the center and formed the sun.

4. Some of the rock and metal pieces smashed together. They formed planets, moons, and other solid bodies.

Make a solar system mobile

What you need:

- 4 dowel rods, ⅛ inch (0.3 cm) in diameter:
  one 17-inch (43-cm) long
  one 21-inch (53-cm) long
  one 35-inch (89-cm) long
  one 43-inch (109-cm) long
- a spool of "invisible" nylon thread
- 4 plastic or metal rings, ¾ inch (2 cm) in diameter
- crayons or markers
- a large piece of white posterboard
- a compass
- scissors
- glue
- tape
- hole punch
- yardstick or meter stick
- large paper plate
- a hanging hook

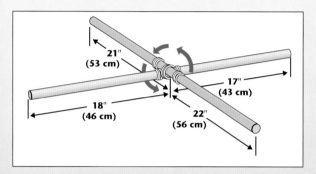

1. Cross the two longer dowel rods so one end of each rod sticks out 1 inch (2.5 centimeters) farther than the other end, as shown above. Tie them together with nylon thread. Do the same with the two shorter rods. Tie a ring above and below each pair of rods at the points where the rods cross.

2. Cut an 8-inch (20-centimeter) piece of nylon thread. Tie one end of the thread to the ring below the longer rods and the other end to the ring on top of the shorter rods. Leave 6 inches (15 centimeters) of thread between the rings.

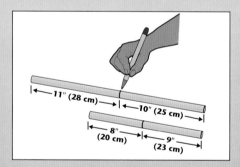

3. Cut one 32-inch (81-centimeter) piece of thread and nine 16-inch (41-centimeter) pieces of thread. Tie the longer thread to the ring on top of the longer rods. Tie one of the shorter threads to the ring below the shorter rods. Hang the mobile from the longer thread on a hook. Then tie one thread to the end of each rod.

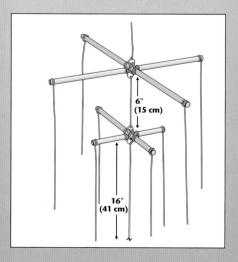

4. To make the planets and the sun, draw nine circles on the posterboard using a compass. Set your compass to the following radii (ask a teacher or other adult to help you if you don't know how to use a compass):

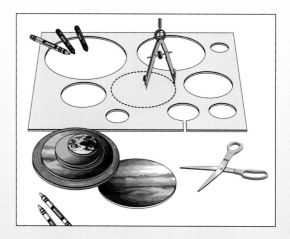

Sun: 4 ½ inches (11.5 centimeters)
Jupiter: 3 ¾ inches (9.5 centimeters)
Saturn: 3 ¼ inches (8.5 centimeters)
Neptune: 2 ½ inches (6.5 centimeters)
Uranus: 2 ¼ inches (6 centimeters)
Earth: 1 ½ inches (4 centimeters)
Venus: 1 ¼ inches (3.5 centimeters)
Mars: 1 ⅛ inches (3 centimeters)
Mercury: 1 inch (2.5 centimeters)

Cut out and label each circle.

5. Color both sides of your sun and planet circles. Use pictures of planets from articles in the Student Discovery Science set to guide you, or find other pictures of planets to use.

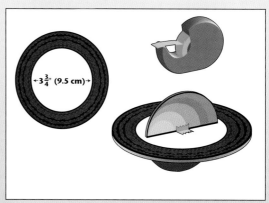

6. Use the large paper plate for Saturn's ring. Color just the outer edge of the plate, as shown at right. Cut a 3 ¾-inch-(9.5-centimeter)-long slit in the middle of the plate, slip the Saturn model through the slit, and tape it in place.

7. Punch a hole near the top of your sun and each planet. Tie your sun and planets to the mobile as shown above. Mercury, the planet closest to the sun, should hang from the shortest section of rod, Venus from the next shortest section, and so on, in each planet's order from the sun. Uranus and Neptune should hang from the longest rod. Look at the picture of the finished mobile (right) for help.

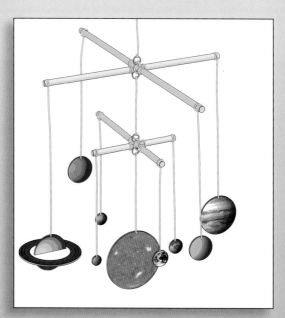

http://bit.ly/YuRwB7

Solar wind

The solar wind is a constant flow of tiny particles from the sun. These particles mainly come from the *corona,* the sun's outer layer.

High temperatures in the corona heat gases. The heat causes the gases to *expand* (grow bigger). Many of the atoms in the gas collide. In the collisions, the atoms lose particles called *electrons.* The atoms gain an electrical charge in the process, becoming *ions.* The electrons and ions—mostly hydrogen ions—stream away from the sun. These particles make up the solar wind.

The particles of the solar wind travel very fast. Their speed ranges from 155 to 625 miles (250 to 1,000 kilometers) per second.

The vast bubble around the solar system made by the solar wind is called the *heliosphere.* The end of the heliosphere is at least 10 billion miles (16 billion kilometers) away from the sun. Near the end of the heliosphere, the solar wind begins to slow and eventually stops.

In 1959, the Soviet Luna 2 spacecraft proved that the solar wind exists and made the first measurements of its properties. Several American spacecraft have also studied this wind.

The solar wind plays a major role in the creation of *auroras.* The wind squeezes Earth's *magnetosphere* (area around Earth affected by the planet's magnetic field). The particles in the wind cause the electrically charged particles already in the magnetosphere to collide with particles in Earth's *atmosphere* (blanket of air surrounding the planet). This collision releases energy in the form of light.

Other articles to read include: **Aurora; Corona; Heliosphere; Sun.**

The shimmering green ribbons of an aurora are light given off by atoms in the atmosphere that have been struck by energetic particles in the solar wind.

Southern Cross

The Southern Cross is a *constellation (KON stuh LAY shuhn)* in the Southern Hemisphere. A constellation is a grouping of stars in the night sky.

The Southern Cross gets its name from the cross made by its four brightest stars. The star farthest to the south in the Southern Cross is of the *first magnitude.* The term *magnitude (MAG nuh tood)* refers to how bright a star is. A star of the first magnitude is brighter than other stars.

The four stars of the Southern Cross are not arranged in the exact form of a cross. The upper and lower stars form the "upright" of the cross. They point to the South Pole of the sky. The Southern Cross appears too far south to be seen in the United States, except in a few places.

Other articles to read include: **Constellation; Magnitude; Star.**

The Southern Cross is also known as the *Crux,* which is Latin for *cross.*

Space

Space is the area between stars, planets, and other objects in the universe. All objects in the universe move through space. Space is so vast that it can never be directly measured. Scientists have discovered that no part of space is truly empty.

For Earth, space begins at the top of the *atmosphere* (blanket of air surrounding the planet). There is no clear boundary between the atmosphere and outer space. But most scientists agree that space begins somewhere beyond 60 miles (95 kilometers) above Earth.

Outer space just above the atmosphere is not completely empty. It contains some particles of air, as well as space dust and occasional chunks of metallic or stony matter called *meteoroids.* Different kinds of *radiation* (high-speed particles and energy) flow freely. Thousands of spacecraft known as *artificial satellites* have been launched into this region of space.

Space between the planets is called *interplanetary space.* Huge distances usually separate objects moving through interplanetary space. For example, Earth *revolves* (travels) around

Continued on the next page

Space *Continued from the previous page*

the sun at a distance of about 93 million miles (150 million kilometers). Neptune, the most distant planet from the sun, is about 30 times as far from the sun as Earth is.

Space between the stars is called *interstellar space*. Distances in this region are so great that astronomers do not describe them in miles or kilometers. Instead, distances there are measured in units called *light-years*. A light-year equals 5.88 trillion miles (9.46 trillion kilometers). This is the distance light travels in one year in a vacuum at the speed of 186,282 miles (299,792 kilometers) per second.

For example, the nearest star to the sun is Proxima Centauri. It is 4.2 light-years away. This means that if you could travel at the speed of light, it would take you 4.2 years to get to Proxima Centauri. A jetliner traveling at a speed of 500 miles (800 kilometers) per hour would need to fly for 1.34 million years in order to travel one light-year. Various gases, thin clouds of extremely cold dust, and a few escaped comets float between the stars. Interstellar space also contains many objects not yet discovered.

Space is dark for a number of reasons. Stars, which give off most of the direct light in the universe, are far, far away from us. Only a little of their light reaches us. In addition, objects nearer to us, such as the planets and moons, give off reflected light. Reflected light is much dimmer than direct light.

Space has no temperature, though objects moving through it do. The temperature of the object depends on the material it is made of and whether it is in direct sunlight.

Other articles to read include: **Galaxy; Interstellar medium; Light-year; Planet; Proxima Centauri; Space exploration; Space-time; Star; Universe.**

Space debris

Space debris *(duh BREE)* consists of objects made by people that remain in orbit around Earth but serve no purpose. Space debris is sometimes called *space junk*. It ranges from used rocket *stages* (sections) to tiny paint chips that have come off spacecraft.

Continued on the next page

Many space missions leave in orbit such objects as bolts, tools, and protective covers for scientific instruments. Space debris does not include working satellites. It also does not include natural chunks of matter called *meteoroids*.

Scientists have identified thousands of pieces of space debris. Space agencies track some 10,000 objects larger than about 4 inches (10 centimeters) using radar and telescopes. Space experts worry about space debris because collisions with it can damage spacecraft or injure astronauts. A collision with a large piece of debris could destroy a satellite. But most collisions involve small pieces of debris that cause minor damage. The first incident of a working satellite being destroyed by space debris occurred in early 2009. A nonworking Russian satellite collided with an American satellite. The collision destroyed both craft.

Some space debris at high altitudes may remain in orbit indefinitely. Friction with Earth's upper atmosphere may cause debris orbiting at lower altitudes to slow down and fall closer to Earth. Eventually, the debris reenters Earth's atmosphere. There it either burns up due to friction or crashes into the ground or the oceans. Only a few pieces of reentering space debris have ever been found on Earth. Reentering space debris has caused no reported injuries to people or damage to property. Space agencies are exploring ideas to reduce the amount of space debris in orbit.

Other articles to read include: **Satellite, Artificial; Space exploration.**

White dots in a computer-generated image of Earth mark the locations of objects in orbit. About 95 percent of the objects shown are debris. (The dots appear larger than the objects they represent.)

Space exploration

Space exploration is traveling into space to gather information about Earth and the universe beyond Earth. Space exploration is a response to human curiosity. It helps us see Earth in its true relation with the rest of the universe. It has greatly improved our understanding of the history of Earth and other celestial objects in space. It might even help us answer one of the most important questions of all time: Are we alone in the universe?

Human beings have piloted vehicles to the moon and have lived in space stations for long periods. Unpiloted vehicles called *space probes* have visited and studied the

Continued on the next page

United States astronaut Edward
H. White II conducts the first
spacewalk, on June 3, 1965.
A 26-foot (8-meter) cord links
White to his Gemini 4 spacecraft.

Space exploration *Continued from previous page*

sun, the moon, other planets and moons, comets, and asteroids. They have collected information about distant stars
and galaxies. They have even brought samples of celestial
objects back to Earth.

Traveling in space is highly dangerous for humans. Space
has no air, and temperatures reach extremes of heat and cold.
The sun gives off hazardous levels of *radiation* (high-speed
particles and energy). Various types of matter also create
dangers in space. For example, particles of dust threaten
vehicles with destructive high-speed impacts. *Debris* (trash)
from previous space missions can also damage spacecraft.

Spacecraft that carry astronauts must provide everything
people need to survive. They must provide water to drink and
air to breathe. They must also have heating and cooling
controls to keep the temperature comfortable. Special toilets onboard suck body wastes into collection containers. Meals on spacecraft must be easy to make and store. Trash is kept in unused places
on the space vehicle. It is thrown overboard or brought
back to Earth.

Once in space, the crew members carry out the
goals of their mission. They gather information about
Earth, the stars, and the sun. They experiment with the
effects of weightlessness on various materials, plants,
animals, and themselves. They also repair, replace, or
build equipment. Astronauts use radio, television, computers, and other equipment to communicate with
mission control on Earth.

An astronaut wears a special space suit to work
outside the spacecraft. A space suit can keep an astronaut alive for six to eight hours. The suit has many
layers of material. It keeps the astronaut from getting
too hot or cold and protects against impacts.
Equipment in a backpack supplies the astronaut with
air to breathe. A helmet blocks out strong, harmful rays
from the sun. Thin, flexible gloves allow the astronaut
to feel small objects and handle tools. The astronaut
communicates with the crew and mission control
through a radio.

Astronaut Buzz Aldrin walks across the
Sea of Tranquility during the Apollo 11
mission in 1969, the first space misssion
to put people on the lunar surface.
Aldrin landed on the moon with Neil
Armstrong, who took this photograph.

Continued on the next page

All of the space exploration beyond the moon has been carried out by space probes. These human-made vehicles have been exploring other planets since the 1960's. The earliest probes carried simple instruments, such as cameras. Modern probes carry instruments that can carry out more complex tasks. These tasks include revealing the internal structures, sensing the *magnetic fields,* and sampling the atmospheres of other bodies in the solar system. A magnetic field is a region affected by a magnet or electric current.

Space probes *orbit* (travel around) a body or fly past on a longer journey. However, there are some that make it all the way to the planet or moon's surface. Landers set down on the surface and send back information to Earth about the environment around them. Other machines called *rovers* can move around the surface. This enables them to observe many different areas and structures. Landers and rovers have been sent to Earth's moon, Mars, Venus, Saturn's moon Titan, and to asteroids. Sometime in or after 2013, two space probes named Voyager 1 and 2 will become the first spacecraft to venture into *interstellar space,* the space between stars.

The space shuttle Endeavour and the International Space Station (ISS) hang above Earth in the first photograph of a shuttle docked to the orbiting laboratory taken from a Russian Soyuz spacecraft. The photo was taken by an Italian astronaut on May 23, 2011, as he and two crewmates were leaving the ISS aboard a Soyuz vehicle.

The space age began on Oct. 4, 1957. On that day, the Soviet Union (now Russia) launched Sputnik 1, the first artificial satellite to orbit Earth. The United States and other Western countries reacted to the launch of Sputnik with surprise, fear, and respect. United States leaders vowed to do whatever was needed to catch up. The United States launched its first satellite, Explorer 1, on Jan. 31, 1958. In that year, the United States government also created the National Aeronautics and Space Administration (NASA) to plan and carry out American space missions.

In the early years of the space age, success in space became a measure of a country's leadership in science, engineering, and national defense. The United States and the Soviet Union were engaged in an intense rivalry called the Cold War. As a result, the two nations competed with each other in developing space programs. In the 1960's and 1970's, this "space race" drove both nations to tremendous exploratory efforts. The space race had faded by the end of the 1970's.

Yuri A. Gagarin *(gah GAHR ihn),* a Soviet *cosmonaut* (astronaut), was the first human being to travel in space. He made his space flight on April 12, 1961. The first American in space was astronaut Alan B. Shepard, Jr. On May 5, 1961, he flew a 15-minute *suborbital* mission—that is, a mission that did not reach the speed and altitude

Continued on the next page

Space exploration

Continued from the previous page

SpaceShipOne, the first privately funded, piloted craft to reach space, soars skyward with White Knight, an airplane designed to launch the rocket, on June 21, 2004. After launch, SpaceShipOne soared to an altitude of over 62 miles (100 kilometers).

required to orbit Earth. On Feb. 20, 1962, John H. Glenn, Jr., became the first American to orbit Earth.

In 1958, both the United States and the Soviet Union began to launch probes toward the moon. The first probe to come close to the moon was Luna 1, launched by the Soviet Union on Jan. 2, 1959. The first human voyage to the moon was in December 1968, when the United States launched the Apollo 8 spacecraft. It orbited the moon 10 times and returned safely to Earth. In July 1969, U.S. astronauts Neil A. Armstrong and Buzz Aldrin became the first people to set foot on the moon.

The Soviet Union launched the first space station, Salyut (Salute) 1, on April 19, 1971. The country launched another space station called Mir (Peace) in 1986. The first U.S. space station was Skylab, launched into orbit by a Saturn V booster on May 14, 1973. In 1998, the United States and Russia joined with some 13 other countries to launch the first sections of the International Space Station (ISS). The first full-time crew—one American astronaut and two Russian cosmonauts—occupied the station in 2000.

In the 1990's, private companies developed an interest in space. On June 21, 2004, Scaled Composites of Mojave, California, became the first private company to launch a person into space. The company's rocket, called SpaceShipOne, carried American test pilot Michael Melvill more than 62 miles (100 kilometers) above Earth on a brief test flight.

Several companies have partnered with NASA to develop spacecraft. In May 2012, an unpiloted SpaceX cargo capsule became the first privately operated spacecraft to deliver supplies to the International Space Station. It was built by Hawthorne, California-based Space Exploration Technologies Corp.

On April 17, 2013, Orbital Sciences Corporation of Dulles, Virginia, launched its first rocket, called Antares, on a test flight. Like SpaceX, Orbital Sciences has an agreement with NASA to deliver cargo to the ISS. Private companies are also developing spacecraft for longer flights and human-piloted flights.

Other articles to read include: **Aerospace medicine; Astronaut; Canadian Space Agency; Challenger disaster; China National Space Administration; Columbia disaster; European Space Agency; Extraterrestrial intelligence; Indian Space Research Organization; Jet Propulsion Laboratory; Johnson Space Center; Kennedy Space Center; Moon; National Aeronautics and Space Administration; National Air and Space Museum; Observatory; Rocket; Satellite, Artificial; Space; SpaceX; Telescope;** *and those on individual astronauts, astronomers, and spacecraft.*

Space-time

Space-time is a term meant to show how space and time are related. The term *space-time* is a name for a special set of rules established by the German-born American physicist Albert Einstein. In the complex mathematics of Einstein's theories, time and space are not absolutely separate. Instead, space-time is a combination of the dimension of time and the three dimensions of space—length, width, and height. Thus, space-time is four-dimensional.

Einstein first mentioned space-time when describing his ideas called the *theory of special relativity.* The theory describes how space and time are more deeply related than scientists had thought.

One simple way to look at the relation of space and time is to think about a meeting between two people. In order for the two to meet, there must be a location. A location consists of the three dimensions of space. But if the two people do not set a time for the meeting, they probably will not be at that location at the same time. So in order for the meeting to happen, the two must agree on both a time and a place.

Other articles to read include: **Cosmology; Fourth dimension; Space; Universe.**

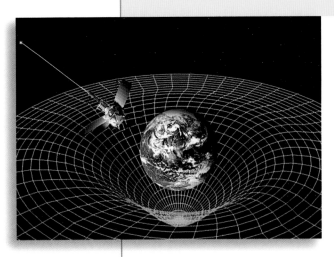

The Gravity B space probe orbits Earth in an illustration showing how our planet distorts space-time with its *mass* (amount of matter). In 2007, evidence from the probe confirmed some of Einstein's ideas about space-time.

SpaceX

SpaceX is a private company that makes spacecraft and rockets. Elon Musk, the creator of the online payment service PayPal, founded the company in 2002. The headquarters of SpaceX are in Hawthorne, California. The company flies missions for NASA, the United States space agency, as well as for private companies and individuals. It is the first private company to fly a supply mission to the International Space Station (ISS).

The first rocket the company attempted to launch was named the Falcon 1. After three failures, the company succeeded in getting

Continued on the next page

The robotic arm of the International Space Station (ISS) reaches for the SpaceX Dragon spacecraft on May 25, 2012. Dragon became the first commerical spacecraft to berth at the ISS.

SpaceX *Continued from the previous page*

the rocket into orbit around Earth. A second rocket developed for flight was the Falcon 9. The Falcon 9 rocket can carry a reuseable space capsule called the Dragon. The Dragon capsule is capable of carrying supplies and cargo into orbit.

SpaceX is working to develop a version of the Dragon capsule that can carry humans into space. The company is also developing larger versions of its rockets to carry a larger payload and to fly farther.

Other articles to read include: **International Space Station; Space exploration.**

Lyman Spitzer, Jr.

Spitzer, Lyman, Jr.

Lyman Spitzer, Jr. (1914-1997), was an American scientist. He made the first convincing suggestion for sending a telescope into space. Spitzer's research focused on *plasmas,* forms of matter made up of atomic particles with electrical charges. He also studied the *interstellar medium,* the gas and dust in the space between the stars.

In 1946, Spitzer argued that having a telescope in space would allow astronomers to avoid problems caused by Earth's *atmosphere.* This blanket of gases around the planet interferes with the light reaching the planet's surface. Spitzer's ideas eventually led to the launch of the Hubble Space Telescope in 1990. The Spitzer Space Telescope, launched by NASA in 2003, was named in his honor.

Spitzer also led efforts to create hot plasmas in laboratories on Earth. He became the founding director of the Princeton Plasma Physics Laboratory in 1951.

Spitzer was born in Toledo, Ohio. In 1938, he earned a Ph.D. degree from Princeton University. He joined the faculty of Yale University in 1939. In 1947, Spitzer returned to Princeton. He worked there until his death in 1997.

Other articles to read include: **Interstellar medium; Hubble Space Telescope; Space exploration; Spitzer Space Telescope; Telescope.**

Spitzer Space Telescope

The Spitzer Space Telescope is a spacecraft that gathers *infrared rays* (heat rays) from distant objects. Some objects give off heat but little visible light. Spitzer can view these objects more clearly than can many other telescopes.

Spitzer follows Earth in its *orbit* (path) around the sun. Because the telescope is in space, it can study objects that ground-based telescopes cannot see. Scientists use Spitzer to study the formation of stars and planets, asteroids and other objects near Earth. and faraway galaxies.

The telescope was launched by NASA, the United States space agency. They named it after the American astronomer Lyman Spitzer, Jr. He was the first to suggest launching large telescopes into space.

Other articles to read include: **Spitzer, Lyman, Jr.; Satellite, Artificial; Telescope.**

The Triangulum Galaxy glitters with color and light in a false-color image made by the Spitzer Space Telescope.

Sputnik

Sputnik *(SPUHT nihk)* is the name of several *artificial satellites* launched by the Soviet Union (now Russia). An artificial satellite is a craft made to *orbit* (circle) Earth or another body in space. Sputnik 1 was the first artificial satellite ever launched. Sputniks did not carry a human crew. The name *Sputnik* means *traveling companion* in Russian.

Sputnik 1 was launched on Oct. 4, 1957. It circled Earth once every 96 minutes at a speed of 18,000 miles (29,000 kilometers) per hour. It fell to Earth on Jan. 4, 1958.

Sputnik 2 was launched Nov. 3, 1957. It carried the first space traveler, a dog named Laika.

The Soviet Union launched several other Sputniks. The last one launched in March 1961.

Continued on the next page

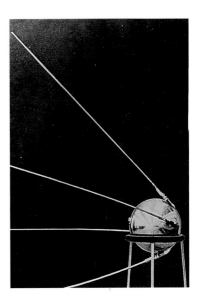

Sputnik 1, the first artificial satellite, was launched by the Soviet Union (now Russia) in 1957. It transmitted radio signals that were received on Earth.

Sputnik   *Continued from the previous page*

The launch of Sputnik 1 stunned the world. Many people in other countries did not believe that the Soviets had the advanced technology needed for space exploration. In the United States, leaders vowed to do whatever was needed to catch up. Thus the *space race* between the United States and the Soviet Union began. The space race drove both nations to tremendous exploratory efforts. Success in space became a measure of a country's leadership in science, engineering, and national defense.

Other articles to read include: **Satellite, Artificial; Space exploration.**

The planet Jupiter and the red dwarf Wolf 359 are much smaller than the sun and Sirius, the brightest star in Earth's night sky.

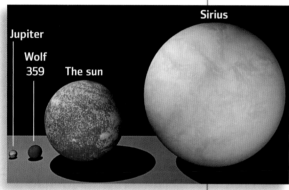

But Sirius is quite small compared with stars classified as giants—including Pollux— and as supergiants—including Arcturus and Aldebaran.

Star

Stars are huge balls of very hot matter in space. They produce a tremendous amount of light and other forms of energy. The sun is the star at the center of the *solar system.* Other stars look like twinkling points of light. The sun looks like a ball because it is much closer to Earth than any other star.

Astronomers (scientists who study the universe) think that from about 50 to 75 percent of all stars are members of a *binary system.* These closely spaced stars *orbit* (travel around) each other. The sun is not a member of a binary system.

Almost all stars are in groups called *galaxies.* The sun belongs to the Milky Way Galaxy. A galaxy consists of hundreds of thousands to trillions of stars. There are billions, possibly even trillions, of galaxies. Thus, billions of trillions of stars may exist.

Bright stars shine because of a process called *fusion.* During this process, energy is created when one type of matter is changed into another. With most stars, including the sun, energy is created when two atoms of hydrogen *fuse* (melt together) into one atom of helium. Most of the energy comes from the sun as heat, *visible light* (light we can see), and a stream of particles called the *solar wind.*

A star has five main characteristics: brightness, color, surface

Continued on the next page

temperature, size, and mass. Astronomers describe a star's brightness in terms of *magnitude* or *luminosity.* The brightest stars are ranked as *first magnitude stars.* Luminosity is the rate at which a star gives off energy.

Stars shine in different colors, including red, orange, and blue. The color of the star depends on its temperature. The hottest stars are blue, and cooler stars are red.

Stars come in many sizes. Astronomers classify the sun as a *dwarf star* because other kinds of stars are much bigger. Some stars, known as *supergiants,* are hundreds of times as wide as the sun. *Neutron stars,* the smallest stars, are only about 12 miles (20 kilometers) across.

A star's *mass* is the amount of matter it has. Astronomers use the mass of the sun to measure all other stars.

The characteristics of stars are related to one another in complex ways. Color depends on surface temperature. Brightness depends on surface temperature and size. A star's mass affects the rate at which a star produces energy. A star's luminosity affects surface temperature.

Stars change as they grow older. They eventually stop shining and grow cool and dim. Stars that have used up their fuel stop shining altogether. The brighter the star, the faster it uses up its fuel and the sooner it dies.

The end of a star's life depends on the size of the star. Smaller stars blow up like a balloon and become many times larger. The star then shrinks and becomes a much smaller, heavier star. Larger stars go through the same steps until the end. But after a large star swells up like a balloon, it does not shrink. Instead, it explodes in a spectacular event called a *supernova.* During the explosion, the star can outshine the light of billions of other stars combined.

After a supernova, a small star turns into a tiny, but incredibly heavy star called a *neutron star.* A bigger star actually shrinks even more. These stars become a *black hole* (a tiny object with extremely strong gravity). The biggest stars explode so violently that nothing is left after the explosion.

Other articles to read include: **Alpha Centauri; Betelgeuse; Binary star; Blue giant; Brown dwarf; Canopus; Constellation; Deneb; Evening star; Galaxy; Neutron star; North Star; Nova; Proxima Centauri; Red dwarf; Red giant; Sirius; Supernova; White dwarf.**

Thousands of newborn and young stars blaze through clouds of dust and gas in the giant nebula NGC 3603, one of the Milky Way's largest "stellar nurseries."

Thin mountain peaks, broad *mesas* (flat-topped hills), and deep areas appear in photographs of the nucleus of Comet Wild 2, taken by the Stardust space probe in 2004. The features suggest that the surface of the nucleus is relatively strong.

Stardust

Stardust was a United States space probe. It was designed to collect material from a comet and return it to Earth. NASA, the United States space agency, launched Stardust on February 7, 1999.

On January 2, 2004, Stardust flew within 147 miles (236 kilometers) of the *nucleus* (solid core) of Comet Wild *(vihlt)* 2. The craft captured thousands of particles from the comet's *coma* (cloud of dust and gas surrounding the nucleus). Stardust then headed back to Earth to release a capsule containing the collected samples. The capsule parachuted to the ground in Utah on January 15, 2006.

In 2011, Stardust became the first probe to revisit a comet. The NASA craft Deep Impact had visited this comet, called Tempel 1, in 2005. The later Stardust mission, called NeXT, gave scientists their first look at how a comet changes after it passes near the sun.

Other articles to read include: **Comet; Space exploration.**

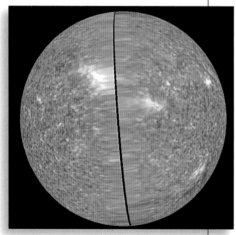

The front and back of the sun appear together in the first three-dimensional image of that star, taken in February 2011 by the two STEREO spacecrafts.

STEREO

STEREO is a pair of *observatories* in space. An observatory is an object or place used to study planets, stars, galaxies, and other objects in space. The two STEREO craft study how the surface of the sun moves and changes. They can also study material given off by the sun. STEREO stands for *S*olar *TE*rrestrial *RE*lations *O*bservatory. NASA, the United States space agency, launched the two spacecraft aboard the same rocket on October 25, 2006.

Each STEREO craft watches the sun from a different angle. Working together, they can study much more of the sun's surface than one craft could. Scientists can also combine images from both craft to create a three-dimensional picture or video of the sun. The STEREO craft roughly follow Earth's *orbit* (path) around the sun.

Other articles to read include: **Observatory; Space exploration; Sun.**

String theory

String theory is an idea about the nature of *matter* and the forces that affect matter. Matter is made of *elementary particles* (particles smaller than an atom). Common theories of physics, together called the Standard Model, treat elementary particles as points. But in string theory, these particles are tiny strings that can *vibrate* (shake) in different ways. Different patterns of shaking would look to us like different particles.

Some scientists hope that string theory might explain all four of the known basic forces of nature. These forces are: (1) the electromagnetic force, (2) the strong nuclear force, (3) the weak nuclear force, and (4) gravitation. Electromagnetism is the force that holds *electrons* (negatively charged particles) to the *nucleus* (core) of atoms. The weak nuclear force is responsible for the breakdown of many kinds of atomic *nuclei* (plural of nucleus). This breakdown is called *radioactivity.* The strong nuclear force binds the nucleus together. Gravitation is the force that attracts objects to one another.

Scientists currently explain the first three forces using an idea called *quantum theories.* They describe gravitation using a theory called *general relativity,* which is not a quantum theory. Since the mid-1980's, physicists have developed many forms of string theory, including a group of superstring theories. However, the theory is still incomplete and providing evidence for it has proved difficult.

Other articles to read include: **Electromagnetic waves; Gravitation.**

Sun

The sun is the star at the center of the solar system. All the objects in the solar system, including Earth, the other seven planets and all their moons, dwarf planets, and many smaller objects *orbit* (travel around) the sun. Life as we know it would not exist without this fiery ball in the sky. Nearly every living thing on Earth, including plants, animals, and people, needs the energy given off by the sun to survive.

Despite its importance to us, the sun is only one of hundreds of billions of stars in just our galaxy, the Milky Way. If we could see the sun from a planet outside the solar system, it would appear as one of many stars in the sky.

Continued on the next page

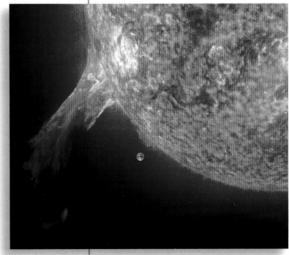

The sun is so huge that about 1 million Earths could fit inside it. (This illustration does not show the true distance of Earth from the sun.)

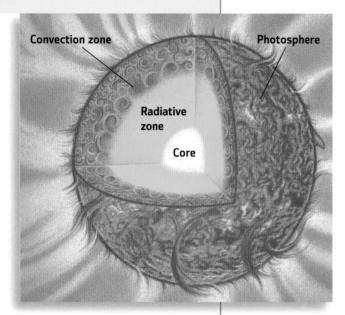

Convection zone

Photosphere

Radiative zone

Core

The sun consists of several layers called *zones*. Energy flows from the *core* (center) through the *radiative zone* and *convection zone*. The thin *photosphere*, which is the lowest part of the solar atmosphere, produces the light we see. Above the photosphere are two other atmospheric zones—the chromosphere and the corona.

Sun   *Continued from the previous page*

It is hard to understand how huge the sun is. The sun contains 99.8 percent of all the *mass* (amount of matter) in the entire solar system. In other words, the sun has more than about 500 times more mass than all the planets, moons, *asteroids* (rocky objects), and other objects in the solar system put together. Because of the sun's tremendous mass, its *gravitational pull* (force of attraction) is very powerful. This pull keeps objects far beyond even the most distant planet, Neptune, in orbit around the sun. The sun's *radius* (distance from its center to the surface) is about 420,000 miles (696,500 kilometers). That is more than 100 times as great as Earth's radius. Moreover, about 1 million Earths could fit inside the sun. But compared with other known stars in the universe, the sun is of an average size.

Most of the energy *emitted* (given off) by the sun is visible light and a related form of radiation known as *infrared rays,* which we feel as heat. Visible light and infrared rays are two forms of *electromagnetic radiation*. The radiation can be thought of as waves of energy or as "packets" of energy called *photons*.

The energy of the sun comes from *nuclear fusion reactions* that occur deep inside the *core* (center). In a fusion reaction, the *nuclei* (centers) of two atoms *fuse* (join together) to create a new nucleus. Fusion produces energy by converting nuclear matter into energy.

The sun is made up almost completely of atoms of hydrogen and helium *plasma*. Plasma is a form of matter electrically charged matter that behaves much like a gas. The plasma forms because the sun's high heat pulls the atoms apart. Because the plasma has an electrical charge, it is sensitive to magnetism. The sun's charged particles flow continually outward in all directions as the *solar wind*.

The part of the sun that we can see is about 10,000 °F (5,500 °C). The inside of the sun is millions of degrees hotter. Also, the atmosphere above the surface, called the *corona,* is many times hotter than the surface.

Continued on the next page

The sun, like Earth, is a magnet and so has a *magnetic field*. This is a region in which a magnetic force can be detected. The sun's magnetic field becomes highly concentrated in small regions. The strength of the field in these regions may be up to 3,000 times as great as the field's typical strength. These regions shape solar matter to create a variety of features on the sun's surface and in its atmosphere. These features range from relatively cool, dark structures known as *sunspots* to spectacular eruptions of matter and energy called *flares* and *coronal mass ejections.*

Scientists believe that the sun was born about 4.6 billion years ago from a huge cloud of gases and dust. Space has many clouds like this. New stars are made when gravity pulls material in these clouds closer together. As the material crowds together, the mass becomes hotter. When the center of the mass becomes hot enough, the collection of gases and dust begins nuclear fusion and shines as a star.

The sun has enough fuel to remain much as it is for another 5 billion years. Then it will grow to become a type of star called a *red giant.* Its outer layers will probably expand past the current orbit of Mercury. Later in the sun's life, it will throw off its outer layers. The remaining core will collapse to become an object called a *white dwarf* and will slowly fade. Eventually, the sun will become a faint, cool object sometimes called a *black dwarf.*

Scientists study the sun by producing images of it. These images are made by cameras mounted on ground-based or space-based telescopes. Scientists also analyze radiation from the sun. This information helps them understand the motions, chemical makeup, and temperature of the sun. Powerful computers are another important tool for scientists studying the sun. The computers allow scientists to *simulate* (represent) how the sun produces radiation. This kind of simulation is similar to the way in which a video game represents a real situation.

Other articles to read include: **Corona; Coronal mass ejection; Eclipse; Gravitation; Heliosphere; Hinode; Magnetic storm; Solar Dynamics Observatory; Solar wind; Star; Sunspot; Transit; White dwarf.**

Electrically charged particles flowing outward from the sun in all directions make up the solar wind. The area of magnetism around Earth, called the *magnetosphere,* prevents most of these particles from reaching Earth.

Magnetosphere

Earth

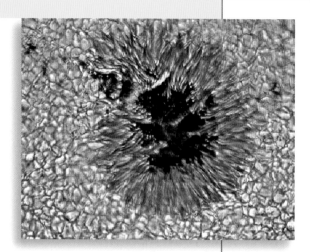

A large sunspot may have a *diameter* (width) of about 20,000 miles (32,000 kilometers) and last for months. Small sunspots may be several hundred miles wide and last only for hours.

Sunspot

A sunspot is a dark area on the surface of the sun. Sunspots appear dark because they are cooler than the rest of the sun's surface that you can see. Sunspots may have a temperature of only about 7,000 °F (4,000 °C), compared with 11,000 °F (6,000 °C) for their surroundings.

A large spot has a dark central region called the *umbra (UHM bruh)* and a lighter area around it called the *penumbra (pih NUHM bruh)*. A small sunspot has no penumbra. The number and location of sunspots varies in a pattern called the *sunspot cycle*. It repeats about every 11 years.

Sunspots have strong *magnetic fields*. A magnetic field is the area of magnetism around a magnet. The fields have a strength up to 3,000 times as great as the average magnetic field of either the sun or Earth. The formation of sunspots is believed to be related to the strong magnetic fields.

Other articles to read include: **Magnetic storm; Sun.**

A supernova can leave behind a very small heavy star called a neutron star. Larger stars may leave behind a black hole. Almost all supernova leave behind a cloud of dust and gas called a nebula such as the Crab Nebula above.

Supernova

A supernova *(SOO puhr NOH vuh)* is an exploding star that can become billions of times as bright as the sun before fading from view. The explosion throws a large cloud of dust and gas into space.

Astronomers recognize two basic types of *supernovae (SOO puhr NOH vee)*. The first type probably occurs in certain pairs of stars that orbit closely around each other. One of the stars pulls matter from the other until the first becomes too large and explodes. The second type of supernovae results from the death of stars much larger than the sun. When such a star begins to burn out, it releases energy. This energy causes the star to burst into a supernova.

Other articles to read include: **Binary star; Neutron star; Nova; Star.**

Tt

Taurus

Taurus is a *constellation* (grouping of stars) also known as the Bull. A constellation is a grouping of stars in the night sky. Taurus can be seen from much of the Northern Hemisphere. It is best viewed from December through February.

Taurus can be drawn in several ways. Often, it includes a Y-shaped group of stars. These stars represent the bull's head and long horns. Other stars may stand for the body.

Several interesting objects appear in Taurus. Just above the bull's back is the Pleiades, a well-known *star cluster* (group held together by gravitation). Taurus also contains a well-known *nebula* (cloud of dust and gas) called the Crab Nebula. The Crab Nebula is the remains of an exploding star. The explosion was seen on Earth in A.D. 1054.

Taurus was among the 48 constellations defined by the ancient Greek mathematician Ptolemy. Today, it is one of 88 constellations recognized by the International Astronomical Union (IAU), the leading authority in the naming of heavenly objects.

Other articles to read include: **Astrology; Constellation; Nebula; Ptolemy; Star; Star cluster; Zodiac.**

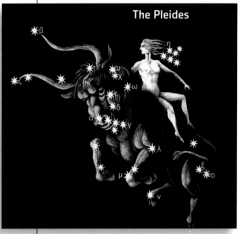

Taurus, the Bull, contains probably the best-known star *cluster* (group), the Pleiades (*PLEE uh deez*).

Telescope

The telescope is a device for seeing faraway things. Objects seen through a telescope appear closer than they really are. Scientists called *astronomers* use large telescopes to study the planets, stars, and other things in space. Without telescopes, people would know little about such things.

The most common kind of telescope is an *optical telescope*. Such a telescope is designed to collect visible light, just as human eyes do. Other kinds of telescopes can detect waves of light that are invisible to human eyes, such as radio waves, microwaves, ultraviolet rays, *infrared* (heat) rays, X rays, and gamma rays. Astronomers use these telescopes to study objects in space that give off these different types of light.

Continued on the next page

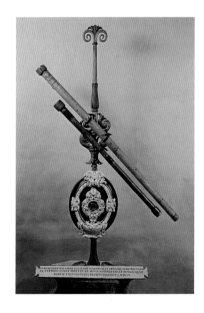

Two telescopes made by the Italian astronomer Galileo in the early 1600's were more powerful than any built previously.

The Horsehead Nebula appears in far greater detail in an image by made an optical telescope in 2008 (above, right) than it does in the first photograph ever taken of the massive cloud of dust and gas (above, left), in 1888.

Telescope *Continued from the previous page*

Telescopes have different sizes and shapes. Some telescopes are small enough to hold in one hand. Huge bowl-shaped radio telescopes may measure 1,000 feet (300 meters) across.

Some telescopes are carried by spacecraft. These space-based telescopes get a sharper image than many telescopes on the ground because they are not affected by the air that surrounds Earth. Although air seems clear, it can make stars and other sky objects look blurry. Some telescopes on the ground have special equipment to overcome the effects of the atmosphere.

People can see objects because light given off or reflected by them enters the eyes. Optical telescopes work by bending this light. One kind of optical telescope has a curved piece of glass called a *lens* at its large end. This lens is the *objective lens*. It bends the light from the object in a way that forms an image of the object inside the telescope. The light from this image then goes through another lens, called the *eyepiece,* at the small end of the telescope. The eyepiece bends the light again, making the object look big. The bending of light by a lens is called *refraction*. Telescopes with such lenses are called *refracting telescopes*.

Another kind of optical telescope uses a mirror instead of a lens to focus the image. The mirror is bowl-shaped. Light from an object bounces off the mirror, forming an image inside the telescope. Light from the image then goes through an eyepiece, making the object look big. A mirror is said to reflect light. Such telescopes are thus called *reflecting telescopes*. A reflecting telescope can generally produce a better image than a refracting telescope. All of the largest modern telescopes are reflecting telescopes.

Objects in space often look dim, even through a telescope. To make them look bright, astronomers use a telescope with a very large lens or mirror. A larger lens gathers more light into the telescope. So objects seen through the telescope look much brighter.

Continued on the next page

The Dutch scientist Hans Lippershey is often given credit for making the first telescope, in 1608. It was made of two glass lenses in a narrow tube. Within a year, the Italian astronomer Galileo built a telescope like Lippershey's. Galileo was the first person to use a telescope in the practical service of astronomy. From then on, the telescope became as astronomer's most important tool.

At first, telescopes were used mainly to observe the planets in the solar system. As telescopes grew bigger and more powerful, astronomers turned their attention to our galaxy, the Milky Way. By the mid-1900's, astronomers were using telescopes to "see" light that is invisible to human eyes. By detecting these kinds of light, these telescopes revealed quasars, black holes, and many other objects no one knew about previously. They also allowed astronomers to probe the deepest reaches of space to calculate how large and how old the universe is.

Other articles to read include: **Astronomy; Galileo** (scientist); **Observatory; Satellite, Artificial;** *and those on individual telescopes.*

Titan

Titan is the largest moon of Saturn. It is about 3,200 miles (5,150 kilometers) wide. It is larger than the planet. It is the second-largest moon in the solar system, after behind only Jupiter's moon Ganymede.

The temperature of Titan's surface is about −290 °F (−179 °C). The surface has seas or lakes of liquid methane, ethane, and other chemicals. Titan may also have a layer of liquid water deep beneath its surface. The surface of the moon shows evidence of *cryovolcanoes,* spots where water and ice have erupted onto the moon's surface.

The Cassini spacecraft began orbiting Saturn in 2004. While in space, it released a probe called *Huygens (HY guhnz).* In early 2005, Huygens dropped through Titan's atmosphere and landed on the surface. It took photographs of a frozen landscape with a large body of liquid.

Other articles to read include: **Cassini; Enceladus; Iapetus; Mimas; Rhea; Satellite; Saturn.**

Titan has a thick atmosphere that forms a haze over the surface. The haze is made up of mainly nitrogen and methane.

Clyde Tombaugh

Tombaugh, Clyde

Tombaugh, Clyde William (1906–1997), was an American astronomer. He discovered Pluto, a *dwarf planet* that orbits far from the sun. He spotted Pluto while examining some photographic plates at the Lowell Observatory in Massachusetts. The American astronomer Percival Lowell had predicted the general location of Pluto 15 years earlier. Tombaugh later became involved in *ballistics,* the study of fast-moving objects, at White Sands (New Mexico) Missile Range in 1946.

Tombaugh was born in Streator, Illinois.

Other articles to read include: **Astronomy; Lowell, Percival; Pluto.**

Transit

A transit takes place when an object in the sky moves in front of another object that looks larger. For example, the planets Mercury and Venus sometimes pass in front of the sun, as seen from Earth. During a transit, the planet looks like a dark dot moving across the sun's disk. People should never look at the sun without wearing eye protection.

Astronomers use transits to find planets around distant stars.

Venus appears as a small black dot as it transits the face of the sun.

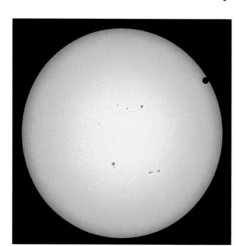

Such planets are too far away to be seen. But when they pass in front of their star, they cause the star's light to dim slightly. Astronomers can detect this dimming.

Other articles to read include: **Eclipse; Mercury; Venus; Sun.**

Triton

Triton is the largest moon of Neptune. It measures about 1,680 miles (2,700 kilometers) across. It is a little smaller than Earth's moon. Triton circles Neptune in the opposite direction of the planet's *rotation* (spin). Triton and Saturn's moon Titan are the only two satellites in the solar system known to have an *atmosphere* (blanket of gases) that is dense enough to have weather. Triton's thin atmosphere contains nitrogen and tiny amounts of methane, carbon monoxide, and carbon dioxide.

Triton was discovered in 1846, just after the discovery of Neptune. In 1984, *astronomers* (scientists who study the universe) discovered nitrogen ice on Triton. In 1989, the space probe Voyager 2 flew by Triton. It sent back images of an icy surface with only a few craters.

Other articles to read include: **Neptune; Satellite; Voyager.**

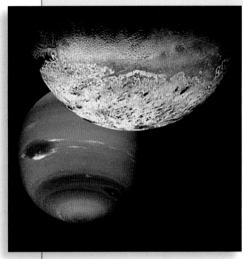

Triton seems to dwarf the much-larger Neptune in an image produced by the Hubble Space Telescope.

Tyson, Neil deGrasse

Neil deGrasse Tyson is an American astronomer. He has been the director of the Hayden Planetarium in New York City since 1996. The planetarium is in the American Museum of Natural History. Tyson also brings science to the public through books, television programs, radio shows, and websites.

Tyson has appeared on several television shows. They include the Public Broadcasting System (PBS) science program *Nova scienceNOW.* Tyson has written several books. The most famous may be *The Pluto Files: The Rise and Fall of America's Favorite Planet* (2009). In 2011, PBS broadcast a program based on this book.

Tyson was born in New York City. He visited the Hayden Planetarium as a child. He then became interested in astronomy. Tyson attended Harvard University in Cambridge, Massachusetts, and Columbia University in New York City. Tyson has studied stars and galaxies.

Other articles to read include: **Astronomy; Planetarium.**

Neil deGrasse Tyson

Unidentified flying object (UFO)

An unidentified flying object (UFO) is a light or object in the air that no one can explain. Some people believe UFO's are spaceships from other planets.

Stories about meetings with beings from UFO's have been told in many books, newspaper articles, movies, and TV programs. Some people have even said they were kidnapped by space aliens in UFO's.

Almost all UFO's can be explained. Many things that people believe are UFO's turn out to be bright stars or planets, airplanes, missiles, satellites, birds, insect swarms, or weather balloons. Scientists say unexplained UFO's are not proof that there is life on other planets.

In 1952, the United States Air Force established Project Blue Book. This program was designed to investigate about 12,000 UFO reports to determine whether UFO's could be a threat to the safety of the United States. The project was cancelled in 1969, after scientists at the University of Colorado advised the Air Force that further study was not likely to produce useful information on this topic. In November 2011, the U.S. government officially stated that it has no knowledge that *extraterrestrial life* (life beyond Earth) exists or that beings from other planets have made contact with humans.

Other articles to read include: **Extraterrestrial intelligence; SETI Institute.**

Universe

The universe is everything that is anywhere in time and space. The universe includes all the matter that we can see with our eyes and scientific instruments. This matter includes the sun and other stars, Earth and other planets, and all other objects in space. The universe is also made up of huge amounts of matter that is invisible to our eyes and even the scientific instruments we use today.

Continued on the next page

A map of the universe taken by a space-based telescope that collects microwave radiation. The map displays differences in temperature from only 380,000 years after the *big bang,* the birth of the universe. The variations show that matter began to clump together in the early universe (orange and red patches). Over millions of years, the clumps began to grow into the galaxies we can see today.

The universe also includes visible and invisible light and other forms of energy also part of the universe. *Gravitation,* electricity, and other *fundamental* (basic) forces are also part of the universe.

The universe combines everything that exists now with everything that has existed in time and space in the past and will exist in the future. But our universe may not be all there is. It is possible that other universes have existed in the past. It is possible that other universes exist now.

Most *cosmologists* agree that an event called the *big bang* marked the beginning of our universe about 13.8 billion years ago. Cosmologists study the development and structure of the universe and the forces that shape it. For the tiniest fraction of a second after the big bang, the entire universe was several thousand times smaller than the head of a pin. A *theory* (idea based on scientific facts) called *inflation theory* explains what happened next. According to inflation theory, the universe grew to the size of a *galaxy* (large collection of stars) in fractions of a second. It then continued to *expand* (grow larger).

Astronomers have found that the universe is still expanding. Nearly all the galaxies in the universe appear to be moving away from the Milky Way, our galaxy, and from one another. Cosmologists believe that this is occuring because space itself is expanding. Furthermore, they believe that this expansion is growing faster and faster all the time. They think that an unknown, mysterious force called *dark energy* is driving this expansion.

Continued on the next page

Universe *Continued from the previous page*

No one knows the size of the universe. Scientists have created maps showing that the universe stretches over billions of *light-years* and includes billions of galaxies. A light-year is the distance light can travel in a vacuum in one year, about 5.88 trillion miles (9.46 trillion kilometers). But scientists have not been able to map the entire universe. They generally agree they will never be able to do so.

Scientists once thought that it was posible that the universe would stay the same forever. But scientific discoveries suggest this is not true. Other scientists thought that all of the matter in the universe could come back together again in a "big crunch." This would happen if the gravitational pull of all of the universe's matter was strong enough to overcome its expansion. The entire universe would eventually collapse back in on itself. Studies also strongly indicate that this will not be the fate of the universe either. Today, many scientists agree that the universe appears to be on a course to expand forever.

Other articles to read include: **Big bang; Cosmology; Dark matter; Galaxy; Hubble constant; Inflation theory; Light-year; Local Group; Milky Way.**

The Milky Way lies on the border between an area of very little matter called a *void* (dark area) and a region dense with matter called the Great Attractor, as shown in a computer-generated image of the distribution of matter within about 300 million light-years of our galaxy.

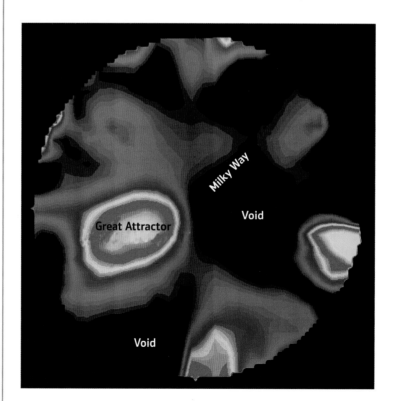

EXPERIMENT

How the universe expands

What you need:

- a felt-tip marker
- balloons
- a ruler
- a pen or pencil
- a notebook

When astronomers look at distant galaxies, they can see them moving away from us. This shows that the universe is getting bigger all the time. Most scientists believe that the universe has been expanding ever since it was created in a huge explosion, called the big bang, 13.8 billion years ago.

You may want to work with a partner on this experiment.

1. Using the marker, draw dots to represent galaxies all over a flat balloon.

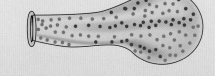

2. Blow up the balloon a little at a time. As you blow it up, the distances between the "galaxies" will grow larger.

3. Stop a few times and measure some of these distances. Record them in your notebook.

What's going on:

Every dot on the balloon moves away from every other dot. This is exactly what happens in space as the universe expands. The galaxies remain the same size, but they get farther and farther apart from each other. Astronomers think that the expansion of the universe is speeding up.

http://bit.ly/18uaFqV

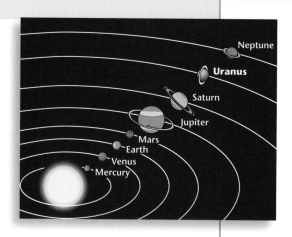

Uranus is the seventh planet from the sun.

Uranus

Uranus *(YUR uh nus* or *yu RAY nuhs)* is the seventh planet from the sun. Only Neptune is farther away from the sun. Uranus can sometimes be seen in the sky without using a telescope. It is about 1,784,860,000 miles (2,872,460,000 kilometers) away from the sun. At that distance, light from the sun takes about 2 hours and 40 minutes to reach Uranus. Light from the sun reaches Earth in about 8 minutes.

Uranus is a giant ball of gas and liquid. It is more than four times as large as Earth. Scientists believe that the *atmosphere* (blanket of gases) around Uranus contains mostly hydrogen. The gas *methane (MEHTH ayn)* in the upper atmosphere gives Uranus a smooth, blue-green appearance. The temperature of the upper atmosphere is about –355 °F (–215 °C). Below the largest part of the atmosphere are clouds made of liquid water and ammonia ice. At the center of Uranus may be a rocky core the size of Earth.

Uranus has bands and spots on its surface. The bans are made of different kinds of *smog,* a gas produced as sunlight breaks down methane gas. The spots are violently swirling masses of gas that resemble a hurricane. Winds howl around the southern half of Uranus at more than 450 miles (720 kilometers) per hour.

Uranus travels around the sun in an *elliptical* (oval-shaped) orbit. It takes about 84 Earth-years for Uranus to go all the way around the sun. The center of Uranus takes 17 hours 14 minutes to spin once on its *axis.* An axis is an imaginary line through the center of a planet around which it rotates. The center of the planet rotates more slowly than the planet's upper atmosphere.

Uranus is tilted so far on its side that its axis lies nearly level with its path around the sun. The axes of other planets point more or less up and away from their paths around the sun. Some scientists think that long ago a planet, perhaps as large as Earth, slammed into Uranus and knocked it on its side. Other scientists think that the *gravitational pull* of a moon that has since disappeared caused Uranus to tilt.

Astronomers have identified at least 27 satellites of Uranus. An astronomer is a scientist who studies the planets and the stars. But the planet probably has more. Astronomers discovered

Continued on the next page

the five largest satellites between 1787 and 1948. Photographs by the United States space probe Voyager 2 in 1985 and 1986 revealed 10 additional satellites. Astronomers later discovered more satellites using Earth-based telescopes. Nearly all of Uranus's satellites are named for characters from the works of the English playwright William Shakespeare.

Uranus is surrounded by a number of rings. Ten of them are dark and narrow. They range in width from less than 3 miles (5 kilometers) to 60 miles (100 kilometers). They are no more than 33 feet (10 meters) thick. Two faint, dusty rings lie well outside the narrow rings. Uranus also has a broad, harder-to-see ring closer to the planet. The exact makeup of the rings is unknown. But they probably consist of small chunks and dust-sized grains of ice, coated in a layer of material that contains carbon.

William Herschel, a British astronomer, discovered Uranus in 1781. Uranus was the first planet discovered since ancient times. Johann E. Bode, a German astronomer, named it Uranus after a sky god in Greek mythology. Scientists learned more about Uranus after Voyager 2 flew close to the planet.

Other articles to read include: **Herschel family; Planet; Planetary ring; Satellite; Voyager.**

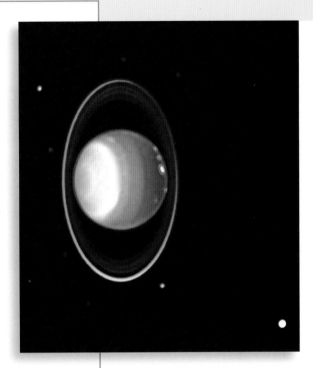

Uranus and its rings appear in a false-color image taken by the Hubble Space Telescope using *infrared* (heat) rays. The bright orange areas represent fast-moving clouds.

Uranus's narrow rings provide a beautiful frame for the planet, in a false-color image taken by the Voyager 2 space probe. In reality, the rings are dark gray.

Van Allen belts

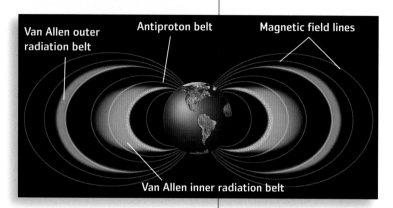

Van Allen outer radiation belt

Antiproton belt

Magnetic field lines

Van Allen inner radiation belt

The Van Allen belts are made of high-energy particles trapped in Earth's magnetic field.

The Van Allen belts are two zones that surround Earth high above its surface. They are also called *radiation belts.* The inner belt extends from about 600 to 3,000 miles (1,000 to 5,000 kilometers) above Earth. The outer belt reaches from about 9,300 to 15,500 miles (15,000 to 25,000 kilometers).

The radiation in the belts consists mainly of high levels of positively charged protons and negatively charged electrons. Earth's *magnetic field* traps these particles and directs them toward the poles. A magnetic field is a region affected by the force of a magnet. The magnetic field can be affected by the sun's magnetism, causing the belts to slightly shift and change shape.

The belts were named for James A. Van Allen, an American scientist, who discovered them in 1958.

Other articles to read include: **Magnetic storm.**

Venus

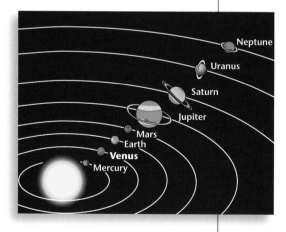

Neptune

Uranus

Saturn

Jupiter

Mars

Earth

Venus

Mercury

Venus is the second planet from the sun.

Venus is the second planet from the sun. Only Mercury is closer. Venus *orbits* (circles) the sun at a distance of about 67.2 million miles (108.2 million kilometers).

People can see Venus in the sky without using a telescope. From Earth, Venus looks brighter than any other planet or any star in the night sky. At certain times during the year, Venus is the last planet or star that can be seen in the eastern sky in the morning. During other times of the year, it is the first planet or star that can be seen in the western sky in the evening. Venus shines with such a dazzling light that early *astronomers* (scientists who study the planets and stars) named the planet for the Roman goddess of love and beauty.

Continued on the next page

Venus is sometimes known as "Earth's twin." Venus is closer to Earth than any other planet. At its closest, it is about 23.7 million miles (38.2 million kilometers) away. Venus and Earth are also about the same size. Unlike Earth, however, Venus has no moon.

Scientists believe that about 4 billion years ago, Venus was much more like Earth. Then, the sun was not as bright and hot as it is today. At that time, Venus could have had mild temperatures, flowing water, and even an ocean. But as the sun got brighter and hotter over time, Venus also got hotter and less like Earth.

Venus is now the hottest planet in the solar system. The planet's *atmosphere* (blanket of gases) is made mostly of carbon dioxide (CO_2) gas. The CO_2 traps heat from the sun close to the planet's surface. The temperature on the surface is about 860 °F (460 °C).

Venus's atmosphere is much thicker and heavier than Earth's atmosphere. The weight of the atmosphere presses down on Venus with incredible pressure. In fact, the pressure is so great that it would quickly crush a person who tried to stand on the surface.

Floating in the atmosphere are thick clouds of *sulfuric acid*. Sulfuric acid is so strong that it can dissolve metals. Some findings from probes sent to Venus suggest that the clouds may produce a "rain" of sulfuric acid. But the heat of the planet is so great, the raindrops *evaporate* (turn to vapor) before they reach the surface.

Venus's clouds make it difficult for astronomers to learn about the planet's surface. To "explore" Venus, scientists have relied on scientific instruments on Earth and on space probes. Using this equipment, astronomers have discovered many interesting features, including plains, mountains, canyons, and valleys. Venus is the flattest planet in the solar system. Smooth plains cover about 65 percent of the surface. Thousands of volcanoes dot these plains. The volcanoes range from about 0.5 to 150 miles (0.8 to 240 kilometers) in diameter. Six mountainous regions make up about 35 percent of the surface of Venus. One mountain range, called Maxwell, rises about 7 miles (11 kilometers) high—higher than Mt. Everest, the tallest mountain on Earth. It stretches about 540 miles (870 kilometers) long. It is the highest feature on the planet.

Some *impact craters* also mark the surface of Venus. These bowl-shaped holes form when an asteroid or other small body strikes a planet. Venus has fewer craters than do the moon, Mars,

Continued on the next page

Features on the surface of Venus are highlighted in a computer-generated image based on information gathered by the Soviet Venera 13 and 14 spacecraft.

This crater on the surface of Venus is about 23 miles (37 kilometers) wide, across the low, dark area in its center. The crater was made when a large meteorite slammed into the surface long ago.

Venus *Continued from the previous page*

and Mercury. This fact suggests that Venus's present surface is less than 1 billion years old.

Many surface features on Venus are unlike anything on Earth. For example, Venus has *coronae* (crowns). These ringlike structures range from about 95 to 360 miles (150 to 580 kilometers) in diameter. Scientists think that coronae form when hot material inside the planet rises to the surface. Venus also has *tesserae* (tiles). The tesserae are raised areas in which many ridges and valleys have formed in different directions.

Venus's orbit round the sun is almost a perfect circle. All of the other planets in the solar system follow a more *elliptical* (oval-shaped) orbits. A day on Venus is longer than the planet's year. That is, Venus takes about 225 Earth days, or 7 ½ months, to orbit the sun. But Venus spins very slowly on its *axis*. An axis is an imaginary line through the center of the planet. Venus takes 243 Earth days to spin once. So on Venus, a day is about 18 Earth days longer than a year.

No space traveler has been to Venus. However, scientists have sent robotic spacecraft to explore the planet. The first spacecraft to pass near Venus was Mariner 2, in 1962. The United States and the Soviet Union (now Russia) each sent several other spacecraft to orbit Venus. Some Soviet spacecraft even landed on the surface.

In 2005, the European Space Agency launched the Venus Express probe. The probe was designed to study Venus's atmosphere and to scan the planet's surface for volcanoes. The probe began orbiting the planet in April 2006. In 2010, Venus Express scientists announced that they had found evidence of "recent" volcanic activity. They said the activity may have happened just a few hundred years ago. But they also said the activity may have happened as long ago as 2.5 million years.

Other articles to read include: **Evening star; Impact crater; Planet; Transit; Volcano.**

Very Large Telescope

The Very Large Telescope (VLT) is one of the most powerful telescopes in the world. The VLT is at the Paranal Observatory on Paranal Mountain in Chile.

The VLT actually consists of eight separate telescopes. Astronomers can use these telescopes in combination, as if they were a single telescope. They can also use them separately. The four largest telescopes of the VLT are called *unit telescopes.* The mirrors of these telescopes are each 27 feet (8.2 meters) wide. Four *auxiliary (awg ZIHL yuhr ee) telescopes* have mirrors that are 71 inches (1.8 meters) wide.

Scientists made the first observations through a unit telescope in May 1998. Construction of the VLT was completed in 2006.

Other articles to read include: **Observatory; Telescope.**

The Very Large Telescope consists of eight separate telescopes that can be used as one single instrument. Here one uses a laser to help "see" through Earth's atmosphere.

Vesta

Vesta ranks as the third-largest *asteroid* in the *Main Belt.* An asteroid is a rocky or metallic object smaller than a planet that *orbits* (travels around) the sun. The Main Belt is a region of probably millions of asteroids between the orbits of Mars and Jupiter. Only the Main Belt asteroids Ceres and Pallas are larger in volume than Vesta. Vesta also has the second-greatest *mass* (amount of matter) of any asteroid, after Ceres. Vesta is about 330 miles (530 kilometers) in diameter. Vesta circles the sun every 3.63 Earth years at an average distance of about 219 million miles (353 million kilometers).

Vesta is the solar system's only known surviving *planetesimal (PLAN uh TEHS uh muh).* Planetesimals are also known as *proto-planets.* They were rocky asteroid-sized bodies about that collided and stuck together to form the planets, moons, and other solid or mostly solid bodies in the solar system. Most scientists believe that all other planetesimals in the early solar system

Vesta is the solar system's only known surviving *planetesimal,* one of many rocky bodies that collided to build the planets and moons.

Continued on the next page

Vesta *Continued from previous page*

either combined to become full-sized planets or were destroyed in a collision with another object.

NASA, the United States space agency, launched the Dawn spacecraft in 2007 to explore Vesta and Ceres. The craft entered orbit around Vesta in 2011. In 2012, Dawn scientists revealed that Vesta is unlike any other asteroid they know of. Vesta has a layered internal structure similar to that of Earth and the moon. Other asteroids are usually made of the same materials throughout. Like Earth and the moon, however, Vesta has a rocky crust and mantle and an iron core. This structure suggests that Vesta is left over from the early formation of the solar system almost 5 billion years ago. Scientists think Vesta may not have grown larger the way other planetesimals did because of the *gravitational pull* of Jupiter, the largest planet. Jupiter's gravity probably prevented Vesta from combining with other planetesimals.

The German astronomer Heinrich Wilhelm Olbers discovered Vesta in 1807. The asteroid was named for the Roman goddess of the household. Vesta ranks as the only Main Belt asteroid that can be seen from Earth with the unaided eye. However, the sky must be dark, and an observer must know where in the sky to look for it.

Other articles to read include: **Asteroid; Ceres; Dawn; Main Belt.**

Virgo is one of the largest constellations.

Virgo

Virgo is a *constellation* also known as the Virgin. A constellation is a grouping of stars in the night sky. Virgo can be seen from much of the Northern and Southern hemispheres.

Virgo can be drawn in several ways. It commonly resembles a line drawing or stick figure of a person. A group of four stars forms the head.

The brightest *quasar* in Earth's sky can be seen in Virgo. A quasar is a very bright object at the center of some galaxies.

Virgo was among the 48 constellations defined by the ancient Greek mathematician Ptolemy. Today, it is one of 88 constellations recognized by the International Astronomical Union (IAU), the leading authority in the naming of heavenly objects.

Other articles to read include: **Astrology; Constellation; Ptolemy; Quasar; Star; Zodiac.**

Volcano

A volcano is an opening in the surface of a planet or moon through which hot rocks or other material shoots out. This blast of material is called an *eruption (ih RUHP shuhn)*. Earth is not the only body in the solar system with volcanoes and volcanic activity. The other three rocky planets—Mercury, Venus, Earth, and Mars—have had volcanic eruptions in their histories. Scientists have also found evidence of volcanic activity on several moons around other planets in addition to Earth's moon.

A plume of mostly water ice and water vapor erupt from Saturn's moon Enceladus.

Images taken by the Messenger space probe in 2011 revealed that the volcanic activity on Mercury was more violent and widespread than scientists had believed. From 4 billion to 3.5 billion years ago, thick rivers of *lava* (melted rock) gushed from cracks up to 15 miles (25 kilometers) long in Mercury's already scorching surface. The lava flows filled impact craters and flooded areas around the planet's north pole. They created smooth plains that cover much of Mercury's northern hemisphere.

Venus has evidence of more recent eruptions. Many scientists believe Venus may still have occasional eruptions. But none have been observed.

Mars has the largest volcanoes in the solar system. The tallest one, Olympus Mons (Latin for *Mount Olympus*), rises about 16 miles (25 kilometers) above the surrounding plains. It is more than 370 miles (600 kilometers) in diameter. Three other large volcanoes, called Arsia Mons, Ascraeus Mons, and Pavonis Mons, sit atop a broad uplifted region called Tharsis. All of these volcanoes have slopes that rise gradually, much like the slopes of Hawaiian volcanoes. Both the Martian and Hawaiian volcanoes are *shield volcanoes*. They formed from eruptions of lavas that can flow for long distances before becoming solid.

Mars also has many other types of volcanic landforms. These range from small, steep-sided cones to enormous plains covered in solidified lava. Scientists do not know how recently the last volcano erupted on Mars—some minor eruptions may still occur.

Evidence of volcanic eruptions early in the history of Earth's moon can be seen in dark areas known as *maria (MAHR ee uh)*.

Continued on the next page

Solidified flows of lava sweep down the slopes of Maat Mons, a volcano on Venus, in a computer-generated three-dimensional image.

A bright red ring circles Pele, an active volcano on Jupiter's moon Io.

Volcano *Continued from previous page*

The word *maria* is Latin for *seas*. The term comes from the smoothness of the dark areas and their resemblance to bodies of water. The maria are cratered landscapes that were partly flooded by lava when volcanoes erupted. The lava then froze, forming rock.

Io, Jupiter's closest large satellite, is the most geologically active body in the solar system. Volcanoes send clouds of dust up to 300 miles (500 kilometers) above its surface. Constant eruptions create so much new land that Io's surface is covered in lava flows, mountains, and pits rather than craters. The cause of Io's volcanic activity is *tidal interactions* with Jupiter and with the planet's other large satellites. The gravitational pull of these objects squeezes Io's interior in different directions. This creates immense heat.

Lava is not the only material to come out of a volcano in the solar system. Titan, a moon of Saturn, has volcanic eruptions of ice. The surface of Titan is very cold. Liquid deep within the moon can work its way to the surface. The liquid then freezes on the moon's frigid surface. Such volcanoes are called *cryovolcanoes*.

Scientists have also observed a plume of particles erupting from the south pole of Enceladus, another moon of Saturn. The plume is fed by several individual jets on the surface of the moon that release mostly water vapor and grains of water ice. But they also release some *organic* (carbon-containing) molecules.

Other articles to read include: **Enceladus; Io; Maria; Mars; Mercury; Moon; Olympus Mons; Venus.**

Voyager

Voyager is the name of two robotic space probes launched by NASA, the United States space agency. The Voyagers were expected to be the first space probes to leave the *solar system*.

The Voyagers were designed for a five-year mission, enough time for each to reach Jupiter and Saturn. Voyager 1 was

Continued on the next page

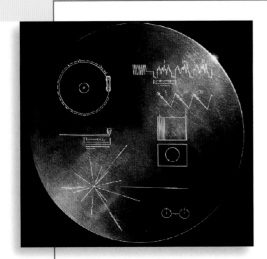

Each Voyager carries a metallic disk, called the Golden Record, that holds greetings in 55 languages. The disks also hold 115 images and a variety of sounds of life on Earth.

launched in September 1977. It passed Jupiter in 1979 and Saturn in 1980. Voyager 2 was launched on August 1977. It visited Jupiter in 1979 and Saturn in 1981. After the spacecraft successfully accomplished this task, NASA engineers sent the probes on longer missions to explore the outer solar system and beyond. Voyager 2 became the first— and, so far, only—spacecraft to visit Uranus (1986) and Neptune (1989).

The probes found proof of volcanoes on Jupiter's moon Io. They detected icy fountains on Neptune's moon Triton. They also sent back information about the atmosphere of Saturn's moon Titan.

Scientists expect the Voyagers to continue sending information back to Earth until about 2020. At that time, their power supplies will become too weak to send signals to NASA's listening equipment.

Other articles to read include: **Jupiter; Neptune; Saturn; Space exploration; Uranus.**

White dwarf

A white dwarf is a star that has run out of fuel. During most of its lifetime, a star burns element hydrogen in a process called *nuclear fusion*. Nuclear fusion releases energy in the forms of light and heat. This is what makes a star shine.

Eventually, a star runs out of hydrogen. It may then swell up, becoming a huge star called a *red giant*. A red giant throws off its outer layers of material. The remaining *core* (center) of the star shrinks and becomes a white dwarf.

Continued on the next page

White dwarf *Continued from previous page*

A white dwarf continues to cool and shrink until it no longer shines. It ends its life as a *black dwarf.*

In certain cases, a white dwarf may have another companion star. These two stars orbit each other and are called *binary stars.* Sometimes the white dwarf will pull material away from the other star. This material settles on the white dwarf's surface. If enough material gets pulled onto the white dwarf, the star will explode in a huge event called a *supernova.*

Other articles to read include: **Binary star; Red giant; Star; Supernova.**

XMM-Newton

XMM-Newton is a satellite observatory. It studies the universe in *X rays* as well as *visible* and *ultraviolet* light. X rays are an invisible form of light. They have more energy than visible light. Visible light is the form of light humans can see. Ultraviolet light is an invisible form of light with slightly more energy than visible light, but less energy than X rays.

XMM-Newton is named in honor of the English scientist Sir Isaac Newton. The abbreviation XMM stands for X-ray Multi-Mirror mission. XMM-Newton uses three X-ray telescopes, each with its own mirror, to gather X rays. The observatory also carries one visible light and one ultraviolet telescope.

XMM-Newton in 2012 made the first discovery of low-energy *cosmic rays* (electrically charged, fast-moving particles) coming from outside the solar system.

The European Space Agency (ESA) built the observatory. It was launched by the ESA on December 10, 1999. Since then, astronomers have used the observatory to observe many different kinds of objects, from comets in the solar system to distant clusters of galaxies.

XMM-Newton moves around Earth in a highly *elliptical* (oval-shaped) orbit. It ranges from 6,000 to 68,000 miles (10,000 to 110,000 kilometers) in altitude, completing one orbit every 48 hours.

Other articles to read include: **Newton, Sir Isaac; Observatory; Satellite, Artificial; Space exploration.**

Yang Liwei

Yang Liwei (1965-) was the first astronaut launched into space by China. Yang spent 21 hours in space in October 2003. He *orbited* (circled) Earth 14 times, traveling more than 373,000 miles (600,000 kilometers). Yang landed safely in Mongolia after the flight. Before flying into space, Yang was a Chinese air force pilot.

People in China call Yang a *taikonaut (TY koh nawt)*. That is Chinese for *astronaut*. Russia and the United States are the only other countries to have launched people into space.

Other articles to read include: **Astronaut; China National Space Administration; Space exploration.**

Yang Liwei

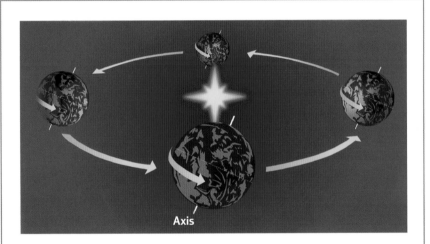

Axis

Year

A year is the amount of time it takes Earth to make one complete trip around the sun. A year is 365 days long, plus a few extra hours. Our calendar year is based on this way of measuring a year. Another way of measuring a year is based on the moon and is called the lunar year. The lunar year has 12 lunar months. The ancient Greeks used a lunar year of 354 days. Today, the Chinese use a lunar calendar. A lunar calendar is also used in the religions of Judaism and Islam. The Christian calendar is based partly on the sun and partly on the moon.

The tilt of Earth on its axis causes the seasons. The tilt also causes the stars in the night sky to appear to change positions throughout the year.

Continued on the next page

Year *Continued from previous page*

Other planets in the solar system also have "years" or the length of time they take to orbit the sun once. The length of a planet's year is related to how far away from the sun it orbits. The closest planet to the sun, Mercury, orbits the sun in 88 Earth days. The farthest planet from the sun, Neptune, orbits the sun every 165 Earth years.

Other articles to read include: **Equinox; Orbit; Sun.**

Yerkes Observatory

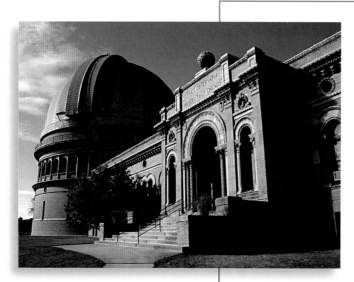

The Yerkes Observatory in Williams Bay, Wisconsin, offers visitors tours and the opportunity to look through a telescope.

The Yerkes *(YUR keez)* Observatory is a place for studying *astronomy* that is operated by the University of Chicago. Astronomy is the study of the universe and objects in it. Yerkes is located in Williams Bay, Wisconsin.

The observatory houses five telescopes. Three are *reflecting telescopes,* which use mirrors to gather and focus light. The fourth is a *refracting telescope,* which uses lenses to gather and focus light. The refracting telescope, the largest of its kind in the world, is 63 feet (19 meters) long. The fifth telescope is a *Schmidt camera,* a device made with both a lens and a mirror.

American astronomer George E. Hale founded the observatory in 1895 with a large donation from Chicago businessman Charles T. Yerkes. Hale, the observatory's first director, made advances there in the study of the sun. American astronomer Frank Schlesinger developed ways to measure the distances to stars.

In 2006, the university announced plans to sell the observatory site to a private land developer. Opposition from the community of Williams Bay prompted the university to reconsider its plan. Along with research, Yerkes provides public tours, workshops for educators, and opportunities for the public to observe through a telescope.

Other articles to read include: **Hale, George Ellery; Observatory; Telescope.**

Zodiac

The zodiac *(ZOH dee ak)* is a band-shaped section of the sky that has 12 *constellations* (groups of stars). The zodiac has special meaning to people who follow *astrology,* the belief that stars and other heavenly bodies influence people's lives. Astrologers divide the zodiac into 12 equal parts called *signs,* named after the 12 constellations. They believe that each person comes under the special influence of a particular sign, depending on when the person was born. The 12 signs are Aries, Taurus, Gemini, Cancer, Leo, Virgo, Libra, Scorpio, Sagittarius, Capricorn, Aquarius, and Pisces.

The Eastern, or Chinese, zodiac, is a set of symbols used since ancient times in some Asian countries. It does not involve constellations and has no historical connection with the Western zodiac. However, both zodiacs have 12 symbols. And in both zodiacs, a person's birth date is believed to affect his or her character and fate. The 12 symbols of the Eastern zodiac are animals. Scientists and many other people consider astrology to be no more than a superstition.

Other articles to read include: **Aquarius; Aries; Astrology; Cancer; Capricornus; Constellation; Gemini; Leo; Libra; Pisces; Sagittarius; Scorpius; Taurus; Virgo.**

The belief that the signs of the zodiac play a role in a person's character and fate is part of astrology. But scientists have found no scientific evidence for astrology.

The index is an alphabetical list of important topics covered in this book. It will help you find information given in both words and pictures. The page number or numbers after a heading tell you where to look for information about a topic. For example, there is a reference to **Adaptive optics** on page 164.

When there is an article on a topic in *The Discovery Science Encyclopedia,* the page number or numbers appear in **boldface.** For example, the boldface page for the article on **Andromeda Galaxy** appears along with references to that topic in other encyclopedia articles. When there are many references to a topic, they are sometimes organized under subtopics, as they are under **Atmosphere.**

Sometimes, an index heading refers you to information in other headings in the index. For example, **Asteroid** has a "See also" reference to additional information on this topic under **Main Belt.** The "See" reference for **Alpha Orionis** tells you that all the information on this topic will be found under **Betelgeuse.**

When an entry can mean more than one thing, there are words in parentheses to help you distinguish between these different meanings—for example, **Antares** (rocket) and **Antares** (star).

A page number in *italics* refers to an illustration only. For example, a picture for **Cassini** (spacecraft) appears on 20, but there is no other reference to this topic in the text on this page or the facing page.

The publisher gratefully acknowledges the following sources for photographs. All maps and illustrations unless otherwise noted are the exclusive property of World Book, Inc.

6-7 NASA; © Shutterstock

8-9 Jan Robrade/ESA; © Shutterstock; © Thinkstock; Bill Schoening, Vanessa Harvey/REU program/NOAO/AURA/NSF

10-11 © Shutterstock; © David Parker, Science Photo Library

12-13 © Shutterstock; NASA

14-15 NASA/Hubble; NASA/JPL-Caltech/MSSS

16-17 © Shutterstock; NASA

18-19 NASA

20-21 NRAO; © James King-Holmes, Science Source

22-23 NASA/JPL; © Shutterstock; Yerkes Observatory; A. Dupree (Cfa), NASA/ESA

24-25 © Rick Fischer, Masterfile; Alan Watson, John Krist, Karl Stapelfeldt, Jeff Hester, Chris Burrows, NASA

26-27 NASA; © Science Photo Library/Alamy; Bill Ingalls, NASA

28-29 NASA; Bill Ingalls, NASA; NASA; © Thinkstock

30-31 NASA/STSci; NASA

32-33 NASA; © Shutterstock

34-35 Smithsonian Institution; NASA/JPL-Caltech/UCLA; © Shutterstock

36-37 NASA/JPL

38-39 © Mary Evans Picture Library/Alamy; © Shutterstock; NASA/ESA/STSci

40-41 NASA; TRW Space & Technology Group/NASA; NASA

42-43 Astra Rocket Company; AP

44-45 © David White, Alamy; NASA; NASA

46-47 NASA; European Southern Observatory

48-49 Globalstar

50-51 NASA; NASA/ESA/STSci

52-53 © Shutterstock; Williams College/EIT Consortium

54-55 NASA/SDO/AIA; D. Ducros, CNES

56-57 Alcatel-Lucent; J. Yang/NSF

58-59 NASA/WMAP Science Team; NASA/GSFC; © Shutterstock

60-61 D. Clow, M. Markevitch, NASA/CXC/CfA/ESO/WFI/Magellan/U. Arizona; William K. Hartmann, UCLA/NASA

62-63 © Jeff Poskanzer; NASA/JPL-Caltech/University of Arizona; A. Fujii, NASA/ESA

64-65 NASA/JPL/Space Science Institute; © Shutterstock

66-67 Caltech/NASA

68-69 NASA/JPL/Space Science Institute

70-71 Mike Brown, Caltech/NASA; NASA/JPL/University of Arizona

72-73 ESA; © Thinkstock

74-75 © Ron Miller

76-77 NASA/DOE/Fermi LAT; NASA; E. O'Sullivan, NASA/CXC/CfA/Coelum

78-79 S. Beckwith, NASA/ESA/STScI/Hubble Heritage Team/AURA; G. Bacon, NASA/ESA/STScI; European Southern Observatory

80-81 © Shutterstock; NASA

82-83 Mary Pat Hrybyk-Keith, John Jones, NASA/Swift

84-85 NASA/JPL; Canadian Space Agency; Lunar & Planetary Institute

86-87 © Shutterstock; NASA; © Shutterstock

88-89 NASA/ESA; NASA

90-91 Chester Harman, PHL/UPR Arecibo/NASA/JPL/APL/Arizona; © Science and Society/SuperStock; © Shutterstock

92-93 Lick Observatory; © Max Alexander, Lord Egremont/Science Source

94-95 NASA

96-97 © Shutterstock; © Science and Society/SuperStock; © Shutterstock; ESA/AOES Medialab

98-99 © Mary Evans Picture Library/Alamy; JAXA/NASA/PPARC; © Pantheon/SuperStock

100-101 H.E. Bond, NASA/ESA/STScI; NASA/ERO Team

102-103 NASA; M. Regan, B. Whitmore, R. Chandar, NASA/ESA/STScI/University of Toledo; STScI/AURA/NASA/ESA/Hubble Heritage Team; © Margaret Bourke-White, Time & Life Pictures/Getty

104-105 © Shutterstock; NASA/JPL/SSI

106-107 © D. Van Ravenswaay, Science Photo Library; © Shutterstock

108-109 AP; NASA

110-111 NASA; NASA; NASA/The Hubble Heritage Team; University of Arizona/LPL/NASA

112-113 © Shutterstock; NASA

114-115 NRAO; NASA; NASA/JPL-Caltech

116-117 © Anthony Holloway, Jodrell Bank; NASA; NASA/JPL/Space Science Institute

118-119 R. Evans, J. Trauger, H. Hammel, HST Comet Science Team/NASA; W. M. Keck Observatory

120-121 George Shelton, NASA; Tim Jacobs, NASA

122-123 © Shutterstock

124-125 © Classic Image/Alamy; John Hill, Large Binocular Telescope Observatory

126-127 © Shutterstock; Juan Carlos Casado, TWAN/NASA; © Shutterstock; WORLD BOOK Photo

130-131 © Shutterstock; Bill Schoening, Vanessa Harvey/REU program/NOAO/AURA/NSF

132-133 © Everett Collection Inc/Alamy; © Shutterstock; NASA/ESA/Hubble Heritage Site

134-135 NASA; NASA/JPL

136-137 © Stocktrek Images/Thinkstock; NASA/JPL; NASA

138-139 NASA; NASA/GSFC

140-141 JPL/NASA; NASA

142-143 NASA/JPL-Caltech/MSSS; © Universal Images Group Limited/Alamy; NASA

144-145 NASA; James Dickson, Jim Head NASA/JHUAPL/CIW-DTM/GSFC; © Meteor Crater Enterprises

146-147 © Shutterstock; NASA/JPL/SSI

148-149 NASA; NASA; NOAA

150-151 Lunar & Planetary Institute; ISRO/NASA/JPL/Caltech; R. Hurt, NASA/JPL-Caltech/SSC; NASA/JPL/Caltech/MITIGSFC

152-153 © Shutterstock; NASA

154-155 NASA; © Shutterstock; T. A. Rector, H. Schweiker, U of Alaska/WIYN/NOAO/AURA/NSF

156-157 NRAO/AUI; NASA/JPL-Caltech

158-159 NOAO/AURA/NSF; NASA/JPL; © Science Source

160-161 D. Leahy, Asaoka & Aschenbach, B. Gaensler, NASA/CXC/ROSAT/NRC/DRAO/NRAO/VLA/DSS; JHUAPL/SwRI; © Shutterstock

162-163 © Shutterstock; NASA/JPL-Caltech

164-165 © Thinkstock; © Shutterstock; NASA; NASA

166-167 NASA; A. Feild, NASA/STSI

168-169 Space.Com/Starry Night; © Shutterstock

170-171 © Shutterstock; © Roy Kaltschmidt, LBNL; © Shutterstock; NASA/JPL

172-173 Pierre Auger Observatory; © Shutterstock; ESA

174-175 © Pictorial Press/Alamy; NASA; NASA/Mariner 10/Astrogeology Team/U.S. Geological Survey; NASA/JPL-Caltech/MSSS

176-177 NASA; © UCAR/University of Michigan; © Carl Zeiss; © Shutterstock

180-181 NASA/JPL-Caltech/Keck; NASA/ESA/JUH/APL; NASA; ESA; M. Showalter, SETI Institute

182-183 AURA/STScl/NASA/Hubble Team; © Shutterstock

184-185 NASA/CXC/SAO/P. Slane; NASA; K. Luhman, NASA/ESA/Penn State

186-187 G. Illingworth, R. Bouwens, UC Santa Cruz/HUDF09 Team; NASA; W. Kirk, The Johns Hopkins University/STScI/NASA

188-189 George Roberts, NASA; Clark University Archives

190-191 © Richard T. Nowitz, Photo Researchers; © Shutterstock; F. K. Baganoff, NASA/CXC/MIT

192-193 JPL/NASA; NASA/Johns Hopkins University/SRI/Goddard Center; Jacques Descloitres, MODIS/NASA/GSFC

194-195 NASA/JPL-Caltech/SSI

196-197 © Belinda Pratten; © Shutterstock

198-199 NASA; NASA; AP

200-201 NASA/ESA/University of Leicester; SDSS

202-203 NASA/SDO/AIA; R. Hurt, NASA/JPL-Caltech/SSC

208-209 © Shutterstock; © Galaxy Picture Library/Alamy

210-211 NASA

212-213 NASA

214-215 © Shutterstock; NASA

216-217 NASA; Denise Applewhite, NASA/Princeton University; NASA/ JPL; © Sovfoto

218-219 NASA/ESA/Hubble Heritage/STScI/AURA

220-221 NASA/JPL/Caltech/Cornell; NASA; SOHO-EIT Consortium/ESA/NASA

222-223 NASA/SOHO

224-225 NOAO; J. Hester, A. Loll, NASA/ESA/Arizona State University; © Shutterstock; © Scala/Art Resource

226-227 © Harvard Observatory; © Adam Block, Mt. Lemmon SkyCenter; NASA

228-229 © Don Smetzer, Alamy; NASA/SDO/AIA/EVE/HMI; NASA/JPL; AP

230-231 ESA/Planck Collaboration

232-233 ESO

234-235 Kenneth Seidelmann, U.S. Naval Observatory/NASA; © A. Tayfun Oner, Calvin Hamilton

236-237 NASA

238-239 NASA/JPL; © Serge Brunier, ESO; NASA/JPL/MPS/DLR/IDA

240-241 © Shutterstock; NASA/JPL/Caltech/SSI

242-243 NASA/JPL; NASA/JPL/University of Arizona; NASA

244-245 ESA; CNSA

246-247 © Shutterstock